T0323882

Bury My Heart at Conference Room B Awards and Top Lists

1. *New York Times* bestseller
2. *Wall Street Journal* bestseller
3. *USA Today* bestseller
4. 800-CEO-READ best in category
5. *Inc.* Best of the Year list
6. *Fast Company* Best of the Year list
7. *Miami Herald* Top 10 business books list
8. *Soundview* Top 30 best list
9. *Booklist* Top Ten Business Books of the Year: Starred Review
10. *Publisher's Weekly:* "must read"

Praise for the *New York Times* bestseller
Bury My Heart at Conference Room B by Stan Slap

"I urge you to follow where Stan Slap fearlessly leads us. He has the answer to making a career in management actually bring you a fuller, richer, better life." **—GEOFF COLVIN,**
author of *Talent Is Overrated*; senior editor at large, *Fortune*

"A subversively radical triumph of a book that uniquely and definitively demonstrates the mystery of how organizations succeed."

—WARREN BENNIS, distinguished professor
of business at the University of Southern California; author of
Still Surprised: A Memoir of a Life in Leadership

"Slap has written the holy grail for companies seeking the most from their managers and for managers seeking the most from their companies. It is fascinating, thought provoking, and actionable. This book is not just a 'must read' but a 'must experience.'"

—JACK CALHOUN, president, Banana Republic

"This book has the answer for any manager who thinks there must be a better way to do the job without hating the job. The single most powerful management book I've read in years."

—JASON JENNINGS, author of
Hit the Ground Running; Think Big, Act Small; and Less Is More

"Stan Slap's approach for developing managers who care resonates deeply with the principles we at Four Seasons strive to embody. There are great insights here for creating a true culture of ethics, integrity, and heartfelt service." **—ISADORE SHARP,**
founder, chairman, and CEO, Four Seasons Hotels and Resorts

"Whether you are a first time supervisor or a CEO, reading this book will allow you to tap into the secret that will drive organizational success."

—**JULIA STEWART**, CEO, DineEquity

"You have to read *Bury My Heart at Conference Room B*. Stan Slap covers all the bases. A warm, witty book that will take you and your organization to a better place." —**KEN BLANCHARD**, coauthor of *The One Minute Manager* ® and *Leading at a Higher Level*

"This book is game changing in a way I have never seen in a business book. I learned about myself and gained new insights into the work I've been doing for thirty years. It is a spectacular read."

—**JOHN RICCITIELLO**, CEO, Electronic Arts

"Humanity in any organization, whether professional or political, is what will save us. The world needs this book."

—**AMIR A. DOSSAL**, executive director
United Nations Office for Partnerships

"A provocative read sure to appeal to managers who want to connect with their employees in a fresh, meaningful, and lasting way."

—*Publisher's Weekly*

"The notion that values matter––in the workplace as well as at home––is certainly not new to the ranks of management gurus and corporate leaders. What are novel in consultant Stan Slap's first book are his passion for the subject, which bleeds from every page, and his easy-to-use framework for identifying and promoting values throughout the business world. . . . In a passion-infused narrative, Slap gives every manager the tools to change." —*Booklist*, starred review

"With humor, pointed anecdotes and historical allusions, [Slap] has delivered a readable, realistic guidebook for organizational leaders and managers at all levels that has a lot of heart in it.'
—*Fort Worth Star Telegram*

UNDER THE HOOD

STAN SLAP

UNDER THE HOOD

FIRE UP AND FINE-TUNE YOUR EMPLOYEE CULTURE

PORTFOLIO / PENGUIN

PORTFOLIO / PENGUIN
An imprint of Penguin Random House LLC
penguinrandomhouse.com

USA | Canada | UK | Ireland | Australia | New Zealand | India | South Africa | China
A Penguin Random House Company
First published by Portfolio / Penguin, a member of Penguin Random House LLC, 2015

LIBRARY OF CONGRESS CATALOGING-IN-PUBLICATION DATA

Slap, Stan.
  Under the hood : fire up and fine-tune your employee culture / Stan Slap.
    pages cm
  Includes bibliographical references and index.
  ISBN 978-1-59184-502-7 (hardback)
  1. Employees—Attitudes. 2. Management—Employee participation. 3. Organizational behavior. I. Title.
  HF5548.8.S543 2015
  658.3'12—dc23

                    2014038640

Paperback ISBN: 979-8-217-04580-8

Set in Whitman LF
Designed by Elyse Strongin, Neuwirth & Associates, Inc.

148720106

For Sawyer Rocket

1, 2 . . . 5!

A NOTE TO MANAGERS
WHO DON'T EVEN HAVE TIME TO READ
THIS SENTENCE

ALL STUFF, NO FLUFF

Your employee culture is not the same thing as your employees and it is far more important as a driver of business impact. This book will finally explain how an employee culture actually works and exactly how to work it. It will provide plenty of new insight for you, and it will allow you to get an astonishing level of commitment from your own culture, along with the flexibility, resiliency, accountability, and innovation that come with it. This is a book about results.

MAKE IT YOUR OWN

Of course I want you to cancel every listing on your calendar, bar the doors, and read this book start to finish in one jaw-dropping, life-changing lost weekend of epiphanies. That will give you the ultimate understanding of culture, which is the ultimate key to your success as a manager. But if you're facing an urgent performance issue, you can also self-curate these pages for focused help.

Go right to the Original Sin to get the essential explanation of what your employee culture really is, and why it chooses to buy or reject any management plan. Go right to any of the other Seven Sins for fast tactical steps you can take around issues like change, communication, and compensation. Go right to any of the Four Vulnerabilities to fix circumstances of unusual stress on your company.

What I want most for you is the success you want for yourself.

Let's go.

CONTENTS

MAINTAINING CULTURAL COMMITMENT UNDER PRESSURE

HOW to get your employee culture's support when the company is in trouble.

PART 3 THE WHOLE POINT

PART 4 RESEARCH NOTES AND TANGENTS

CONTACT. LIFTOFF.

I'm always interested in hearing from you.

AT A LOSS FOR WORDS

Thanks to all of the people who made this book happen for me and for you.

SELECTED RESEARCH NOTES

Sources, proof and data points; related and completely unrelated facts; and anthropological jungle cred.

Your great ideas? Your grand theories?
Those are parlor furniture.
Come with me . . .
I'm going to take you down to the
   cellar and show you how the house
   really works.

—SIGMUND FREUD

UNDER
THE
HOOD

INTRODUCTION

THURSDAY MORNING. 7:30 a.m. I've been asked to an urgent meeting with the senior strategic team of a very well-known IT company.* They are not happy.

"Seriously, this strategy could be a matter of life and death for us," one of them explains earnestly. "We've made some mistakes, okay? And we've been slow. We've got one big move left, and if we don't get it right we're going to be irrelevant in a competitive market and never recover.

"We do have a turnaround plan, and we know it's really good," he insists confidently. "We've actually had it for a while, but we've waited to implement it until we got the whole company on board. It's going to need a lot of change from our people."

"So we did everything right," chimes in another. "The big strategy kickoff, then the regional strategy road shows, then the employee intranet strategy site. We did the strategy T-shirts, the strategy posters,

---

* You'd know the company right away—it's a multibillion-dollar iconic enterprise—but in this one case only, I'm not going to ID it. As of this writing, their strategy is still live. Besides, the point of the book isn't to make managers feel dumb; it's to make them even smarter.

the strategy mouse pads, the strategy screen savers, and the strategy wallet cards."

"We did those balloons," adds a third.

"That's right! We did the strategy balloons for everybody."

■ ■ ■

"On the eve of execution we decided to audit our employee culture," they continue. "Not because people didn't know about the strategy. You'd have to be brain-dead not to know about the strategy; it's all we'd been talking about for eight months. It's that we're sure our turn-around is going to work. This is going to be taught as a case study someday, and we figured some proof about all the patience we showed under pressure would make it even better."

"So we polled our entire employee population and asked only one question: Do you understand our new strategy? When the answer came back, it was overwhelming."

"No."

"What is *wrong* with these people?" they moan.

■ ■ ■

Nothing is wrong with the employee culture. What's wrong is that the executive team didn't read the whole response. The employee culture wasn't actually saying, "We don't understand the strategy. You're using too many big words."

The employee culture was saying, "We don't understand why we should get up for making the strategy happen."

With all the rah-rah and blah-blah, management forgot to acknowledge the mantra of successful selling: You must respect why your customer buys. And the mantra of this book:

You can't sell it outside if you can't sell it inside.

1, 2 . . . *10!*

Increase revenue. Increase margin. Don't just make market share; take it. Improve customer reputation. Improve product quality. Get to market faster. Put major distance between you and the competition. Become one united team across business units.

What employee could argue with the irrefutable logic of these corporate performance strategies? In a perfect world, your own employees would immediately grasp the logic and devote themselves wholeheartedly to achieving them.

Wake up, wipe the drool from your desk, and say "hi" to reality.

In the real world, neither business logic nor management authority nor any compelling competitive urgency will convince an employee culture to adopt a corporate cause as if it were its own. In the killing field between company concept and employee commitment lies many a failed strategic plan.

Want your employees to buy a new management goal? You have to know how to sell it to them. This means selling to your employee culture—knowing how the culture works and how to work the culture.

We're not just talking about a bunch of employees. When they form a relationship with a company, employees become a culture and are far more self-protective, far more intelligent, and far more resistant to standard corporate methods of influence. A culture is a distinct organizing framework that gives your people a motivation fundamentally different from the company's motivation.

It's not late-breaking news that you *have* employees, but it's only when you truly understand them as a culture that problems once considered chronic are finally resolved, and opportunities once considered unattainable are finally realized. The difference between understanding your employees and understanding your employee culture is the difference between whether your performance goals succeed or fail.

FROM MACRO TO UH-OH

You're going to need that understanding. Like any company, your company regularly bets its life on the ability to roll out new strategies to the marketplace—ahead of schedule, ahead of budget, on the heads of your competitors. Yet most strategies in most companies don't really work. They don't really do what they were supposed to do, don't really cost what they were supposed to cost, and don't really happen when they were supposed to happen. They only look like they're moving forward because they're being slammed from behind by the next strategy.

This is because even the smartest companies subscribe to the most dangerous strategic myth: A strategy has to be planned well to be successful. In fact, a strategy has to be implemented well to be successful.

Successful implementation starts with being able to enroll your employee culture in fierce support of the strategy. If you can do this, you're well on the way to achieving strategic insurance. If you can't, and you think any strategic or performance goal will be successful without the hard-core support of this particular group, you're building a base camp on Mt. Delusional.

WHAT THIS BOOK WILL DO FOR YOU

This isn't another book about how to successfully manage employees; it is a unique book about how to successfully manage an employee culture, which is a whole different thing.

Yet an employee culture is the *same* thing whether you have two employees, 200, or 20,000, or whether your employee culture is located in Manhattan, Mumbai, or Machu Picchu. And the best ways to gain its ultimate commitment are the same, whether you are a senior manager with responsibility for the entire company or you are a line manager with responsibility for a single team.

If you have a wonderful employee culture, this book will help you scale it. If you have a troubled employee culture, this book will help you fix it. If you have an employee culture under pressure, this book will help you protect it. If you have a new employee culture, this book will help you shape it. And if you are investing in a company, this book will help you protect your greatest purchasable asset.

There is often frustration among managers about why an employee culture acts the way it does: Why can't it just dependably support what's important to the business? But it's not up to an employee culture to understand the business logic; it's up to the business to understand an employee culture's logic. This book will explain exactly why your own employee culture may choose to resist supporting a strategy or performance goal and explain practically and tactically what to do about it. Not just to gain your employee culture's support. To gain your employee culture's maximum, dependable, adrenalized support.

Along with frustration, there is a belief among some managers that there's a genetic limit to an employee culture's willingness to give sustained commitment and loyalty. There's not, of course, but this book is going to blow the cap right off *any* limitation. You'll learn how to get whatever you want from your employee culture, whether it's greater commitment to the company and its goals, increased accountability, increased innovation, rapid acceptance of change, improved speed and accuracy of execution, or representation of your company's best intentions to your customers. Whatever plan you have for increased performance, I can assure you it will be far better protected and promoted by your people.

I can assure you because for years I have been applying these same proprietary methods in many of the world's most successful, demanding organizations in information technology, financial services, entertainment, mobile, manufacturing, and retail—creating large, sustained metrics impact for companies that don't include "Patience" on their list of corporate values.

MYSTERY ACHIEVEMENT

As a kid I was notorious in my family for certain behaviors. One of them was being very hard to bluff: Parents: "Eat your vegetables; there are people starving in China." Me: "Name one." Another was an obsessive curiosity about how and why things work. How did it come to be? Where is the power? How can it go faster, do more, or do something new? How do you fire it up, fine-tune or fix it? What is under the hood?

I carried this obsession into adulthood and into business. It causes the results my company gets for our clients today. That's because I found the ultimate answer to how and why things work. An employee culture is the power that drives the enterprise engine. Fire it up and it will take you wherever you want to go; fine-tune or fix it and it will take you there faster. You want maximum business performance? Look under the hood and you'll find your employee culture.

Under the hood there is both power and mystery. To harness the rumbling power of your employee culture you've got to solve the mystery of what that culture actually is, how it operates, and how to move it forward. These are the keys that this book is going to put right in your hands and that's a real good thing. A company that will achieve long-term progressive success without them? Name one.

LET'S MAKE IT PERSONAL

My company is renowned for achieving maximum commitment in manager, employee, and customer cultures. That's what we do; the reason I do it is because I believe that, short of homicide, the worst thing one human being can do to another is to make them feel small: *You're not. You can't. You won't ever be.* This is a killing of the soul, of hope, and of potential. Domination and disregard drive me absolutely nuts, whether it's committed by individuals or by organizations.

The world works, and it is affected by work. A person made to feel small on the job doesn't stay on the job. These same people are parents, partners, neighbors, and voters: The toxic impact is incalculable. Nothing—no motive, no circumstance, and no position of authority—grants the right to cause it.

The passion that fuels my work is that nobody should be diminished by business—working in it or buying from it. This may be a noble sentiment, but it's too unproductive to interest the typical profitable enterprise, so I long ago translated it into a series of high-impact ROI methods that most definitely do.

When an employee culture is repositioned as a newly precious, workable asset, a company will naturally protect it, same as with any asset. An employee culture can't be protected without protecting the humanity it represents and without managers reclaiming their own humanity where it may have disappeared in the labyrinth of their job descriptions.

If we lose humanity in business, we're all doomed. If we save it—company by company and manager by manager—we will have saved ourselves.

In case you fear this icy hand of altruism will grip your own company by the throat and choke the life out of revenue, not to worry: We're talking here about making the business case for humanity. In any environment where meaning is determined by metrics, the point of view and processes in this book are going to cause measurable, sustainable results.

BETTER YET, LET'S MAKE IT PERSONAL TO YOU

James Bond is strapped to the table as a laser beam relentlessly moves to cut him in half. As it's about to reorganize critical parts of his anatomy, Bond frantically offers, "If you kill me, they'll just send another agent to take my place." Goldfinger gives him the villainous eye roll. "I don't think so, Mr. Bond."

"Can you afford to take that chance?" Bond counters, and the laser is shut off.

If you're a senior manager and all the last major strategies or critical performance goals in your company worked just like they were supposed to, maybe you don't need to leverage the true motivations of your employee culture. But they probably didn't, and considering that your company's success in a hypercompetitive market—as well as your own success and legacy—could depend on the next one, can you afford to take that chance?

If you're a manager at any level, you're going to constantly be given a strategic handoff to drive over the line—your part of a financial goal or organizational change. Considering that your job success involves achieving results through others and that those others work for you, an unerringly accurate understanding of an employee culture is the most important information you can possibly have. You could gamble on achieving results without it. But can you afford to take that chance?

SEVEN THINGS. AND ONE MORE THING.

Despite constant reminders that it won't work, enterprise strategies and performance goals remain front-loaded on the planning side, with implementation expected to be carried out by the logic that calls for them or the bribery that pays for them. Let's call this 1, 2 . . . *10!* In between 1, 2, and *10!* are the Seven Deadly Sins of Cultural Commitment that cause employees to limit or deny their support.

Note to overachieving managers: The key is to avoid all Seven Sins, not to accomplish them.

Commitment is an act, not a word.

—John–Paul Sartre

PART 1
THE SEVEN DEADLY SINS OF CULTURAL COMMITMENT

Take me to the river.

—Al Green

> Give them freedom from above or they will take it from below.
>
> —Alexander II (1865)

THE ORIGINAL SIN

FAILURE TO RESPECT THE POWER OF AN EMPLOYEE CULTURE

> Heat the beat, and the rest will turn sweet.
>
> —James Brown (1965)

THE MYSTERY OF AN EMPLOYEE CULTURE IS SOLVED. THE POWER IS CONFIRMED.

All of the Seven Sins are important, so they're not listed here in any particular order, except for the first one. The Original Sin, from which all others are born: a failure to respect the absolute power of an employee culture to make or break any management goal—and any manager right along with it.

If you're a manager with a deep preference for control, the idea of surrendering it to an employee culture around issues as critical as the execution of strategies and performance goals may seem difficult or dangerously counterintuitive. Oh, don't worry about that: The control isn't yours to surrender anyway. Who is going to decide the success of your company or team's goals? If you're the one running it, start by scratching yourself right off the list. Your employee culture has the first vote. If the culture wants something to happen in your business, it will. If it doesn't, it won't.

Wait, it gets worse: Your customers are employees somewhere, too, so they belong to the overall employee culture. They'll decide to protect or reject your company in part based on how they perceive your company treats people just like themselves. Unless there are flagrant circumstances—you're renowned as the best employer or the worst—this perception will be an intuitive mind meld between your employees and your customers. It's going to be based on what kind of legitimate enthusiasm your people show for your products, pricing, and policies. As employees somewhere themselves, your customers know they themselves would never show the same legitimate enthusiasm unless they were being treated with deep understanding and respect.

All of this should cross your mind when considering the win/loss odds of any important management objective. Or cross your legs, if you really think about it.

WELCOME TO THE JUNGLE

Culture may be the most overused but least understood concept in business. Many managers sling around the word, although few have an accurate working definition of what an employee culture is and how it makes decisions. Even fewer have the proper respect for the power of an employee culture to bury them and their filthy little strategies if it wants to.

Let's make really sure you're not either one of those. You're already smart, or you wouldn't be reading a book about how to get smarter. Getting smarter about an employee culture starts where the biggest implications for business first started.

The concept of culture has been around for a while and has been examined by a number of esteemed intellects* including Margaret Mead, who famously field-researched primitive native tribes in the Samoan jungle around the turn of the last century, reaching formative anthropological conclusions.

Margaret, or "Dinner" as she was known to the natives, discovered that what appeared to be the simplest of societies, without any modern methods of communication, were actually highly developed communities with specific rules of behavior and complex rituals governing birth rites, death rites, celebratory feasts for the Chief, relationships with other tribes, and locations of safe watering holes. Remarkably, everybody in the tribe obeyed these rules faithfully and practiced these rituals accurately.

---

* Important thinkers include Bastian, Benedict, and Boas, and that's just the B's. There's more information about anthropological science in the Research Notes and Tangents section at the end of this book. I put it at the end because you need to know what your employee culture is up to before you get distracted by reading those pages.

"How can these primitive societies originate, stay together, and pass accurate information from person to person?" Maggie wondered, as she was being bound hand and foot and sprinkled with salt. Her answer, and none too soon, by God, was that the social system that brought the natives together, created their ability to communicate, and maintained their willingness to abide by the same behavioral standards was something called a "culture." Culture, Mead said, "is the body of learned behavior by which a group of people who share the same tradition, environment and lifestyle transmit that knowledge . . . among themselves and members of society."

The natives weren't sure what to do with that either.

Here's the bottom line: *A culture is your employees' shared beliefs about the rules of survival and emotional prosperity.* "How do I survive—in this company, on this team, working for you—and once I know I'm going to be okay, how do I get rewarded emotionally and avoid punishment?"

Whenever people share the same basic living conditions, they band together to share beliefs about how best to survive. The more people there are looking for the safe watering hole, the safer it is for everyone. The conditions Mead noted in that Samoan jungle are therefore the same conditions present in any organizational environment.

In your own organizational environment, you have a group of people who share the same basic lifestyle, environment, and traditions. They all work in the same industry. They all work in the same company. They all work in the same line of business. They all work on the same team. They all work for you. They are all part of your employee culture.

There are two important things you need to know about this. Right away.

THE FIRST IMPORTANT THING

An employee culture isn't just self-protective. An employee culture exists to protect itself. Once you get this, your employee culture becomes the simplest operating system in the world. It is an information-gathering organism, designed to assure its own survival.

That's its *own* survival—not yours, and not the company's. Even though it seems that a through line logically links success for the enterprise with survival and emotional prosperity for the culture, that logic would depend on the employee culture perceiving a reliable connection between what happens to the company and what happens to the culture. As you'll discover in this book, this is rarely the case, and it is rarely the culture's fault.

Because it's self-protective, it's a little crazy. Even on its best days an employee culture is neurotic and prone to hypochondria. How could it not be? It is trying to understand how to survive in an environment it can't reliably anticipate or control. On its worst days—which ironically can be some of the company's best days—it's in a snarly, hostage-taking mood. Ignore this, and that decision will come back to bite you—and the culture will, too. Snippy and Pissy aren't cartoon characters; it's your employee culture under pressure.

THE SECOND IMPORTANT THING

You are not part of your employee culture. As a manager, you may be friendly with your people. Maybe you're friends with some of your people. Maybe you used to be one of your people and got promoted. But you're not part of your people's culture—you're management, standing outside of the culture, trying to sell it something. You do have a special place in the culture, though, as the key influencer of its survival and emotional prosperity. It's a lonely place, but it's special.

True, you are also an employee if you are a manager, but in the relationship with your employee culture you are foremost a member of the culture of management, be it executive, middle, or entry level. The rules of survival and emotional prosperity for managers, and within each of these manager levels, are distinct unto themselves and distinct in many ways from those of the general employee population. The considerable influence of managers over their employee culture further isolates managers, keeping them from being part of it.

THE CULTURE'S VISION STATEMENT: KEEP A WARY EYE ON YOU

The implication of this for you as a manager is that your employee culture's antennae are constantly working, tracking you and seeking information. The culture's credibility detector is infallible. Its perceptions are alarmingly accurate. Its memory is everlasting. Quick recap: the prodigious recall of a wizened elephant combined with the impact potential of a rabid wolverine.

There isn't much that goes on that the culture doesn't know about; it's always watching, always gathering and sifting information, always updating its perceptions. It knows when you've been naughty. It knows when you've been nice. It knows that you're reading this page of this book. You can't sweep anything under the rug to hide it from an employee culture. A culture *lives* under the rug.

Your employee culture will notice what you emphasize, what you reward, what you give priority attention to, what you ignore. It will observe why you protect and promote, why you punish. It will watch to see whether you defend what's important to you under stress or temptation to compromise. The culture will use all of these impressions to form beliefs about how to behave in order to best serve itself.

It won't ever tell you what it believes—and don't think you can send a spy into the employee culture with orders to infiltrate and report; the culture will mail you back the body parts—but it will show you what it believes by its actions or its hesitancy to act.

There is no indecipherable algorithm here: It is not that your employee culture's behavior is unpredictable; it is that the culture perceives critical information as unpredictable and so isn't sure how to regularly behave. The culture rarely gets all the information it wants, the backstory, or the chance to confirm directly with the source.

Does your employee culture ever get it wrong? Sure. Not intentionally and not very often, but since it can't always confirm the accuracy of the information it's collecting it has to take a best guess at interpreting the meaning and implications. Like any human organism, once it reaches a conclusion it tends to seek further information as confirmation of its existing belief system, which can compound the error.

An employee culture cannot survive with any sanity in a state of complete unknown. It needs to believe that *something* is real so it can take action to regulate its circumstances. The culture is going to act on its perceptions: Inaction isn't the wisest option when pursuing safety in an uncertain world. Your employee culture's perceptions are not just its reality. They're going to be your reality, too, unless you understand where they came from and how to recalibrate them as needed.

How, then, do you manage an employee culture? The more you know about how it works, the more it may seem unmanageable.

You can't bribe, bluff, or bully an employee culture into sustainably doing anything. You can't tell the culture what to believe. You can't stop it from existing. But you can take comfort from knowing that an employee culture is the utmost rational system, agnostic and objective about everything except its own survival. And it isn't static—it is focused on survival, so it must remain constantly open to receiving and evaluating new information. Nothing is fixed in a culture's belief system except why it needs to believe something.

Based on its own perceptions, an employee culture rarely does anything illogical or unpredictable. Neither is it asking for motivational fairy tales. It is asking for management demands to be imbedded with respect for what is most important to the culture that is expected to deliver on them. And while it is naturally suspicious, it isn't naturally hostile to business goals. Your employee culture wants to do the right thing. It believes that the right thing is to protect itself. Don't fight this; honor it, and you're on the way to the culture linking its own protection to protection of the business.

HOW I FIRST LEARNED ABOUT CULTURE

▶ Every executive should work in retail at some point. It's a great way to learn that every strategy, no matter how daring or darling, has to make the cash register ring. And it permanently imbeds images of customers and employees connecting at the sales counter—the magic moment—which is what business is all about.

My own retail experience began when I left home at sixteen and worked as temporary Christmas help in a record store and nine years later concluded as part of the executive management team of a retail bakery chain called Mrs. Fields Cookies, as we built it from nineteen stores to over 300 and took it into four countries. That was a long time ago, so if you've had a bad cookie since, gimme a break.

Those cookie store jobs weren't rocket science, but then again, rocket scientists don't have to build the entire rocket, sell it, and clean the factory when they're done. Our thousands of employees, largely unskilled labor, were responsible for making the cookies from scratch, selling them, collecting the cash, and maintaining the facilities. Anything and everything could go wrong if they weren't motivated to do their best.

The stores' performance was the company's performance, so the metric I always looked at was our customer average sale. It was a single key indicator that showed multiple forms of operational readiness: For that number to be high, the product had to be good and available, the service had to be fast and friendly, the staff had to be sufficient and happy—and they had to be cross-selling milk with the cookies. The customer average sale was nowhere near where I wanted it to be, mostly because the selling of milk wasn't happening.

I sent memos to the district managers, then I sent the district managers to the stores, then I called the stores personally with an explanation that simply suggesting milk could increase the average sale by as much as thirty percent. Multiplied by a hundred thousand cookies a day in stores open every day, this was a big revenue number.

But our employees wouldn't do it.

Finally I hit the road myself to meet personally with every store team. "You eat cookies at home with what?" I asked them. "Milk," they responded immediately. "When I say 'warm cookies,' what do you think of?" I asked them. "Milk," they responded immediately.

But they wouldn't do it.

Exasperated, I started thinking less about what I wanted our employees to do than about who they were. Most were just turning eighteen, and everything in their lives was subject to change. Relationships were ending or getting more serious. School was harder and more important. Money, once provided to them, now had to be earned. Decisions about the future were expected and carried more weight. As a result, our employees had pretty much lost the mirror that confirmed who they were, which could be frightening.

I wanted to make the case that all of that uncertainty didn't matter in one circumstance: If you were allowed behind the counter at one of our stores, it was because you were something special. And if you wanted to believe that about yourself, you would perform to a certain standard. So one day on a tour of the San Francisco stores I had large posters printed and installed in the back rooms of all of them:

WE ARE QUALITY.
We will serve nothing less than perfect cookies.
We will treat our customers like family.
We will work as a team and win as a team.
We will keep this store so clean it sparkles.
We will beat all sales projections.

It wasn't exactly a big initiative. Took me about ten minutes to write, a minor attempt to address a major problem that I was running out of ways to solve. I knew it was cheesy and I didn't really think it would work. I didn't think about it at all after the posters were installed.

Until weeks later, when I was back in San Francisco and noticed that not only were the posters still up, employees in every store had voluntarily signed them. As I entered one store, they were in the midst of singing "We Are Family" to customers. What? Wait a minute. What?

Ever have one of those experiences that you are aware is being etched permanently into your memory right as it's occurring? It wasn't on the store visits but later that night in the cab back to my hotel. All these years later, I still remember riding in that taxi, knowing that I had been taught a tremendous lesson. Some sort of secret door to influence had briefly revealed itself, but how? What had happened?

What had happened is that this was the first time I had unknowingly stopped thinking of employees and started thinking of an employee culture. A life force with its own purpose, logic, and source of energy that had to be met on its own terms.

And the forty-one percent increase in average sale. That happened, too.

KEY TO THE HIGHWAY

The defining characteristic of the relationship between a company and its employee culture is tension. It is a tension based on different perspectives about priorities, power, pressure, and definitions of success. Without real understanding of the other's deep-set views, the motives and process of an employee culture often remain unfathomable to management, and the motives and process of management often remain unfathomable to its employee culture.

This chronic unease about the difficulty of forecasting the other party's decisions translates into threat conditions for both. It makes the risk to survival and emotional prosperity a front-and-center priority for an employee culture, which causes the culture to detach emotionally from the company's goals and assurances. The culture remains suspicious and resistant to embracing the unknown. That's too bad, because "unknown" happens to be territory that a company frequently has to occupy, and the employee culture's commitment is what's most needed to conquer it.

The very thing that management uses to define enterprise success—the relentless drive forward—isn't determined by a strategic map that reveals the destination but by the engine that makes the trip possible.

THE COST AND EFFECT

Management generally considers three types of resources on hand for strategic execution: time, talent, and dollars. But there's a fourth that trumps the three: commitment of the employee culture. There are many bad decisions a company can make, but few that can't be made good by an employee culture's decision to course-correct it. There are many good decisions that a company can make, but few that can't be made great by an employee culture's decision to protect it and promote it to customers with its own good name.

Those once-august companies who are now stories of faded glory have lost the willingness of their employee cultures to protect the flag it once planted. Groovy new companies are planting the flag in shallow ground if they think that plenty of stock and snacks will buy their employee cultures' enduring devotion. When things go wrong, these kinds of companies will shift blame to the employee culture for its failure to commit—labeling it as change-resistant, willing to sell allegiance to the highest bidder, intellectually incapable of understanding the finer points of business cause and effect, and emotionally incapable of sustained loyalty.

None of this is true. Your own employee culture will give you everything you want, but you have to give it what it wants first. This is the difference between defiance and compliance and, once you know how, it won't cost you much to do.

Not doing it will cost you plenty.

DO THIS NOW
GIVE YOUR CULTURE ENERGY

A culture is an organism. Like any organism, its first priority is to survive. In order to survive, it needs energy, which it prizes as a priority. An employee culture has an extraordinary need for energy, which it uses to fuel its constant work of taking in information—announcements, facts, rumors, patterns, what is said and left unsaid—crunching it to extract relevant implications and simultaneously maintaining defense shields against the unknown.

Uncertainty costs an employee culture plenty of its energy. The more unsure it perceives its environment to be, the more fuel it must expend translating messages into meaning and the more formidable those defense shields have to be. Even if there's no actual threat, hunkering down in constant anticipation of the unanticipated takes a lot of effort. The more exhausted your employee culture gets, the more it will use its remaining energy to protect itself, not your business goals.

If this were some sort of video game a culture could play on the couch, it would still be exhausting. It's not: Your company is forcing its employee culture into constant forward motion. It needs to move quickly while fighting the urge to slow down and ensure the path ahead is safe, and that costs the culture even more energy.

Why would this uncertainty exist in an organizational environment where, say, the demands for performance are constant, the metrics are established, the compensation systems are intact, and the company values are clearly stated? Because that's what *management* says. The perceptions of an employee culture about what is dependably true may be very different based on its acute focus on what the company and its managers say versus what they do.

There are three dimensions of an employee culture's healthy energy—the regenerative kind that translates into productivity and loyalty:

■ Context (looking backward)

If your employee culture can easily understand why something is happening, it needs less energy to probe management actions and announcements for implications.

■ Predictability (looking forward)

The more your employee culture can forecast how the company will act, the less energy it requires to classify the future as reliable.

■ Sense of self (looking inward)

If what your company does—and, more important, how and why it does it—is a positive force in the world, being part of it boosts your employee culture's sense of self, which it converts into energy.

Align the reinforcement of these energy dimensions with what you really want from your culture. If, for example, your employee culture is encouraged to take its sense of self from constantly making the diving catch—last-minute saves of something about to go horribly wrong—the culture won't suggest or welcome any proactive controls that could stop this sort of risky organizational behavior.

Demand all the energy you need from your culture, but protect these three dimensions by constantly stockpiling and resupplying them. Should its energy get exhausted, your employee culture will become resistant, inflexible, cynical, slow, detached, suspicious, and incessant in demands for financial rewards. And you'll want to work from home.

1. HOW TO GIVE YOUR CULTURE CONTEXT.

● REVISIT DECISIONS MADE AND UNMADE

An employee culture hears decisions from management all the time, but rarely hears what happened when those decisions are revised or discarded. Did the dog eat them?

Understandably, your culture then believes that things rarely work out the way they were promised and that what executives say in speeches rarely comes true. Both of these perceptions are stone-cold context killers. Avoid this by regularly explaining what happened to at least some of the plans that didn't proceed as announced, especially if they were originally announced directly from the C-suite.

● DON'T FOCUS EXCLUSIVELY ON REVENUE

Whoa, now—down, down. Of course revenue is the driver of the enterprise. It's just not suitable as the sole driver of context for your employee culture. For cultural context to exist, it has to be benchmarked to something that rarely changes rather than focused entirely on performance goals, which change constantly. You don't want your culture to wonder, "Now that we've made the number, who are we?"

You can—you must—continue to talk revenue expectations to your culture, but base that talk on fundamental company beliefs that remain stable regardless of any revenue fluctuation. Position quarterly revenue results as a way of keeping score about what the company always stands for: goals met as a result of upholding product performance and customer relationship standards, and the company's belief in its employee culture. No margin? No mission. Don't explain how your world was improved when the company exceeded its target; explain how *the* world was improved by receiving more of what you do. This same context is necessary when revenue targets are missed: How a company protects what it stands for when things go wrong is sure to be noticed by its employee culture.

2. HOW TO GIVE YOUR CULTURE PREDICTABILITY.

● PROVIDE SIMPLE RULES FOR LIVING

Take what is most uncompromising about your company's standards, personality, and performance ethic and translate it into simple guidelines—one page, total—that your employee culture can use to prioritize and make decisions: This is what the company believes is absolutely most important, so always do this, and never do that. Assure your culture that any decision it makes in concert with these essential guidelines will be supported.

Fair is fair: You can then point out that anyone violating these essential guidelines will be held immediately and fully accountable. This will allow your culture to predict the consequences of its own behavior.

● HOLD PREDICTABILITY DRILLS

Conduct regular predictability Q&A exercises with your employee culture, as a company and by individual business units. Propose various scenarios about performance, values, mistakes, good times, and bad times and explore how your culture believes the company would react. What would the company always do? What would the company always refuse to do? Make these predictability exercises part of introducing any major new strategy or performance goal.

Don't bother arguing if your culture doesn't yet agree the company will actually protect what it says is most important or if it can't identify much in the way of predictable enterprise behavior. You can't win using logic against a belief system, and your culture has its own sound logic for everything it believes. Instead, use these exercises to uncover the causes of those beliefs (why and when did they happen?) and read-just with credible action.

3. HOW TO GIVE YOUR CULTURE A SENSE OF SELF.

Anybody who works has to constantly answer two questions. From those who don't know you, it is *What do you do?* From those who know you best, it is *What did you do today?* The key to an employee culture's sense of self is helping it answer both in a way that makes its members feel good—and look good to others—because they work for you.

● **HELP TO ANSWER *WHAT DO YOU DO?***

Any company can spin its business model into some sort of sniffle-inducing noble purpose: ACME manufactures a flange that supports one of the gears in machines that fold boxes that hold the food that some company ships to all those starving kids in Africa = *ACME Feeds the World!*

A noble purpose helps maintain a positive sense of self for the culture—if your company really has a reason for being in business besides making money, it is seriously imbedded in the enterprise, and it is actually a driver for many decisions. Energy-producing pride of affiliation is created if the company declares such a larger raison d'être* and then protects it.

It's well known that Apple's iconic *"Think Different"* campaign was first aimed at the company's employee culture, not its customer culture. "It was a way of signaling to employees, This is what we believe in. This is what we think. And we make products for people who think like this," says Alan Olivo, who was Apple's senior vice president of worldwide marketing at the time of the launch.

---

* Don't ever use such a pretentious term with your employee culture.

"People don't remember that Apple was almost out of business when we launched this campaign," Olivo asserts. "We had rapidly declining revenue, some troubled products, a lack of focus, an OS licensing deal that was killing us, no presence at all in the enterprise, and four CEOs in four years. *'Think Different'* was not a signal to non-customers by any means. It was a signal to the Mac world, to people who made Apple stuff, and people who used Apple stuff, in that order.

"Steve felt that Apple made computers for people who do not care what the computers can do; they care about what they can do with computers," he explains. "And Apple had in some ways lost that purpose, that sense of what we do being so important to what others can do, that faith that we will produce only innovative, highest-quality products. The Apple employee culture no longer knew how to act like Apple. Restoring what you call 'sense of self' was what *'Think Different'* was about."*

Even if your company has that kind of noble purpose, or even if it doesn't, your employee culture's sense of self is pegged to who your company (or team) *is* far more than to what it *does*. What matters to your culture is your company's true character—how it treats people inside and outside. This is where you need to give your employee culture bragging rights: Make sure every member of the culture learns about company decisions that show empathy and decency to people within the company; delightful features of the customer experience; how the company treats its vendors and partners; how it supports its local communities and conducts itself as a national and global citizen; and, most important, how it treats its employee culture.

Sometimes these examples are extraordinary. You're a member of the Google employee culture and you have given yourself an impres-

---

* After Alan left Apple, he headed the brand consulting (customer culture) division of my company. I knew he was very fond of Jobs and knew also the extraordinary pressure of working directly for him that Alan endured for many years. On the day Jobs died, I offered my condolences. "Yeah," sighed Alan. "I've been sitting here thinking of all of those one-on-one meetings with Steve, just me and him in his office. I'm remembering all of the times I left that office thinking of the magical, revolutionary ways . . . *I could kill myself.*"

sive stretch goal: You're stretching for that box of free licorice on the topmost shelf of one of the snack cabinets. The cabinet suddenly topples and fatally flattens you. Here's what happens next: Your spouse or domestic partner continues to receive fifty percent of your full salary for a decade, along with your company stock, which is vested immediately, and each of your kids receives $1,000 a month until they're nineteen, or until they're twenty-three if they remain full-time students. Even if you survive your assault on the north face of the snack cabinet, the bragging rights about how the company conducts itself and values you make you look a lot more valuable when you explain it to others.

The same cultural impact is still there for your company even if you can't afford this kind of munificent policy or can't even fund the free licorice. There are many smaller opportunities in business to do the right thing, as established policy or in unexpected situations, and these become storied proof points that members of your culture can use in discussions with others. Do enough of these small things and they add up to a huge thing: People outside of the company will often have heard good things about your company even if they don't recall how. This reflects well on anyone who works there: If you're employed by a company that obviously cares about you, you must be worth caring about.

Every day there are reports of companies that are apparently hellbent on proving they *don't* care. It's worth noting to your employee culture how your own company chooses to act differently. What your company chooses not to do is as important as what it does.

HELP TO ANSWER *WHAT DID YOU DO TODAY?*

The constant seduction of key influencers is critical—those family, friends, and business contacts outside of the company whose opinions matter most to members of your employee culture. This should start as soon as any new member of the culture starts:

- Buy dinner for them, their partner, and a couple of close friends as the company's celebration of their joining the company.
- Send a package to their home that includes FAQs with which they can easily explain the importance of the company and its role in their personal community.
- Have your CEO and your team sign "Why You Were Hired" welcome letters.
- Produce a company comic book that explains to kids what the enterprise does and how their dad's or mom's job makes them a superhero.
- Give a donation in their name to a company-sponsored charity.

On an ongoing basis, move from sending stuff to sending messages. Continue to explain the impact of what the company does and why the company has made recent decisions—especially those decisions where there was a more expedient and less costly way to solve a problem. The company's veracity means the culture can take pride in both representing the integrity of the enterprise and in being allowed to act with integrity itself. At the end of the day, what could be more important to tell someone close to you than that your company allowed you to protect your own good name?

HO, HO, *WHOA*

▶ Founded in the late 1990s, GoDaddy is an Internet beast, offering website hosting to more than twelve million customers worldwide and managing about fifty-five million domains.

Taking care of business like this for other companies is a 24/7 operation, every single day of the year, including holidays. It's hard to staff for holidays and hard to keep the staff you do have from being glum and grumbling to customers who don't like to hear it, since it reminds them that they're working on the holiday, too.

In GoDaddy's early years, the company relied entirely on volunteer staffing for major holidays like Christmas. The basic principle: Since nobody wants to work on Christmas Day, let's find out who wants to work on Christmas Day. This sounds like some Zen wisdom that has been seriously lost in translation, but GoDaddy's logic was sound. "A lot of people are alone during the holidays, and they would never think of coming to work," says Bob Olson, GoDaddy's vice president of Customer Strategies and Business Operations from 2003 to 2007. "By coming into the office, they actually had a better time than they would have had sitting all alone on a couch at home."

Holidays at work became a tradition at GoDaddy, beloved by members of the culture and affectionately curated by management, and were regularly overstaffed. For many, GoDaddy was the place to be during the holidays.

"Every Christmas, my children knew that they couldn't open any gifts until I had delivered donuts to every GoDaddy work site," recalls Bob. "I would shake every single person's hand, wish them happy holidays, and thank them for being there. Then I'd go home, and after the kids had opened their presents I would go back to work with more donuts for the second shift."

Codependence Day

Fast-forward to June 2012. GoDaddy's revenue picture was dim. The company had been seriously missing projections, and in order to recover it needed to generate a flat-out impossible 280 percent of quota in three days. Flat-out impossible made worse: It had to be done during the three days of the Fourth of July holiday weekend.

As good luck would have it, Bob Olson had just returned to the company after a five-year absence. This didn't seem to be particularly good luck for Bob Olson, since he had been given the responsibility of making the aforementioned nutso revenue target. "No problem," thought the Holiday King, thinking he would crank up his all-volunteer army, and take that money hill. Except that while he was away, his volunteer staffing program had gone away, too. Seems it was just too much of an administrative burden for HR, so the company had returned to mandatory staffing, where the normal weekend shifts were required to staff customer service centers on all major holidays.

Olson persuaded the company to try it one more time and sent out the call for volunteers. He got 630 of them—more than forty percent of the entire company culture that would have been scheduled to work if it weren't a holiday. Over the Fourth of July holiday weekend of 2012, Olson and his fellow managers threw a nonstop party for the volunteers, with plenty of food, gifts, and even contests where managers dropped and did push-ups to honor employees who made their sales quotas. As the weekend went on, employees who weren't even scheduled to work over the holiday started coming in just to cheer on their friends.

Those 630 members of the employee culture ate, drank, laughed, talked to customers, danced, sang, talked to customers, *made up the entire 280 percent revenue shortfall and put the company back on track for the year*, ate some more, and talked to some more customers.

Olson is very clear that GoDaddy's volunteer staffing policy was about meaning, not metrics. "The purpose was a higher calling," he says today. GoDaddy could have simply ordered employees to work on the Fourth of July. If those employees needed their jobs, they would have come into work. But GoDaddy figured out that the holidays weren't always a celebration for some of their employee culture, and that some members of the culture were closest to the people they worked with. So why not spend those special days with each other? Why couldn't the company celebrate *that*?

On Independence Day and the holidays that followed, GoDaddy sent an unmistakable message to its employee culture: We take care of business by taking care of our own.

THE END OF SIN: TACTICAL RECAP

THE ORIGINAL SIN: FAILURE TO RESPECT THE POWER OF AN EMPLOYEE CULTURE

Your employee culture will give you anything you want; you just have to give it what it wants first. A culture has an extraordinary need for energy, which it uses to defend itself in a world it cannot reliably anticipate or control. Demand whatever energy you need, but be sure to replenish it as you go, because your employee culture's energy translates into its flexibility, resilience, commitment, and productivity.

1. Give your culture context: Why is this happening?
- Revisit decisions made and unmade
- Don't focus context exclusively on revenue goals

2. Give your culture predictability: What will happen next?
- Provide simple rules for living
- Hold predictability drills

3. Give your culture a sense of self: Who am I as part of this?
- Help to answer the question What do you do?
- Help to answer the question What did you do today?

BOTTOM LINE:
Give your Employee Culture ENERGY

Growth demands a temporary surrender of
security.

—Gail Sheehy

THE SECOND DEADLY SIN
PRESUMPTION OF RAPID BEHAVIORAL CHANGE

Lightnin' change when Lightnin' want to
change.

—Lightnin' Hopkins to ZZ Top

ATTEMPT TO implement strategic or organizational change, and you'll get one of two kinds of resistance from your employee culture:

1. OVERT adj. |ōvərt, 'ovərt|
    It's too late to prevent it.

2. COVERT adj. |'kōvərt, kō'vərt, 'kəvərt|
    You don't realize it's too late to prevent it.

Any performance strategy that requires rapid cultural change to succeed probably won't. Your employee culture won't suddenly become one happy team by Q2 to make Q3 numbers. These kinds of serious behavioral transformations take awhile, and not because a culture is naturally slow to react. Its cheetah-like speed is reserved for lunging after the new and different, pinning it to the ground, and leaving it lifeless.

Why does an employee culture notoriously resist change? Now that you know why the culture exists, you can finally answer this question. What is an employee culture concerned about? Protecting the known rules of survival and emotional prosperity. What does any strategic or organizational change do? Messes with the known rules of survival and emotional prosperity. This is true for tough, necessary change, but it's also true for change that would seem to be of obvious, direct benefit to the culture.

You don't like change is a patronizing and inaccurate charge when leveled against an employee culture. An employee culture doesn't hate change. It hates the loss that change represents: the loss of the known.

Your culture used to know its job; now you're changing that job, and it has to relearn then re-earn its competence. Your culture used to have relationships it understood and could depend on; now it's being reorganized and it doesn't have those relationships. Your culture used to understand its compensation; now there's some fabulous new bonus program, but the culture doesn't know what it means when it earns it and, more important, when it doesn't.

HOW TOP DOWN BECOMES TOPPLE DOWN

I've been in countless meetings with company executives who are frustrated by the hesitant employee acceptance of change. Many believe that their own positions are earned in part by the ability to fearlessly embrace The New and The Different. "We don't have a problem with change," they say. "Must be why we're senior management." But let's face it: Change is a whole lot easier to deal with when you invented the change yourself, when that change isn't going to happen until you're ready for it to happen, and when you have a bunch of resources to heave at that change to help make it happen.

The change clock in the C-suite starts earlier, runs faster, and ends sooner than the employee culture's clock. By the time that change hits the employee culture, it's live—the clock has already started, and the goal is in motion. The culture is expected to understand it, embrace it, and translate it into action within approximately the same minute it officially hears about it. And your employee culture *is* the "bunch of resources" required to make the change happen.

You can't reasonably blame the culture for resisting this process. It was just whistling down the street when *whomp!* A ten-ton change safe has fallen on the sidewalk from the top floor. The culture is going to be hesitant about continuing quickly down the same path.

Because the culture didn't have the luxury of seeing the change develop, it loses perspective. Who knows what else might change?

Maybe anything, maybe everything. Any strategic or organizational change serves as an uncomfortable reminder of how little control an employee culture has over its life at work.

Meanwhile, the executive team has begun busily plotting the next change, secure that the last one went over just fine. "Sure, there was some bitching at first, but that's all gone now. We don't hear that anymore."

That's right. It's all gone now. That's right. You don't hear it anymore. It's all gone underground to the employee culture, where management can't hear it anymore. Meanwhile, the culture has activated its guerilla networks—it's dynamiting bridges, issuing commands, and reaching out to conscript the entire supply chain, sometimes including your customers, to help slow or stop the change.

It's not that the culture refuses to come together in response to a big new company strategy. It will definitely come together—for the purpose of resisting coming together. Then it will promptly head back to its own cave.

YOU CAN'T HURRY LOVE

You can't start with the action you want your employee culture to take. Action is at the end of the schematic:

RELEVANCY + TRUST + PROOF = ACTION

RELEVANCY: You're on your culture's frequency, putting your request for action in terms most important to an employee culture. The culture may not agree that the change is worthwhile, based on its own concerns. But it has stopped just hearing you and started listening.

TRUST: Your culture believes that you believe in the change, and that it will be good, or at least survivable, for the culture..

PROOF: Your culture is actively looking for proof points that the change is real and safe. And your culture is finding them.

Even if the change you seek is relatively minor, was relatively well socialized by your company, and appears to be relatively well received by your culture, there will be some grade of resistance. Should your company not have a lot of tolerance for a candid cultural response, you may not hear about it directly. You may not feel the resistance directly either: It could be revealed by a subtle lack of speed, uniform action, and discretionary effort. But no employee culture is left immune to the unsettling impact, and even the most reasonable change causes the fur to stand up on the back of its neck.

Some companies brag about their insatiable hunger for change, with a culture evidently comprised of vampire bats that feast on what nauseates normal creatures. The enterprise claims to thrive on change not just as an industry imperative but also as a source of pride and excitement for their employee culture. It *is* exciting to be in an environment of such endless alteration: The culture doesn't have to really commit to anything, since everything will soon be replaced.

Still, no matter how well a culture appears to tolerate it, constant change means constant detachment. Employee cultures in these kinds of companies operate in a state of manic disinterest; commitment to goals is fast and loud but not deep and dependable. They're not Masters of Change; they're Masters of Putting Up with Change. Not the same thing.

DO THIS NOW
GIVE YOUR EMPLOYEE CULTURE PERSPECTIVE

Change is a necessary fact of life for any successful organization, but even good, obvious change creates negative echoes for an employee culture, which last long after the announcement. If change is presented with the same casual presumption of receptivity as a wedding

Please join The Enterprise on the occasion of the revamping of your reality.

announcement, then the honeymoon is over before it's begun for your culture, and the culture is pretty sure who's going to get screwed.

Change feeds your employee culture's neurotic fear of uncertainty around every corner. This fear makes your culture fast but stupid, as it shifts its reaction from cognitive to feral. Fast-stupid is not the ideal way to move an organization forward. It's hard to be in a relationship with someone who's losing their mind without losing yours.

NOW, HERE'S HOW TO DO IT

1. EXPLAIN WHAT ISN'T CHANGING.

The key to an employee culture's acceptance of change is to restore its perspective. In the face of unforeseen change, its entire foundation is considered susceptible to sudden revision. Your culture has more than enough spiritual strength to accommodate any change if it's not using that capacity to defend against a larger perceived threat.

The solution isn't complicated, but it's rarely considered by companies that are constantly tilted toward new, better, bigger, and more: To reduce the negative impact of change, you must explain to your culture what *isn't* changing. Don't focus solely on the unknown; focus on the known. To move your culture forward, start by moving it backward to what is and what will always be.

If you introduce five PowerPoint slides that say, "This is changing," follow it with ten that say, "Here's who we have always been, here's who we still are, and here's who we will always be." Talk about uncompromising consistency of product focus, quality standards, customer relationships, and anything else, big and small, that qualifies as stable.

2. SELL CHANGE LIKE A CONSUMER PRODUCT.

It's generally a mistake to try to sell an employee culture on a new strategy en masse. The culture will vote with the culture, so get to the early adopters in your organization first, transform them into disciples of the change, and let the culture sell to the culture. A message from the employee culture to the employee culture has more credibility than anything you'll send from your position outside of the culture.

Pick those subsidiary organizations or teams that will benefit most from the change. Ensure that the change is viable for them: that there are no obstacles to execution, and they will receive the support and resources they need and the recognition due them for being the first. Let them prove success is feasible; you can then let their endorsement happen naturally, or ask for it, if you need to speed the change enterprise-wide.

OF THE PEOPLE, BY THE PEOPLE

▶ When senior executives of your government call with a direct request for services, I believe that you have to come running—or start running away from routine tax audits and anal cavity searches at the airport.

Among my company's clients at various times have been very powerful branches of the federal government in intelligence and administration. I've found that the public sector is very often comprised of talented people dedicated to a founding organizational mission who do their best to ignore the political leanings of any

Yet Another Cultural Learning Experience

given administration; they've usually been there longer and know that change at the top is inevitable. Their employee cultures want to serve the purpose, not the politics.

But they sure do envy the private sector for what they perceive as a faster acceptance of change, which they believe has cured problems they continue to suffer. In one particularly intense Washington, D.C., meeting, I heard the complaint, "We have silos of excellence." "What does that mean?" I asked. "Buried underground with only two people allowed in at a time and a complex code required to activate?"

I didn't want to be the one to break their hearts: It's the same all over, because an employee culture and how it is managed is pretty much the same all over.

The first thing I ever did for one of our government clients—the IRS—was a keynote speech. They were insistent that "We want you to talk to us like we are a business, not the government." I accordingly ended my speech by advising, "Let me tell you the most important rule for managing a successful business." Fourteen hundred pens poised anxiously, ready to etch imminent words of wisdom from the other side. "Pay your taxes!" I declared. Standing ovation. Sometimes my job is as easy as shooting fish in a barrel.

THE SECOND DEADLY SIN: PRESUMPTION OF RAPID BEHAVIORAL CHANGE

An employee culture doesn't hate change. It hates the loss of the known rules of survival and emotional prosperity that change represents. Even good, logical change produces anxiety, and the culture moves to stop or slow the change.

1. Explain what isn't changing.

Focus on the security of the known as you introduce the excitement of the unknown.

2. Sell it like a consumer product.

Don't go for mass buy-in. Sell to early adopters first, and let them sell it culture to culture.

BOTTOM LINE:

Give Your Employee Culture PERSPECTIVE

Caution: Cape does not enable user to fly.

—Instructions on Kenner Products Superman costume

THE THIRD DEADLY SIN

PLENTY OF MANAGEMENT WHERE LEADERSHIP IS NEEDED

It ain't easy to get it so I'm not hand twirling when the others are doing some hip thing!

—Barbara Lee, The Chiffons

A CULTURE IS never more united than when it is aroused, either by attack or inspiration.

Uncertainty is perceived as an attack on the known rules of survival and emotional prosperity. Under these conditions, your employee culture is unusually receptive to inspiration—to leadership.

Of course, that would have to be *real* leadership. Most of what passes for leadership in the enterprise is a corporate subversion of a beautiful concept, much more adept at getting a company what it wants if the company doesn't mess with it like companies usually do. And while a big, new goal can bring out the leaders in an organization, it often just brings out management who has crowned themselves leaders in the name of the latest strategic intent. Nothing like royalty self-decreed in a vacuum to stir the masses to a fevered pitch . . .

In fact, leadership and management are different things. They are different for your company, different for your employee culture, and different for you as a manager.

This is a subject I explored in depth in my first book, *Bury My Heart at Conference Room B*, which is about the greatest commitment by a *manager* culture and the real leadership behavior that happens as a result. That writing took eight years, was backed by a twenty-three-person research team, and is based on work with tens of thousands of managers, so I'm not going to try to cram the whole thing into this chapter. But your employee culture needs real leadership to move it forward, so here are some key points, plus new information.

THE BIGGEST MYTH OF BUSINESS LEADERSHIP: IT IS IMPORTANT

Is leadership, as it's commonly defined, some sort of all-purpose, miracle panacea for the enterprise? No. Is *real* leadership? Pretty much, yeah.

There are over 400,000 leadership book titles in print, and U.S.-based Fortune 500 companies alone spend an estimated $12.3 billion each year on leadership development for their managers. It's a safe bet that you've been preached at about it, screeched at about it, and had leadership behaviors routinely imbedded into your job description. Ever wonder where the incessant babble about leadership in the enterprise comes from? It comes from the one thing that any company wants most from its managers: emotional commitment.

Your emotional commitment is the ultimate trigger for your discretionary effort, worth more than your financial, intellectual, and physical commitment combined. A manager's emotional commitment is what solves problems that are unsolvable; creates energy when all energy has been expended; and ignites emotional commitment in others, like employees, teams, and customers. Leaders are those rare human beings who have emotional commitment and can inspire it at will in others. Legendary organizational success is at its root the result of a bunch of emotionally committed managers who protect and promote the company like a personal cause.

Any manager can appear fully productive and enthusiastic simply because they're financially, intellectually, and physically committed. But if you've ever witnessed a human being emotionally committed to a cause—working like they're being paid a million when they're not being paid a dime—you know there's a difference, and you know it's big.

IT MAY BE BIG, BUT IT'S NOT EASY

The key neurobiological source of emotional commitment is the ability to live your own deepest values in whatever relationship or environment you're involved in. As a manager, this would be in the relationship with your company and the environment at work.

"Manager" may be a great job to have, and you may be having a great time doing that job, but imbedded in any manager's job description is the constant requirement to subordinate or compromise personal values in favor of company priorities. I'm not saying you're out there committing heinous acts as part of some Faustian bargain—although even if you are, listen up—but what your company wants done and how it wants it done must regularly take precedence over your own deep priorities. That's what it means to be a manager: Serve your company first.

Put any human being in the position of having to regularly subordinate personal convictions, and they will detach emotionally to protect themselves. In a bad company that cares little about its managers' welfare, this detachment is a conscious choice. Managers in those toxic kinds of companies knowingly suit up every day for the detachment factory, leaving the best of who they are at home and hoping it will still be there when they get back.

But even in a good company that tries to do the right thing for its managers, the detachment happens anyway because of the constant tension between corporate focus and deep personal preferences that so few companies handle well. It seems disloyal even to talk about in a company that you admire so much and that does so much for you. If anything, manager detachment is more dangerous in good companies because financial, intellectual, and physical commitment combine to masquerade as the missing type: emotional commitment.

LEADERSHIP HAS TO BE SELFISH TO BE SELFLESS

Nobody is born a leader, nor are you the big swinging desk simply because you hold an elevated position in the organizational hierarchy. You don't have followers because you have head count or leadership vision because you have a bold go-to-market strategy. People only become leaders by doing the things that leaders do for the reasons that leaders do them.

Leadership is a purpose before it's ever a practice. Those 400,000 leadership books will tell you that the purpose of leadership is to increase shareholder value and team productivity. Leadership will do those things in a company, but that's not the true purpose of leadership. It never has been and it never will be. The irreducible essence of leadership is that leaders are human beings who live their own deepest values without compromise and use those values to make life better for other people. That's why people become leaders and why people follow leaders.

There isn't any leadership school that can claim history's greatest leaders as alumni. They all started somewhere and figured it out. A leader begins with an acute awareness of what's most important to them. They know their values, so they know the type of world they want to live in. Since they can't make that happen all by their lonesome, they have to turn their values into a compelling cause for others.

For all the selfless acts that leaders commit, their motivation is self-centered: They have to do something for you because they need you to do something for them. If a leader knew who they were, so they knew where they wanted to go, and knew how to go there, they'd just go. They'd send you a postcard from the Promised Land: *I have a dream. You're not in it.*

AN EXCELLENT QUESTION TO ASK— IF YOUR ATTORNEYS ARE PLANNING AN INSANITY DEFENSE

Why do you need to live your values at work? You are spending over half your waking hours at work. If you're not living those values at work, you're not living them in life. Values are your very own definition of what life looks like when you live it exactly the way you want to. Work-life balance isn't a matter of escaping from work; it's a matter of living the way you want to, whether you're at work or not.

Your values are your very own source of safety, hope, and renewal. Campaigning to live them at work is not a subversive act; it's the most supportive corporate action you can take. Your company has to really work for you before you'll really work for your company. But even if it weren't of such direct benefit to your organization, it would still be critical. If you don't know what's true for you, everyone else has unusual influence. This is your one and only precious life. Somebody's going to decide how it's going to be lived, and that person had better be you.

What do you want from your job? What do you want from your life? If these are two very different things you're going to have a problem getting either.

LET'S PUT THE "THINKING" IN NEW THINKING

The corporate purpose of leadership is essentially about getting managers to do the things that leaders *do*, like model selfless acts of devotion and inspire a group of sullen individuals to make a bloody charge up the enemy's hill and capture the fourth-quarter flag. Yet the enterprise rarely encourages the uncompromising personal motivation that provably creates leadership in the first place. If what the enterprise wants most is its managers' emotional commitment, which manifests as leadership, why resist the driver?

The great fear of the corporate organism is that if it sets managers free to pursue their own deepest priorities, they won't prioritize company goals and objectives. The intuitive organizational concern is that *real* leaders won't carry the company values wallet card; they'll carry their own, and they'll burn the corporate house down to advance their cause. This concern can be defined as reasonable. That's what iconic social leaders have often done throughout history. But only if destroying the system was the purpose of their leadership.

What if it were to protect the system? What if real leaders in your company, transformed from throughout the ranks of its managers, flourished in the belief that to protect the company was to protect their ability to gain the personal benefits of leadership—to live their most important personal values every day at work?

For this to happen, the company cannot always be the first cause. Managers' ability to practice deep personal fulfillment must also be a cause. This isn't licensing chaos; it is ensuring control. There is no better way for the company to become the cause than by not always insisting on being the cause.

A company will buy any reasonable manager action that produces business results. The companies that are most intense about performance become the most maternal about those who deliver the performance. The key to getting enterprise sanction for living your own values is to be able to tell a new story of results because you did. Monetize that story without risk to the company, and you can keep the key.

And monetize it you will: When you turn your job into a mechanism for fulfilling your deepest personal values, you'll seek to protect that mechanism by making your company even more successful. You'll think twice about leaving, since this is a rare and beautiful mechanism to have in place.

There are many empirical metrics of emotional commitment, but the biggest impact won't be seen until managers need to show it. If the company gets into trouble, only emotionally committed managers will step up to save it. If that happens even one time, your company won't be dismissing the concept again.

WE HAVE MET THE ENEMY. THEY WERE AT THE MONDAY MANAGERS' MEETING.

Amazingly, one of the reasons that emotional commitment doesn't happen naturally in managers comes from managers themselves. Put any couple of managers into a room and ask them about how they want to live and work, and how they want to live at work. They're generally sane and sensible about it; they want to bring the best of what life gives them to the job and to be able to use personal values to execute performance goals. Put those same couple of managers into a room with a bunch of other managers, and some bizarre herd mentality takes over, and they start legislating against their own best interests.

There is no evil brain in a jar behind the curtain. The conditions that managers deplore most on the job, like not being able to live their own values without hesitation or qualification, are created and maintained by managers, acting as *management*, the honor guard of the corporate organism. Noble work, but this is facing backward, guarding the wrong thing: In order to really get emotional commitment from its manager culture, a company has to allow managers to live and act according to their personal codes.

IF YOUR EMPLOYEE CULTURE HASN'T BOUGHT IT, YOU HAVEN'T SOLD IT

Buy it? Your culture is dying for your leadership, dying for the certainty and meaning that leadership provides.

In a world where everything is changing, a leader's values never do. If you can say, "This may be changing in our company, but here is who I have always been and who I will always be," then your leadership becomes a lifeline of consistency amid swirling seas of uncertainty. You may change your mind, but not your heart. True leadership is emotional coherency easily understood by an employee culture.

This declaration of what you stand for is a gift from the gods to your employee culture, because it allows the culture to put you in the middle and put itself in safe orbit around you. It always knew that if it protected what you considered most important, it protected itself—now it knows what that is.

An employee culture doesn't even mind bad news; it minds whether it can trust who is giving it the news. It is even more concerned about understanding you than understanding the company; a culture prioritizes proximity, not position. Your CEO has a bad day? That's of mild interest to your culture. *You* have a bad day? That's of wild interest to your culture. It's you who directly impacts the culture's survival and emotional prosperity.

THE NEW MATH

No matter how eloquently or expensively delivered, whether on the small screen via email or the big screen via an off-site, every management message to an employee culture is an equation that ends only one way:

$$= \text{work harder}$$

Nothing wrong with that, but it's different from a real leadership message. Every real leadership message is also an equation that ends only one way:

$$= \text{live better}$$

Your employee culture is not going to work harder unless it's convinced that this will allow it to live better. An employee culture doesn't trust strategies; it trusts leaders who bring it strategies. It can tell the difference between *I have a dream* and *I have a scheme.*

THIS IS LEADERSHIP.

"I have a dream . . ."

"With this faith . . ."

". . . hew out of the mountain of despair a stone of hope."

"The rough places will be made plain and the crooked places will be made straight . . ."

". . . transform the jangling discords of our nation into a beautiful symphony of brotherhood."

"Free at last, free at last . . ."

THIS IS MANAGEMENT.

SENT: AUGUST 21, 1963
FROM: THE REVEREND MARTIN LUTHER KING JR.
TO: ALL MARCH COORDINATORS
SUBJECT: WASHINGTON OFF-SITE

In one week's time, we will execute on our Q3 plan to increase awareness of mission-critical goals (see FY63 Organizational Objectives) required for implementation of a new civil rights strategic paradigm.

Let us never forget what is important: Preparation and seamless execution will be the keys to the success or failure of this strategy. Therefore it is imperative that all March Coordinators be responsible for verifying that KPI components of the plan are in place and dissemination of information is handled in a timely manner. I know you're busy—we're all busy—but this will allow us to stay on budget and simultaneously achieve our dream of a referenceable event.

TRANSPORTATION: Buses and other forms of public and quasi-public transportation will depart from previously announced points according to schedule. With this rate, we will all arrive in the prescribed order. With this rate, there will be little unnecessary congestion. With this rate, you won't be left behind as long as you are at the departure point on time.

CROWD CONTROL: Over 200,000 marchers are expected. Sanitation facilities adequate for maximum utilization by the number of participants will be located behind the Lincoln Memorial. Think customer-centric: Audience comforts are our concern here, not our own. Use the facilities before arriving at the event site; our own people will pee at last, pee at last.

CLEAN UP: Event permits clearly state that the coalition is solely responsible for post-event sanitation, and we want to be able to come back here for next year's strategy kick-off. We need synergy in our efforts so designated M.C.s must deputize as many "Freedom Volunteers" as they deem necessary to fulfill the coalition's responsibilities. Together, we will hew out of the mountain of trash a stone of organized, packaged waste. Make sure to explain that if they are going to be janitors, be the very best janitors, etc.

DRESS CODE: Suit and tie for presenters, march casual for everyone else.

REHEARSAL: Members of the Broadcast Subcommittee will hold a rehearsal meeting at the venue on August 27, immediately prior to the event. This will include a sound check and full run-through of all presentations. The rough places will be made plain and the crooked places will be made straight. I want all jangling discords transformed.

BOTTOM LINE: Let me say how very proud I am to be in the fellowship of dedicated professionals such as yourselves. If God is in the details, you all surely hold a special place on His logistics team.

I'll be in meetings up until event day and not checking messages. Should you have any questions, please don't hesitate to contact Jesse, Ralph or any other member of the Executive Committee.

Carry on.

BR for MLK Jr.

MLK

GIVE YOUR CULTURE INSPIRATION

In the same way that you will protect your company when it affords you the opportunity to live your values, your employee culture will protect you when you translate those values into greater certainty of the rules of survival and emotional prosperity. You have become of far greater worth to the culture, no longer an easily replaceable component as its manager.

How is your culture going to protect you? It will deliver on your strategies and performance goals. The culture has a lot of its own commitment held in reserve; giving it to you as a leader will be judged a fair price to pay for what it gets in return.

NOW, HERE'S HOW TO DO IT

1. UNDERSTAND YOUR OWN VALUES.

Your own top values will become the unshakable motivation that drives your leadership results. The first step is to figure out what those values are. Use whatever enlightenment method works best for you: books; tapes; meditation; spiritual practice; discussions with family, friends, and mentors; or stuff I can't really condone here, other than to suggest a great accompanying playlist and selection of snacks.

Don't take the process of discovery lightly or make the decision hastily: This is tricky stuff to figure out. Anyone trying to sell us something stands to profit from our not having a strong sense of self. We are trapped in a relentless, seductive fog as consumers, voters, and managers while others try to replace our priorities with theirs. Even if you admire your company's values, don't ride on its coattails—figure out your own. Also, your morals may not be the same as your values; one is the right thing to do, the other is the right thing for you to do.

Where do your values come from?

- ➤ Early upbringing
- ➤ Big decisions and the consequences of those decisions
- ➤ Personal beliefs and priorities placed under extreme pressure
- ➤ Religious and spiritual doctrines
- ➤ Intimate mentors and role models
- ➤ Significant life events
- ➤ www.tellmemyvalues.com

The most profound method for understanding your—wait a minute: the www.tellmemyvalues.com thing was a *joke*; get back here—for understanding your deepest values is called Life. Other good methods include:

- ➤ You can look at a list of common human values—not just Family and Integrity, but also Adventure, Compassion, Courage, Enlightenment, Fun, Passion, Service, Spirituality, Security, Tradition, Wisdom, and many others. See which resonate the strongest.
- ➤ You can consider what circumstances—in your own life or in the world—drive you the craziest, since this is most likely a reaction to your values being challenged.
- ➤ You can ask yourself questions both tough and tender. What have been your hardest decisions to make that felt the best? What are the three things most important to living a fulfilled life that you would tell a child?
- ➤ You can look at your life. The decisions you've made, the ones you've consciously or instinctively avoided, and the road nobody but you has seriously considered traveling.
- ➤ You can talk to others. Ask the mentors and the inspirations in your life about how they first realized what was truly important to them.

➤ You can listen to others. Do people close to you keep saying they know you better than you know yourself? Make them prove it.

➤ You can do all of these things. You knew that was coming.

2. PICK YOUR TOP THREE VALUES.

You're going to need to take a stand on just a few values. The longer your list, the less able you're going to be to even remember it, let alone get your employee culture to remember. Pick the three values that are absolutely the most important to you, that define you most as a human being, and that you'd least like to live without.

Yes, it's an artificial construct but real leaders maintain an intense focus on a few things—you know what they care about and they show a marked lack of interest in anything they don't care about. Think eating habits of a cat.

3. TURN YOUR VALUES INTO THE PROMISE OF BETTER WORKING CONDITIONS FOR YOUR CULTURE.

If you were a world leader, your leadership would be taking place on the world stage, and your promise of a better place for followers would be improved global circumstances in the name of your values. As a manager, the stage you're playing on is the work organization you supervise, and the circumstances you're promising to change as a reflection of your values are the working conditions for your employee culture.

Your definition of a better place is what life looks like with your values fully realized. The definition of a better place for your employee culture is vastly improved working conditions based on those values.

Building your vision of a better place starts with a deeper under-standing of what your values really mean to you. What makes them your top three values? Beyond the literal definitions of the words, what do these values *give* you that cause them to be so important?

If you picked Family as a value, it doesn't simply mean that you love your partner, children, or parents. Look beyond this to what those rela-tionships provide that is of such high personal priority. Is "family" a place where you are assured of unconditional support, open and honest com-munication, and when you need it, tough love? Is it a place that you can always go home to, where you can stumble and fall and still be forgiven, where you can rage on about your passions and be listened to without judgment? Is it a place where you are surrounded by people who often put your welfare ahead of their own, inspiring you to do the same for them?

This is the transferable currency you can use to define the better place for your employee culture.

MY VALUE: FAMILY

SAY TO YOURSELF: *WHAT IT GIVES ME THAT MAKES IT SO IMPORTANT*

- ➤ Unconditional support
- ➤ Open, honest communication
- ➤ Honest feedback
- ➤ Support if I make a mistake
- ➤ Involvement in and contribution to the lives of others
- ➤ Protection if something goes wrong
- ➤ Feeling good—reasons to celebrate

SAY TO YOUR EMPLOYEE CULTURE: *LET ME TAKE YOU TO A BETTER PLACE*

"This will be a place where you will never again put your job and your family into conflict without giving me the chance to do something about it. Your job and your family will be strangers no more; you're doing good, important work here, and as we celebrate that for you, we're going to roll that celebration right out to your family—the people who make it possible for you to get in here every day and do that good work. When you have something great going on at home, I don't want you to have to leave it locked up at home; you roll it in here, and we will cheer you on. Know this: If something ever seriously goes wrong at home, you will have the strength and support of this family during your hard time.

"Because we're family here, too; we're together all the time, so it's time we started acting like a family. I mean the very best of families: This team will have open, honest communication. This team will have unconditional support. When we need it, this team will have tough love, but if you ever stumble, this team will help pick you up. Under pressure, this team will never turn on this team. Instead, this team will come together to protect this team, because that's what families do, and family is very important to me."

■ ■ ■

The ultimate importance of any value is that living it allows you to feel safe, confident, and inspired. This is your better place and your employee culture is going to want to go to that better place; it would have to be crazy not to. In order to get there, the culture has to drag your values right along with it. Your culture has to manifest the very behaviors you are describing, and it has to create the very conditions in which it wants to live. If it wants open and honest communication, it's going to have to be open and honest when it communicates. If it wants unconditional support, members of the culture are going to have to support each other unconditionally.

And it will. Your employee culture just needs the focus, the sanction, and the deep commitment from you. It needs your help to "see" the better place. As soon as it sees it and decides that's what it wants, its movement forward will create the spark that ignites your leadership. If you have five people in your employee culture, that's now 500 percent more horsepower aimed at getting to your better place. If you have fifty people, that's now 5,000 percent more horsepower. If you have 500 people, hang on: You're strapped tight to a herd of hungry, nostril-twitching thoroughbreds that has just sensed far better grazing potential over the next big hill.

But remember: Your vision of a better place should not directly be a financial one. Your better place isn't about market share; it's about what your team shares. It's not about customers, financial goals, or anything else pointed outside. It's about the quality of working conditions based upon achievement of your values. It's pointed inside.

Don't worry about the financial part—remember that leadership is the first and best way of delivering on any enterprise financial objective. Instead of focusing on how the business results are going to happen, focus on getting your employee culture to want those results to happen for their own deepest reasons.

■ ■ ■

There is more mythology, misdirection, superstition, and generalized academic babble about leadership than most business subjects. You can cut through all of it by remembering this:

1. The primary *purpose* of leadership is to change the world around you in the name of your values so you can live those values more fully.
2. The primary *process* of leadership is to turn your values into a compelling cause for others so you can gain resources to help you do that.

Sure, there is much more to leadership than these steps, but these are the essential first two. Every good thing that will follow for you and your employee culture is the result of putting them into action.

THE END OF SIN: TACTICAL RECAP

THE THIRD DEADLY SIN: PLENTY OF MANAGEMENT WHERE LEADERSHIP IS NEEDED

An employee culture doesn't trust strategies; it trusts leaders who bring it strategies. But that would be real leadership, which comes from a manager's sure understanding of their deepest personal values and the translation of those values into the promise of better working conditions.

1. Bring your own values to work.

Take the time to be certain what they are, refuse to subordinate them on the job, and earn the room to move by turning them into the story of how you got increased performance.

2. Pick your top three values.

You have a lot of values but the longer your list the harder it will be for you to evangelize it and your culture to remember it. Pick the three values that are absolutely the most important to you. The three that define you most as a human being and that you could not imaging living without.

3. Turn your values into the promise of better working conditions for your culture.

This is how you'll get that increased performance: Move beyond the literal definition of those values to what they give you that makes them so important. Build an environment for your culture that gives it this same benefit.

BOTTOM LINE:
Give Your Employee Culture INSPIRATION

All I was doing was appealing for an endorsement, not suggesting you endorse it.

—George H. W. Bush

THE FOURTH DEADLY SIN
SAY WHAT?

I heard it through the grapevine.

—Marvin Gaye

OMMUNICATING TO an employee culture and convincing it are different concepts, and the first doesn't guarantee the second. The purpose of communication to employees is to inform; the purpose of communication to an employee culture is to persuade.

To be persuasive, management communication has to be sincere, heartfelt, and empathetic to the lives of those receiving it. There's not much point in talking to the culture in a formal, detached manner, unless you're seeking a formal, detached response.

It also has to be simple. Managers often attempt to engage the culture with an obscure, proprietary management buzz lexicon in the belief that it makes them sound intelligent, but you sound intelligent only when people understand what you're talking about. Your employee culture won't join you in the thrilling hunt for the elusive Bird of Meaning. If the culture can't immediately make management communication relevant to its own concerns, it will ignore you or make up its own definition. Any language perceived as an attempt to obscure a message will be perceived as an attempt to deceive.

An employee culture won't pay attention just to what you say. It will note how often you say it, to whom you say it, how you prioritize it, and whether you regularly relate it to happenings in the business. Your culture is wondering whether to care about the message by deciding how much you care about it yourself. If what you're saying was driven by your real passion, you would never stop talking about it and you would always talk about it first. If it's another transient "life as we know it will come to an end unless . . ." phlegmy bellow from management, an employee culture will wait disinterestedly for the End of Days while it turns its attention elsewhere.

An employee culture will also consider the placement it receives within the message. Take any list of organizational priorities, from a new go-to-market model or revenue goal to the "one company" initiative that is routinely foisted on an employee culture like the predictable reappearance of hurricane season and tax debt: The welfare and value of the employee culture is inevitably the last bullet point on the PowerPoint slide, listed after the need to satisfy enterprise, analyst, investor and customer constituencies. Those constituencies are vital to the company, but it is the employee culture that will shoulder much of the burden to satisfy them, and when it is again reminded of its place at the bottom of the totem pole, it disengages some due to the implied lack of respect.*

WHY YOUR CULTURE KEEPS YOU WAITING

If you do your level best to communicate sincerely and endearingly, and the reaction is . . . *crickets* . . . the culture isn't dismissing the message. Unless your employee culture is actively angry about something, lack of an immediate response isn't a hostile response. Your culture is also listening to what else it's hearing at the same time and what else it has heard before, and it's up to its knees in the management message Dumpster, sifting through all those banana peels and used diapers for the probable truth.

Wildly mixing metaphors isn't the brightest thing for me to do when advising you about effective communication, but to further make this important point: The culture will take your message to its own jury room for deliberation before delivering you a veracity verdict.

Don't despair if the culture's verdict is a cynical one. Cynicism doesn't mean your employee culture doesn't care. Apathy would mean your employee culture doesn't care. Cynicism means it hurts to care, and the culture still has plenty of commitment to give if it can be convinced it's safe and sane to give it.

When corporate communication meets cynical with chirpy, it only reinforces the hurt. The culture translates this perky propaganda as intimating: "There's nothing else happening in your world, and we've

---

* The bottom of the totem pole? That's the sharp end.

never tried to sell you something that didn't work out as promised. Let's go!"

Much of the communication to an employee culture is talking, not listening; it's all about telling and selling. You are expecting your employee culture to perform like an adult; don't talk to it like a child.

If you want an employee culture to take you to a new place, you've got to talk to it like it really talks to itself. You don't have to agree with the culture's reluctance to immediately embrace a message, but you have to respect the reluctance. Don't debate the cynicism; acknowledge it in order to transform it into optimism.

THE SOUNDS OF SILENCE

A culture doesn't love to communicate; a culture *lives* to communicate. What does it mean, then, if your employee culture tends toward quiet? It may mean nothing at all: The culture isn't talking to you all the time, but it's always talking to itself, so your demands are still being socialized.

Quiet isn't the same as silent. A restrained employee culture is saying little: It's a manner. A *silent* employee culture is saying a lot: It's a message. Don't worry if the culture isn't constantly babbling, but listen hard if it stops making any sound at all when it should be talking to you. Never misinterpret lingering cultural silence as agreement, compliance, or an indication that the culture has nothing to say. The culture is saying something loudly, and its silence is an action that you should investigate.

Cultural silence is a protective organizational response that could indicate big mistrust of you or the company. If the relationship with the company or its management is perceived as incurably erratic or autocratic, what's the point in the culture contributing to the dialogue?

Should some members of an employee culture believe the relationship goes far enough to compromise their personal values, silence becomes a withdrawal behavior, and this can quickly spread throughout the culture, which won't be silent at all about it—among itself. The employee culture's attention is then focused on monitoring heightened threat conditions, and it's operating in a state of aggressive detachment. The silence is now both defensive and offensive: Sorry, no time to chat.

You can't stay stuck in a silent world with your employee culture. If all of your efforts to herd it to greater productivity are met with a bovine stare, you're going to have to find out why and fix it. As with all things cultural, look to yourself first, and consider what behaviors may have caused your employee culture to believe that silence is the only language you'll understand. Feedback from your culture is a valuable gift—when the culture speaks and when it doesn't.

Just like you're considering the implications of your culture's silence, the culture will be considering the implications of yours. Aristotle said nature abhors a vacuum* and so does an employee culture: It assumes that management silence is deliberate, a choice to not explain something, which is viewed by the culture as disrespect or cause for alarm.

An employee culture figures that management silence could also indicate the lowering of a priority. An impassioned message about product or process quality that is front-loaded during employee onboarding, then rarely mentioned again, isn't translated by the culture as being so imbedded into the fabric of the company that it need not be spoken about. It is translated as "Quality must no longer be an enterprise obsession." The culture then becomes less confident about protecting it as a guideline for its own safety and less willing to represent it to customers as a source of its positive sense of self.

Your employee culture may attempt to rectify management silence with questions, but they aren't often questions in a literal sense. The culture is looking for information, not answers. How will you respond when it asks you? Will you tell the truth, admit if you don't know, care enough to answer carefully and completely, return with a better expla-

---

* He meant that nature requires every space to be filled with something, which is a typically astute observation from someone who many historians consider the smartest person to ever walk the land (if he was so smart why didn't he drive?). Aristotle also licked his hands to go to sleep. Presumably the key to our modern application of that breakthrough experiment is in the estimated two-thirds of his writings that have never been recovered.

nation as promised? This is cultural sonar seeking to identify whether you can be trusted.

THE BEST WAY TO TALK TO YOUR CULTURE . . . IS NOT TO

There are a lot of ways to communicate with an employee culture. Oddly enough, directly isn't the best. The best way to talk to your culture is to get it to talk to itself.

An employee culture communicates through legends—true stories that can be transmitted immediately within the culture, stored for quick retrieval, and even bequeathed to the next generation. A story attains legend status when it serves as a clear proof point about the culture's survival or emotional prosperity. Legends are a carefully vetted and curated database and the culture's most protected asset.

OKAY SO FAR? CLING TO THAT, BECAUSE HERE WE GO

A culture legend will reliably happen whenever you do something significant to protect or violate what you say is most important. Once the culture perceives that as credible and telling, it will communicate it among its own population. A legend is spread rapidly and completely. It's listened to carefully, taken seriously, and considered true by everyone, although the irony of cultural legends is that something has to be exaggerated to be believable.

That's what becomes a legend—something prominent enough to be worth adding to the survival database. Yet one of the remarkable things about cultural legends is that the legends themselves aren't exaggerated at all when passed from one employee to another. These aren't fish stories (except among fish cultures).

There will never be hardware, software, satellite, or Internet technology that spreads information faster and more accurately than an employee culture. A cultural legend is a bullet train on the Underground Railroad. Legends remain in the culture's database as a relevant survival guide unless new ones are accepted that update or replace them. Over a period of years, even when you've diligently hunted down and dispatched all the original witnesses, a cultural legend will retain all the meaning and nuances of the actual event. These legends have life spans beyond the lives involved when they originally occurred. Your employee culture will believe stories about you even if not a single current member was around when the story was first generated.

This. Is. Survival. Information.

It doesn't matter what you demand from your employee culture. The combined power of these legends greatly decides what the culture will do and what it won't do. Members of your employee culture know the legends by heart, and they refer to them constantly.

Who are these legends most often about? They are most often about you, due to your unique position of influence on the culture's survival and emotional prosperity. You are the Chief—but don't get a swelled head about that or the culture will shrink it right down for you. As with the granting of many titles in the corporate jungle, this one's not all it's cracked up to be. It's just short for "chief subject of all the stories."

When will you hear these legends? You will never hear these legends, because they represent what your employee culture has figured out are the rules of survival and emotional prosperity in your world. If it were to reveal to you what it has figured out are the rules when working for you, what is the first thing you would do? Change the rules. What is the possible upside for your employee culture to reveal to you that it's collected this information?

YOU'RE NEW? THE CULTURE TALKS FAST

If you're fresh to the company or even just fresh as manager to the team, the culture will collect the information fast. The For-Culture-

Ears-Only dossier will arrive well before you do, crammed with juicy info gleaned by probing your prior employee cultures for legends of your personal veracity, supervisory style, and emotional hot buttons. It will be communicated thoroughly within the culture by that first day, when you innocently pull into the parking lot in anticipation of introducing your bevy of potential followers to their new leader.

THEY'RE NEW? THE CULTURE TALKS FAST

What if a member of the culture is new to you? Let's say you've decided to take control and start your next new employee off right, avoiding the risk of germy contamination from the general population. You invite this fresh meat, Bob, to your office, first thing in the morning of his first day. "Bob, welcome to the most important company in the most important industry in the world," you proclaim grandly. "Your arrival is so vital—to me, to our company, to our industry, to our solar system—that I've decided to take the whole day off to personally orient you to the company." True to your word, you guide him through every perk and policy, from stock options to registering his own stapler.

Are you done? You're just getting started. "Bob, when I say the words 'strategic intent,' what does that mean to you?" you ask. Without waiting for a stuttering response from your naïve new vessel, you pivot swiftly to the projector and big screen, then proceed to fill him to the brim with the company's epic strategy for conquest, including an explanation of every competency, table stake, milestone, and benchmark necessary to achieve it. "A *very* smart strategy, I think you'll agree," you whisper dramatically, and then you pounce: "Bob, *you* are the linchpin on which this entire strategy depends!"

Are you done? No, you leap onto the desk, and thrust out an arm. "Take my hand and let me take you to a better place!" you implore and proceed to deliver an impassioned leadership speech about how, together, you and he will vanquish formidable obstacles and scale great heights.

Are you done? Yes, you are confident at last that you have taken Bob to the river and evangelically stuffed his head underwater in what must surely have been a transformational organizational baptism. He's bonded to your worldview now, and his faith won't easily be sullied by any confrontations with workplace reality. As you walk him to the door, you apply one final dollop of cultural cement by assuring him that "The door to my office—no, scratch that—the door to my *heart* is always open to you."

Has Bob listened to this message? Definitely. He is new to this world, and what he wants to know most are the rules of survival and emotional prosperity in an unfamiliar jungle. There are two ways he can learn: step wrong and land in the quicksand, or be lucky enough to get a primer directly from the Chief, who has explicitly defined those rules.

So he holds on tightly to this information, walking out of your office. He holds on tightly to it, walking around the corner. He holds on tightly to it, sitting down in his cubicle for the first time. He holds on tightly to it, until two heads stick around the corner, and say, "You're the new guy? Let's go to lunch."

Uh-oh. Your new disciple has just been paid a visit by the cultural welcome wagon. The employee culture knows that the more people in the culture looking out for its safety, the better. It's not going to let a new arrival orbit out there alone; it's going to bring them in to begin contributing. It's going to do it by gifting them with a legend that affords essential protection.

That legend will be about you. It will be a true story about how you've declared what is most important to you and, when under pressure or temptation to compromise, you've proved you mean it. This would be *great* for you, because this is culture-to-culture advocacy of how you want your organization to run.

Or . . .

Your employee culture will tell them a true story about how you've declared what is most important to you and, when under pressure or temptation to compromise, you failed to support it. This would be the *opposite of great* for you, because this is culture-to-culture dismissal of how you want your organization to run.

Good legend or bad, all those hours you spent filling up Bob's emotional hard drive didn't matter. That drive has just been wiped clean in the time it took for the culture to talk to the culture.

Whether you're new or they're new, it isn't how long the relationship is that matters most; it's how long it takes your employee culture to trust you. While certainly preferred, your culture doesn't even have to like you to trust you. It has to be able to confirm the dependable rules of survival and emotional prosperity when it's working for you.

DO THIS NOW
GIVE YOUR CULTURE BELIEVABILITY

Much has been made of the special language and rituals of a culture. Forget all of that; that's what the tourists see. You won't ever witness the real stuff, and besides, that's not what's most important. You'll never affect how the culture communicates. What you must affect is *what* the culture communicates.

NOW, HERE'S HOW TO DO IT

This is a matter of deliberately causing cultural legends that reinforce what you want from the culture: in essence, writing the script the culture reads to itself when considering what behavior will best impact its survival and emotional prosperity. A legend is information inserted by the culture into the pipe that flows dependably into its own belief system. A culture's obsession with its own well-being ensures that it will adjust its behavior to take advantage of any information it perceives is beneficial.

Your employee culture will give you all sorts of indications of its true perceptions. You just have to know how to read them, which is a whole lot easier if you're the one who wrote them.

Grand acts alone won't convince your employee culture of anything. A culture is focused on its survival and so it places a premium on consistency—it's looking for a pattern of management behavior, so the small things in between the big things are most important to the culture in gauging dependability. However, legends are critical to getting the culture's attention and creating awareness of linkage to important management behaviors that might otherwise go unnoticed.

1. MAKE IT VERY CLEAR WHAT YOU STAND FOR.

There are two ways to create cultural legends: Declare what is most important to you, then prove it, or prove it first, then retroactively point out the linkage between what you do and what you say.

Both methods have to be reliable to work, but the first is more expedient. Be emphatic, then dramatic. If you go with talk-it-before-you-walk-it, you'll need to undeniably declare your intention in order to set the legend process in motion. Explain very clearly what is important to you—as a person, as a manager. No matter which method you use to set a legend in motion, though, make sure that the intention you declare comes from a deep conviction that you'll support intuitively, rapidly, and consistently.

This will make it easier to remember to say it, which is important, because your employee culture is going to have to remember you said it. Redundancy is your friend here: Say what you have to say again, and again, and again, and again. Your culture won't think, "We're hearing this again, and it's patronizing." It will think, "We're hearing this again, and it could be valuable."

2. DO SOMETHING SIGNIFICANT TO PROVE THAT YOU MEAN IT.

Manager actions that become legendary are usually memorable to your culture from the outset: They are provocative or profound, unexpected, never-thought-we'd-see-it, and sometimes flat-out loony. But they are always linked to that declaration of what's important to you and so they are always relevant to the culture.

You can cut through the chronic red tape that your culture has always viewed as a punishing obstacle to getting its job done. You can provide creative reinforcement for protecting what you've declared is most important. You can climb deep into the customer or product development experience—or whatever organizational end point most of the culture regularly deals with, with its own good name. You can take swift disciplinary action for violations of what you've declared is most important, even if it's aimed at someone with sacred cow status. You can protect what you say is most important under stress or temptation to compromise. You can be willing to play the fool in order to make a point of appreciation for success.

When you declare that anything is especially important, have a legendary action in your pocket, ready to be announced. Do it right then or within weeks, so the culture links what you've said with what you're willing to do to support it. Before announcing it to your employee culture, look ahead to see where it's most likely to encounter pressure and prepare to deal with it. Your unshakable commitment and decisive action when the hammer falls will become the stuff of legend.

One of the biggest opportunities to create a legend is when the hammer falls right on the culture and someone has to go. It doesn't matter if it was individually deserved and your decision, or if was enterprise-justified but not your decision. Letting someone go is rarely a happy experience, is rarely well handled by managers, and is rarely well received by the rest of the employee culture.

If the person leaving did a good job when they worked for you, ask them to provide their top few recommendations about how best to work in the organization, and circulate these to the culture as a legacy statement. Send a note to their family confirming the quality and importance of their work and how much they'll be missed. Keep them at least somewhat connected to the team instead of pretending like they never existed the day after they left. Pick a date on the calendar to check in with them. Celebrate with your culture their success in finding another job. If you can officially help them, do it. If you can't officially help them, do it any way you can.

If you believe the person leaving was the employee from hell, sent as your karmic payback for transgressions on a scale you can't imagine having committed in a hundred lifetimes—and even your *culture* begged you to get rid of them—treat that person well anyway. The treatment is simultaneously being noted by the rest of your employee culture, which is still closer to one of its own than to you. Bury your dead with dignity. Your behavior here is considered a trustworthy indicator of how you truly value the rest of the culture. No matter how justified, choke down those "Let the doorknob hit you where the good Lord split you" comments; focus on your own accountability and the departing person's dignity instead. Overtly wish them better days and never, ever talk badly about them after they've gone. If they've done damage to the culture, focus efforts where they belong—making that team strong again.

If the RIFs are big enough to make news outside the company do not release a statement that solely justifies them in anticipation of revenue improvement. That's a message for analysts and major shareholders, intent at winning their pockets. To win the hearts and minds of not only the employee culture inside your company but of all the employee cultures outside your company (a.k.a. your customers), make it clear in that statement that you have sympathy for those who are being sacrificed. Mention highlights of what you're doing for them to aid in their career transition, and offer appreciation of their efforts and best wishes for their future.

To gain the most from those who are left, you have to give the most to those who are leaving. There's only so much you can or should communicate through email. Be present to your employee culture during this period of unpleasantness. The culture realizes that you don't have to do it and probably don't want to do it. Duly noted.

Cultural legends don't have to be outrageous acts; they have to be actions that are noticed as legitimate connections between what you say and what you do—as with all things cultural, real is what matters. On the other hand, no need to rule out outrageous if you can do it.

Nor do they have to always be created solely by the chief executive officer in your company to have impact. Of course, such an act by the CEO would mean something to the employee culture, as an indication of what matters by the person who makes decisions of consequence for the enterprise. Remember, though, that it's your own decisions that have the most immediate consequences for your employee culture. Your culture is closer to you—if not in affection, at least in observation—so the linkage between what you say and what you do means more, because it's easier to confirm.

Having said that, there are some CEOs who are natural-born positive legend machines, and their actions are good to study—admittedly, sometimes from a safe distance. The proof points these folks create for their employee cultures aren't born from Machiavellian calculation; they're born from unshakable personal passion that causes legendary—and occasionally lunatic—acts. Here are a couple examples of cultural legends created by chief executives. One, you could possibly try a version of on your own. One, you should never, ever try a version of on your own.

YOU HAD TO BE THERE. EVEN IF IT WAS A REAL HASSLE

▶ Tom Mendoza was president of technology giant NetApp from 2000 to 2008, and he remains the company's vice chairman. He has a BA in economics from Notre Dame, but let's go ahead and give him an honorary doctorate in cultural legends, for the purity and power of moves like these. I'll let Tom explain them to you:

"I hired a guy to run the Israel division of NetApp who was fantastic for us. His name is Shlomo Nataf, really just a fantastic guy. Number one market share, the whole thing. And then he retired, and our employees in Israel asked if two of the founders, Dave and James, and I, the CEO, would speak on film for a few minutes about what Shlomo has meant to the company, and, of course, we did that.

"So I went to a football game, in South Bend, Indiana, the weekend when they were going to hold his retirement event. And I'm sitting there telling somebody the stories about this guy, and they said, 'He's been with you how long?' I said, 'Only thirteen years, but he made an incredible contribution,' and it hit me that I should go to Israel. And it was one of those things—as soon as I said it, I was embarrassed that I wasn't going.

"Now it's Saturday in South Bend, and Monday is the event in Israel—which is Sunday here—but I still have to see customers that weekend, and I have to be back in Silicon Valley on Tuesday. My assistant said, 'Listen, you won't even land in Israel until five on Monday and the event is at seven, and you'll have to turn right around and fly back.' I said, 'Okay, let's do it.'

"I'd had an exhausting weekend, but I got on the plane, and the whole way, I'm laughing, thinking how cool is this? Nobody in Israel knows I'm coming except one person, because I had to have somebody help me through security. So I get there, I walk backstage right as they're showing the movie. And it's like, we had about 500 people there, including customers, friends, family—I mean, it was a big, big deal. And when that screen came up, I was just sitting there. It didn't matter what I said—I must have given some little talk—but that didn't matter. That I was there meant something to the employee culture, and that it clearly meant something to me mattered even more.

"Another time I was in Singapore and I got a call from the person who ran the North Carolina division, where we run three shifts, and we're having some motivational issues on the late shift. Could I come out there sometime in the next few months? I looked at my calendar and I realized that unless I go now, I can't. I'm in the club that says Singapore Air, and so I said to my admin, 'How would I get to North Carolina?' Unfortunately, there's not a Singapore—North Carolina shuttle service. I flew home seventeen hours to L.A., changed, repacked, and took the red-eye right out again. As people were getting off their shift, I was standing there the next day. And I spent, I'd say, eight hours speaking to groups of fifty every forty minutes—so almost every person. Just talked and listened and let them see me. And the next day, I was in New York City for meetings.

"I think it's as simple as this: The culture doesn't care what you know until it knows that you care. So when you say it, you'd better mean it, and the more uncomfortable it is, the harder it is, the better, because now when your employee culture says, 'What can I give?' you're the example. 'If he's willing to do that, who am I to do less?'"

YOU HAD TO BE THERE. EVEN IF YOU REALLY WISH YOU WEREN'T

▶ Apple and Samsung have always been competitive companies; in technology, against their own former best efforts, and seemingly even in the ability of Steve Jobs versus Lee Kun-Hee to be the best nonstop legend machine to their respective employee cultures.

Jobs was justifiably lauded for his passion and dramatics. But for every painstakingly handcrafted iPod prototype that he purportedly tossed into an aquarium to prove to his engineers that there was room to make it thinner ("See? Bubbles."), there is Gumi.

Sorry, no contest.

First, some background: Lee took over the company when his father died in 1987. On his watch, he's built it into the world's biggest electronics manufacturer, with annual revenue today closing fast on $200 billion. But that's just Samsung Electronics: The Samsung empire also includes construction (it built the Burj Khalifa in Dubai, the world's tallest building), engineering, transportation, health care, life insurance, and shipbuilding (it's the second-largest shipbuilder in the world). All in, Samsung accounts for seventeen percent of South Korea's entire GDP and employs 370,000 people in more than eighty countries.

The company leans heavily Confucian, with deep respect for order and hierarchy in general, and specifically for the mysterious Chairman Lee, who rarely shows up at headquarters these days and never gives interviews. He doesn't need to: Lee has permanent "Dear Leader" status within his company. (You know you want that.)

Okay, so about Gumi, which you can file under "don't try this at your company," but which you can't deny made the point in a legendary way. It happened in March 1996, although the employee culture at Samsung swears it took place yesterday at 8:14 a.m.—it remains that vivid. It seems that for 1995 New Year's gifts, Lee had sent out Samsung's new wireless phone to friends, family, and important business associates. They would have called him to say thanks, but that was difficult: The phones didn't work too well.

Uh-oh.

It is a chilly March morning in the South Korean city of Gumi, where Samsung manufactures its computers, fax machines, TVs, and . . . phones. As they prepare to begin their day, the factory's 2,000 employees are suddenly summoned to the courtyard for a surprise visit from Chairman Lee! They quickly assemble, each wearing a headband with the company's slogan, *Quality First*, and they are quivering in anticipation of a stirring sermon from their leader. It is a brisk 35 degrees outside, but someone has lit a roaring bonfire that warms the entire area. That Chairman Lee, always thinking about his people.

Oddly enough, Chairman Lee is standing in front of a sky-high mountain of consumer electronics equipment. Employees gaze up at it in baffled wonder; it is as if the factory's entire 150,000-piece inventory has been heaped into a towering pile. Wait a minute—that *is* the factory's *entire 150,000-piece inventory heaped into a towering pile*. Lee stares at his employees with steely eyes. They stare wide-eyed back at him. The only sound is the crackling of the fire. Then, suddenly, at Lee's command, ten men with sledgehammers proceed to smash every single piece of equipment to pieces. And toss them onto the blazing flames.

At which point, Chairman Lee finally speaks. "Fix it, or I'll be back," he snarls.

Today, the question of whether *Quality First* was picked out of a slogan book never really comes up within the Samsung employee culture. And the new phones work just fine.

The Frankfurt Declaration

Even before the Gumi Roast there was the Frankfurt Declaration. Chairman Lee already had a reputation for—let's just be charitable and say *focus.* On a world tour of retailers in 1993, he noticed that Samsung was still merchandised as a second-tier product, behind Sony and Panasonic. He was bothered by it first in California; by the time he hit Germany, he was livid.

He summoned several hundred of Samsung's top managers to a meeting at the Falkenstein Grand Kempinski Hotel in Frankfurt, locked them in a meeting room, and delivered a speech lasting three full days—kind of like the Fidel Castro of consumer electronics—outlining his passionate plan to transform Samsung into the biggest and most powerful electronics manufacturer on the planet. The message? Samsung was in crisis and needed to do things differently, and there wasn't a minute to spare. Key quote: "Change everything but your wife and children."

Today this visionary speech is reverently known within all of Samsung as the Frankfurt Declaration. The doctrines that the chairman presented are called "Lee Kun-Hee-isms" and have gospel significance at the company. They are repeated constantly and deeply adhered to by the employee culture.

At Samsung's Human Resources Development Center near Seoul, the company has created an exact replica of that original Frankfurt conference room. It paid the hotel to strip it and ship it, right down to the pink tablecloth, fake flower arrangement, and painting of Venice that was on the wall. Photography is forbidden inside this shrine and employees speak in hushed whispers. The Frankfurt Declaration philosophy is also available in the home version, a 200-page book that all members of the Samsung employee culture are expected to study carefully. And the company has produced a comic book version for the less literate but equally committed.

THE END OF SIN: TACTICAL RECAP

THE FOURTH DEADLY SIN: SAY WHAT?

The purpose of communicating to your employee culture is to persuade, not to inform. Keep it heartfelt, empathetic, and free of management buzz lexicon. Acknowledge the culture's natural cynicism rather than pretending it doesn't or shouldn't exist. It doesn't mean your employee culture doesn't care; it means it hurts to care. And don't assume a lack of response means that your culture has nothing to say; it's often trying to tell you something with its silence.

The best way of communicating to an employee culture is to get it to communicate to itself. A message from the culture to the culture has more credibility than anything you send from your position outside of it. To do this, deliberately create cultural legends that speak on your behalf.

1. Make it very clear what you stand for.

Make your standards, intentions, and point of view very clear to set context for our actions.

2. Do something significant to prove that you mean it.

Take significant, provocative, exaggerated action to support what you say is most important, including advocating it relentlessly, protecting it under threat, and reinforcing support for it. This will create a legend for your employee culture: a clear link between what you say and what you do that serves as a proof point about how it should align its own actions to stay safe in your world.

BOTTOM LINE

Give Your Employee Culture BELIEVABILITY

How can you expect to govern a country that has 246 kinds of cheese?

—Charles de Gaulle

THE FIFTH DEADLY SIN

PAY WHAT?

Them belly full (but we hungry).

—Bob Marley

COMPANIES REGULARLY overestimate the importance an employee culture places on money. It's not that the culture doesn't like money. It likes the money, it will take the money, and it will ask for more money. But a culture's concerns are chronological and specific: Survival comes first, then comes prosperity, which is emotional, not fiscal.

Your employee culture wants to know the meaning of the money. Offering a bonus if your employee culture works harder, works differently? Your culture wants to know if that bonus is a reliable indicator of its increased safety. An employee culture gets really annoyed if it has to sweat to figure this out. After all, it might guess wrong, leaving it vulnerable—in many companies a bonus one day does not ensure job security the next. Besides, it already had to sweat to get the bonus. Now the culture wants to see the company sweat. It wants to see performance reinforcement that shows some respect for what the culture actually cares about.

Most compensation systems focus on money. The better ones focus on what money buys. The best ones—that deliver maximum cultural impact—focus on what money can't buy: security and a sense of self.

Money will get you a lot of things, but it can't get you what it can't buy, and what it can't buy is the most valuable of all to your employee culture. Money will only help your culture survive outside of the company, not inside. Your employee culture wants peace of mind a lot more than it wants a piece of the pie.

GOLDEN SLUMBERS

The war for talent rages on today, as companies seek to secure top performers in a hypercompetitive market, but it's not the first time it's been fought. It happened first about fifteen years ago and was waged mostly by the information technology industry, where the impact of individual contributors is considerable and runaway growth required runaway head count to keep pace. To recruit and retain, IT companies slathered money and stock options on people—any people. You know what I mean if you were there: Some of this talent was well worth it, but ridiculously rich packages were extended to some whose skill set apparently peaked at fogging up a mirror, and only if said mirrors were placed directly under their noses for a considerable length of time.

Many employees became multimillionaires; some of my company's IT clients had problems with a chronically absent employee culture. People weren't calling in sick; they were calling in rich, when managing their multiple new rental properties couldn't be done within a one-hour lunch break.

And yet all that money didn't ground these employee cultures to their companies, didn't halt turnover, and didn't sustainably increase productivity. Instead, people became day traders with their own careers, moving in a constant, restless search for the next-highest bidder to whom they could pledge temporary allegiance. A new class of migrant workers was born: *The Beaujolais Nouveau of Wrath.*

This was because the critical signals linking money to meaning were missing for the employee culture. Fat as it was, compensation was treated by these companies as a commodity, so their cultures treated it like a commodity, too. During this same time, we also had clients who operated good companies in more traditional industries. They initially despaired at being unable to fete their employee cultures in a competitive fashion but found that giving the most they could and attaching dependable linkage between performance reinforcement and safety meant the cultures didn't feel diminished and didn't give diminished loyalty to their companies.

In many companies the connection between compensation and what an employee culture cares about remains inconsistent and undependable—two conditions that are anathema to an employee culture, which prizes consistency and dependability *as* compensation. Cultures in these companies have learned to suck the cactus for whatever emotional nourishment they can find; they get some, but it's exhausting and it hurts.

THE TERROR OF RE-GIFTING

▶ Microsoft has asked me to meet with some of their people in the Taiwan office. The purpose is to improve the customer experience, but that's not what's foremost on their minds when they learn I'm from America. "You need to tell Bill Gates to stop sending us these clocks!" they plead. They are referring to the large gold desk clocks that Microsoft sends employees as anniversary gifts.

They seem like very nice clocks.

And it seems like a thoughtful gesture from Microsoft headquarters in Redmond to employees anywhere in the world who are celebrating their tenth year with the company.

Except in China, where giving someone a clock is considered a grave insult—almost literally. It is intended to remind you of the diminishing minutes of your life, a signal of your impending doom. It's a gift of menace, and presenting this device to an employee is like sending a note saying thanks for all the good work—pinned to a bloody horse's head.

"Have you talked to Redmond about it?" I ask.

"Yes!" they screech.

"What did they say?" I ask.

"They keep sending us these clocks!" they wail.

"What do you do with them?" I ask.

"Oh, we give them to customers. They are very nice clocks," they shrug.

Note: These circumstances occurred a while ago. Microsoft since announced it was "upgrading" to new years of service awards. Presumably with something that downgraded the terror experienced by some of those who used to receive them.

DO THIS NOW

GIVE YOUR CULTURE MEANING

Money is a fickle opiate to an employee culture; it doesn't mean that much if it's provided as a substitute for what really does. Since your employee culture uses that money to buy meaning, might as well skip the middleman and give the meaning directly. The good news is that you have an unlimited budget to provide what money can't buy.

Anything that motivates a human being motivates an employee culture.

+

Anything that motivates an employee culture is compensation.

=

Anything that is compensation should be managed with extraordinary care.

The quality of care that a company gives to compensation is decided by a combination of *attitude* about whether the employee culture deserves to share in the success of the company; the *need* to compete in acquiring talent, keeping it and keeping it productive; and the *resources* an enterprise believes it can use to act on the attitude and need. This whole book is about making the case for the attitude and the need—we're on the Fifth Sin here already. As to the resources, it has been neurobiologically proven that external rewards will not achieve sustained internal motivation in human beings. It doesn't matter whether you can fund it; extraordinarily realized compensation requires moving past the culture's pocket to its heart.

1. FOCUS ON WHAT MONEY CAN'T BUY.

MATCH IT TO THE DNA

Match compensation features to the principles and personality of the company, which presumably resonated enough with members of the employee culture that they joined the company in the first place. Your product is innovative? Make sure performance reinforcement is innovative. You service the world as a global enterprise? Open the world to your culture as a reward. You market the company as having a provocative or whacked personality? Apply the exact same provocation or twisted ethic to reinforcement.

Use compensation to reinforce results, but don't just reinforce the actual achievement; reinforce also the spirit in which it was achieved—celebrate how, not just how much. If results were consistent with the character of your company and your culture made an obvious effort to protect or advocate that character on the way to reaching the goal, pointedly overreact by increasing reinforcement from what it would have been for just meeting the objectives any old way. This will be an energy-producing signal to your culture that the character of the company matters and your return on the spend will be greater.

MAKE MANAGEMENT TRANSPARENT

Every manager of an employee culture has learned some things—somewhere and somehow—that they consider most important about how to do it well. Query your own managers about their most important lesson, including what they wish they'd known before they learned it, then collect these lessons into an online or hard copy book, featuring a single page per manager, with each explaining their epiphany.

Don't make it available only to your managers; make it available to your employee culture.

Some of the lessons are bound to be from making mistakes, managers being human and all, which is bound to elicit a supportive response from the employee culture, it being comprised of humans, too. It will help your culture better understand the pressures and motivations that drive management decisions and behaviors.

This is important knowledge that will help the culture to anticipate management actions and reactions; if there were a store that sold this sure anticipatory sense, your employee culture would be lined up around the block to buy it. As a gift with purchase (for you), this will allow your employee culture to be more empathetic to the experience of a manager as evolutionary, a process of continuous lessons learned.

EXTEND THE IMPACT

Let the reinforcement of performance cascade from your culture to those who surround your culture and to those who are most important to your culture:

- Ensure a connection between those who get top performance reinforcement and the security of their jobs. Well . . . yeah . . . that should exist anyway and usually does for the best performers in sales or engineering organizations, but many a corporate reorganization has washed out good people, recently recognized for good performance, who have less visible profiles. If a recently lauded member of an employee culture in the Manhattan office finds that their job has suddenly moved to Macau without them, they won't be the only one who cares. The rest of the culture will wonder if this is an indication of the company's ultimate plan and true character.

- Include life goals with performance goals, especially if your employee culture is being asked to protect the business as if it were life itself. Imbed these personal growth goals (learning, pursuing personal values satisfaction) into your employee culture's performance objectives—whatever the employee equivalent of an MBO program you have in place (or, you know, should have). Assume that the more personally fulfilled the members of your employee culture are, the more they will support the company that encouraged the fulfillment.

- Erect a huge Heroes of [the Company] monument, onto which any employee whose over-the-top act that protects what the company stands for gets their name etched forever. Put that monument in the executive offices where your CEO and senior team will see it or in the lobby where customers, vendors, and job applicants will see it. Give the honorees a different business card that invites conversation about their special status. Seriously upgrade their workspace to an extent that it causes teeth-gnashing envy in their peers: furniture (there are plenty of ostentatiously overdesigned desk chairs to choose from), technology (the latest and greatest, possibly above their pay grade), and art (let them pick a large, limited-edition photo of a favorite musician or personal cultural inspiration). Have them write a POV piece about your company or industry for your website; if someone made it to the statue, they should make it to the site.

- Use job recruitment collateral to talk to prospective new members about the existing culture. Don't talk solely about the requirements applicants must have or the standard corporate pitch about the company; talk about how you admire and honor your employee culture. Here's the standard to aim for: Printouts of your recruitment advertising should be good enough to be posted on office walls by people who aren't applying for a job with your company but who fantasize about being treated that way by their own company. We often get this kind of response from my own company's recruitment marketing, which we always end with:

We promise to pay you well, work you hard, make you laugh, drive you crazy, treat you with respect, and allow you to be great.

In your own recruitment marketing and job descriptions, show the culture what it's like to be managed in the position they're applying for—what your managers are held accountable for regarding the supervision, growth, and fulfillment of their people. This is not only attractive for potential candidates, it's also more affirmation of corporate intent for your employee culture.

- Issue an annual "human capital" statement on your website and, if possible, in your annual report that brags shamelessly about the accomplishments of your employee culture, including not only academic degrees, but years of experience, other accomplishments, awards and recognitions, and career path progress.

- Include an employee's family in performance rewards. Chances are there was sacrifice of some kind if a member of your culture needed to give the company extra effort, and they deserve something, too. At the very least, provide a letter thanking them for their support and explaining what a great job their partner/parent did. If special accomplishment is being formally celebrated, extend an invitation for their family and friends to attend; even if they can't come, the point has been made. If you are recognizing accomplishment with anything printed or engraved, give them two copies: one to put on their desk and one to put on the mantel at home or to attach to the wall over the bed. (It's up to them where the impact is going to be the greatest.)

- Offer concierge assistance to help busy members of your culture. Managing the business of life is difficult when you're constantly working. Offer support services that research best-rated and -priced schools, vacations, cars, local events, and repair services.

2. SHOW OBVIOUS EFFORT AND CREATIVITY.

How you sweat the quality of your employee culture's performance reinforcement is directly connected to how your employee culture sweats to earn it. Avoid ritualistic performance recognition—no employee of the year, month, or minute, and no generic package of perks aimed at parity with the generic package of perks offered by other companies. Your employee culture will immediately recognize the minimal effort expended on its behalf; it has worked in other companies and knows plenty of people who still do.

LEVERAGE THEIR DISCRETIONARY INCOME

The cultural problems with compensation systems begin with people who approve them usually not having to live under them. When you're ready to create higher-impact performance reinforcement, start by actually *asking* your employee culture what it wants—not money, but what money buys and what it can't. You'll be surprised by your employee culture's answers about what money buys: It won't always be the wildly aspirational big cars and houses but more often the gym memberships, family trips, big concert tickets, and occasional night out that management might take for granted but which can represent a noticeable discretionary spend to members of an employee culture.

You can focus your employee culture's input by asking it to respond in price, lifestyle, and personal values categories, like family, health, adventure, home, and learning. These can be translated into perks like family activities, adventure travel, self-development lessons, home improvement, and yoga classes.

- Start thinking of your employee population as a consumer population to others. Choose retailers who sell these items and offer to encourage the members of your culture to look their way if they will provide exclusive discounts. The smaller your employee population, the smaller and more local retailers you should target.

Provide a proprietary company "credit card"—a debit card identical to the look of a credit card issued exclusively by your company to its employee culture. These private debit cards are available from a number of banks and credit card companies, and they can include your logo or a custom design. Regularly load the cards with funds that pay for special prenegotiated perks, linked to those material goods that your culture most covets.

The color of card and the corresponding selection and amount of the discount can vary by an individual or team's performance review. Green cardholders get tickets to a concert. Gold cardholders get better seats to the concert and the artist's complete MP3 collection. Platinum cardholders get even better seats and backstage for a meet-and-greet. Diamond cardholders get to run away with the band.

This system allows your employee culture to leverage its discretionary income by working for you and by the quality of its work. The credit card is used to validate them to a designated retailer but, much more important, the card is a reminder that their company empathetically cares about them, and is a ready conversation piece to prove it to anyone in their circle outside of the company. That's real validation.

If you devote obvious creativity and concern to compensation, that effort is a major perk for your culture. So make sure that you aim to surprise and delight with the rewards you load onto the cards; keep them fresh, unusual, and hysterically exciting. Don't just offer tennis lessons through the card; offer circus trapeze lessons. Don't just offer a meal at a coveted restaurant; include one of everything on the dessert menu. If your company has the resources, show the power of the mighty enterprise to make the fantastic happen. Everything and everyone is available for a price: Your Fortune 500 company can get Duane Allman exhumed for your 50th birthday.*

---

* We have orchestrated all sorts of insane perks for our clients' employee cultures, including two weeks' stay at Mick Jagger's beach house; hiking through the Costa Rican rain forest with five ex-Playboy playmates; invites to the hottest Oscars, Tonys, and Grammys after-parties; into the pit and onto the track at Le Mans; golf lessons from Tiger Woods' coach; home dinners by Michelin-decorated celebrity chefs—at your home

The leveraging of the culture's discretionary income for family adventures, gym memberships, clothes, toys, shopping sprees, event tickets, and big-buzz restaurants gives members of your employee culture a whole lot of fun and the occasional taste of luxury. Not only that, it gives them memorable lifetime experiences, the opportunity for personal improvement, and the ability to be heroes to their families.

LOCALIZE PERFORMANCE REINFORCEMENT

Performance reinforcement means more when it's relevant to an employee culture's particular lifestyle and heritage. If you're operating in multiple countries or regions, be sure to understand the local environment, conditions, and social norms. This way, you can link rewards to places that people love to go, love to buy from, love to be seen at. And you can shine a light on what's right and wrong with the community, including spotlighting local heroes and helping to repair local problems.

My company recently conducted a cultural audit of one of our global clients to determine its employee culture's willingness to support new performance goals. The positive response from their employee population in Bangalore was so much higher than the rest of the company that we had to back it out from the mean score to get an accurate company picture. What was happening in India? The company was offering zero-interest loans for weddings, days set aside twice a year for employees to bring their entire extended family into headquarters for a visit and special presentation, free use of loaner cars, and community outreach that included food distribution and sponsoring of local high schools with technology days and support. These things may have resonated in New Jersey, too, but they evidenced an especially precise understanding of what is important to an employee culture in Bangalore.

---

or theirs; and band party with front-row seats at Bruce Springsteen's annual private concert at his old high school. Everything and everyone: available.

3. IF YOU'RE BETTING BIG, GO BIG.

MAKE SURE IT SAYS SOMETHING

If your company is depending big-time on the success of a new strategy, goal, or focus, the reward should be big, too—legendary for its creativity and empathy. It can be an individual award or a team award; if it's a team award, each member should receive the equivalent.

As an example, offer a bonus in four parts—the winner or winners get *all* of them—and make it big: depending on your budget, from $2,500 to $5,000 to spend in each category.

1. *Big for them:* Winner's choice, from a list of available categories. The point here is to make it personally indulgent. Categories include the likes of:

   ➤ Clothes: Gift certificate to their favorite store
   ➤ Music: Any instrument or recording device
   ➤ Lessons: Learn anything from a top professional, from golf to fitness to circus trapeze
   ➤ Auto: Any car accessory or improvement
   ➤ Rare and collectible: music, film, posters, historical artifacts, books

2. *Big for family and friends:* Winner's choice, from a list of available categories. The point here is to share the reward with their close friends or apply to their home environment. Categories include the likes of:

   ➤ Home improvement: landscaping, paint, furniture, entertainment system
   ➤ Houseboat vacation for their family and friends
   ➤ Spectacular activities with kids
   ➤ Best seats at the hottest restaurants

➤ Four front-row seats and VIP treatment at sports events or concerts

3. *Big for the world:* Winner's choice, from a list of available categories to improve the lives of others. The point here is to allow them to impact the less fortunate. Categories include the likes of:

   ➤ Donation to charity in their name
   ➤ Scholarship to underprivileged in their name
   ➤ Billboard with personal (company-approved) social message

4. *Big for the company:* Winner's choice, from a list of available categories to address the highest level of management of their choice within your company. The point here is to allow them unusual direct access to provide their passionate POV. General approval of the content is required and includes the likes of:

   ➤ Opportunity to address the board of directors for fifteen minutes at next meeting*
   ➤ Opportunity for a thirty minute meeting with the president of the company
   ➤ Opportunity for a thirty-minute presentation/Q&A to entire C-suite at its next meeting
   ➤ Opportunity for a one-hour meeting with their choice of executives

---

* A good board wouldn't hesitate to make some time for a presentation from a member of the employee culture—direct access to the ideas and concerns of the culture would be important to those directors. I was on the board of a sports clothing company called Patagonia for many years, and one of my fondest memories as a director was deciding the special bonus granted the company's receptionist. His name was Chip, and as a first point of entry to the company, he was an ideal representation: an award-winning athlete with a contagious personality. He had famously answered a customer who had called corporate headquarters to bemoan the destruction of an expensive new Patagonia outfit by her cat. "What should I do?" she asked. "Get a new cat," Chip advised without hesitation. We gave him $10,000.

➤ Opportunity to write an article for the company's external website

PUTTING THE INTUITIVE IN COUNTERINTUITIVE

▶ If you're operating in an intensely competitive, margin-shredding environment, cutting costs to ensure success is a no-brainer—especially employee costs. Yet the team running Costco has combined brains with heart, resulting in the famously generous treatment of its 173,000-person employee culture. It seems to have worked out fine: Today the company is the seventh-largest retailer on the planet, with annual revenue of over $100 billion.

The generosity toward their employee culture extends beyond higher wages and better benefits. There is an attitude of deep respect, of affection, and of encouragement of potential—what money can't buy. Costco has been a client of my company, and I've witnessed this—it is tangible and visceral.

But what was the genesis of the decision to approach performance reinforcement this way? Was it the right thing to do, or simply the right thing to do for the business? I asked Costco co-founder Jim Sinegal and CEO/President Craig Jelinek how the approach originated. And what it means to them professionally and personally.

JIM: It was a business decision when we first started. We knew we were going to get a lot of skepticism, because we're a crazy business—forklifts running around, stuff stacked up to the ceiling, cement floors. We didn't want our customers to think, *They're probably making money off the backs of their employees.*

Today people are seventy cents of every dollar that we spend to run this business . . . and Craig is spending a lot. (Laughing)

CRAIG: Thanks, that's hysterical. (Laughing)

JIM: Any company had better pick some aspect of its business to be good at. Getting productivity is so important to us. If you buy the promise that Costco is the low-cost provider of goods, and we're paying the highest wages and making a profit, we must be getting better productivity.

CRAIG: You can measure this directly in our business.

JIM: An analyst at one time wrote a big, catchy headline, saying that it's better to be a Costco employee or customer than it is to be a shareholder. But if you look at our business, like Craig says, you can measure the impact of how we run it. We went public in 1985. In the twenty-nine years since, we have grown our sales at a compounded rate of about 13.8 percent and profits at a 13.3 percent compounded rate. Our stock value, market value, has grown at a 16.9 percent compounded rate. As we've told the shareholders, it isn't getting any better.

Some Real Bad Times. Some Real Good Moves

JIM: In 2003, our stock took a huge hit. I was shaving that morning when the news broke, so thank God I'm still alive. It wasn't about our performance; we were using a company that, in error, didn't fax all of our detailed reports to everyone, so it looked like a selective release of information.

Our employees were very upset and wanted to know if we were okay, if they were okay. Our response was immediate: We put our arms around them.

CRAIG: In 2008, we were holding a meeting of our seventeen-person executive committee right after the meltdown of the economy, when things were really horrible. We just happened to be redoing our culture's employment agreements at the time. Every single person in that room said, We have to give the employees an increase.

JIM: True. There wasn't anyone who said, Listen, they're going to have *jobs*, they're already the highest-paid employees in retail, and everybody else is going to be adjusting wages downward. Not anyone. That's how deeply imbedded the culture is as a priority in our company.

CRAIG: I watch this all of the time, in every country we do business in. My attitude is, we don't want to just be better than every other retailer in Mexico, as an example. We want to be Costco in Mexico. That means we pay thirty percent to forty percent more than any other retailer in the country. And I know some say, Hey, you don't have to do it. But we want our entire employee culture to understand that we're not going to try to lower wages every time we get the chance.

Sweet Dreams Are Made of This

CRAIG: I'm big on respecting people. What it gets down to is that you have to build trust with your employee culture by trusting it. If you build the trust, then you build the people, and good things are going to happen.

It's been very successful for us.

JIM: To answer your question, Stan, we feel that we have a responsibility to make sure that our employee culture feels secure. That it can sleep at night.

Fulfilling this responsibility is how I sleep at night.

THIS JUST IN: SIZE DOESN'T MATTER

Before there was ever a profusion of VC-funded and IPO-imminent start-ups to work for, employee cultures stood by their small companies that had mighty missions and family-like intimacy. Even if the companies didn't have a lot of money to lavish on them. Whatever the culture got meant more because it cost the organization more to give.

Same as it ever was today. Trust, the sources of cultural energy (context, predictability, sense of self), and, above all, safety are the messages compensation has to send to your employee culture. Some companies can make grand investments to create this, but there are plenty of work-arounds if you can't. Those grand-scale companies make news about their generous sabbatical policies, luxurious lifestyle services, and outrageous feeding troughs. Yet the talk around the Google water cooler is not that it's cucumber-lime today; it's that the company values its employee culture.

Here's where creativity and effort are most needed but also most telling. If you can't afford the best total insurance package, you can afford to help your people be healthy. If you can't afford the employee development, you can afford to have everyone in the company teach what they know to others. If you can't afford the company cafeteria, you can afford to ensure that treats are constant and are painstakingly selected to be the best. If you can't afford to stuff everyone at a company Christmas party, you can afford to sponsor a competition to let people and teams bring their own best recipes. If you can't fund your own charitable foundation, you can afford to pick smaller charitable concerns or start your own, and allow a day or two paid leave to help your culture make a difference in person. If you can't afford the sabbaticals, you can afford to give birthdays off, create an unusual annual holiday, or allow your employee culture to nominate its own.*

BIG SPEND ON A MANAGER'S BUDGET

An employee culture unhappy with its compensation will often decry a lack of creativity and effort from management around rewards. This

---

* No matter how fast we're growing, my company will always be smaller than our Fortune 500 clients. We give our people the same standard benefits they do and extend most beyond what those largest companies offer. Still, it's the little perks that seem to get the most positive response, like the books and music reimbursement, the fanatically chosen constant supply of artisanal chocolate, the 1957 Les Paul and Marshall half stack for anyone who wants to play or learn, each person's choice of any favorite literary or musical quote professionally applied on one wall of their office in very large type, and that our offices are closed every year to celebrate Charlie Parker's birthday.

will often frustrate management, who can point to competitive salaries, bonuses, and benefits. Those are systemic and scheduled components of compensation. The culture believes it is making regular decisions to protect what's most important to the company and it wants to know that you know about them and were moved enough to respond as they occur.

Can you name each of your employee's favorite flowers? Their favorite author or band? The dessert they remember most fondly from childhood or what they used to collect as kids? The new restaurant they most want to try? There's nothing outrageous or particularly creative about these kinds of material reinforcements, but if they're individualized this gives them weight and connotes positive implications for your entire culture: You care enough to know. You don't have to focus just on your people's faves: Sharing your own favorite book, band, or brand of bubblegum cigarette is an intimate act. Either way, the significance is in the obvious effort behind the reward. Don't buy your employee culture a cake; bake it a cake. Can't bake a cake to save your life? Means even more.

Here's something that will take no money at all.* Is a member of your employee culture doing a great job? Stop and spend the time in your hectic day to handwrite them a letter, if it's to one or a few people; if you have more than ten people, type and print it up if you need to, but hand-sign each copy. Mention that you wanted to take the time to tell them how proud you are of their efforts and how much it personally means to you.

Mail the letters to their homes.

The members of your employee culture get home and are flipping through the mail. Magazines, bills, direct mail offers . . . and a letter they didn't expect, with their company's name printed as the return address. Uh-oh. Worse than that, their manager's name is handwritten above it. UH-OH. Until they open the envelope.

---

* I lifted this concept from *Bury My Heart at Conference Room B* when the author wasn't looking.

If they're living with someone, the value of your letter has just gone up one hundred percent. "What's that, honey?" "Oh, nothing. Just a note from my boss telling me how they are *blown away by my fabulous work!*" Even if they just live with a pet: "Get your leash! We're going out!"

SIZE DOESN'T MATTER BUT MARKETING SURE DOES

The best rule of thumb is to approach cultural compensation with a marketing ethic: a constant effort to engage, stimulate, and differentiate, with an understanding of the attitudes, values, and beliefs of your target demographic and an effort to micromarket to specific interests whenever possible. And to remember the first rule of good marketing: Don't say something until you stand for something.

Yet Another Cultural Learning Experience

STAR TIME

▶ Really, it's not that I learned all my business wisdom running a cookie company many years ago, but there is one more lesson from that time that has stuck with me ever since, and it's relevant to the Fifth Deadly Sin.

It had to do with my continuing obsession with the customer average sale as a key metric. One of our stores, in Bellevue, Washington, had suddenly doubled that amount, then tripled it two weeks later, then quadrupled it three weeks after that. This was unheard of company performance, and I was looking forward to mercilessly raising the bar on everyone else when the store suddenly dropped back to its original level, and didn't recover.

I was in the Seattle area the following week and made Bellevue my first stop.

"Tell me everything about this store," I demanded of the Seattle district manager as we were driving to the mall. He explained that a newly hired manager was in charge. She was a grade school teacher who didn't have any retail experience, but he had needed someone to fill a sudden vacancy and figured if she could manage a classroom she could manage a store. "Sounds great," I said. "Hostage-taking incident," I was thinking.

Clare was her name. She was a friendly woman who radiated a manic combination of positive energy and ruthless efficiency. This might make third-grade students pay attention but would certainly fail to touch the too-cool-for-school ennui of the average retail store employee.

We met in the store's back room. "Talk to me about your average sale, Clare," I asked. "Oh, that thing," she said. "Well, I believe a work area should be clean and orderly, so when I first got to the store, I set about straightening up the stockroom. You would not have believed the lack of organization. In this one corner alone . . ."

"The average sale, Clare," I interrupted.

"Yes, well, on one of the shelves I found a little box of gold stars. Rather than waste them, I posted an announcement that anyone who sells a dozen cookies gets a gold star on their time card." "And what?" I said. "What, what?" she asked. "Did the winner get a bonus?" I asked. "No, no, just the gold star."

"And this worked?" I asked incredulously. I glanced at the front of the store where two of our employees were comparing tattoos of what looked like . . . no, that couldn't be.

"At first," she confirmed. "Then it became very competitive and I had to change it to a gold star for every two dozen cookies. Then every three dozen. My goodness."

"But the average sale has dropped, Clare. What happened?" I asked.

"I ran out of stars," she said.

"Oh, my God," I muttered as I lunged for the phone.

THE END OF SIN: TACTICAL RECAP

THE FIFTH DEADLY SIN: PAY WHAT?

An employee culture uses money to buy meaning—skip the middleman, and give it the meaning. You have an unlimited budget to do this, since what the culture cares about most is what money can't buy: the linkage between its performance reinforcement and its safety, and the emotional prosperity that comes from the effort you make to be creative about compensation.

1. Focus on what money can't buy.

Include family and friends—the people that members of your employee culture listen to the most—in performance reinforcement, and make your thanks for great performance something they can see.

Match reinforcement to your company's DNA. Reinforce whatever claims the company makes about its products, customer experience, and larger noble purpose. If you say the company is innovative, make reinforcement innovative. If you say you make the world a better place, focus reinforcement on making the culture's world a better place.

2. Show obvious effort and creativity.

Don't buy your employee culture the cake; bake it. Don't be afraid to be unusual and exaggerated because the effort you spend will mean as much as the reward. Whenever possible, individualize rewards based on members' individual preferences and wish lists.

3. If you're betting big, go big.

If your company is depending big-time on the success of a new strategy, goal, or focus, the reward should be big, too: Match what you want with what you give. But the size of the reward doesn't matter as much as the size of the priority you assigned to making the recognition of performance relevant, thoughtful, and exciting.

BOTTOM LINE

Give Your Employee Culture MEANING

We have to distrust each other. It is our only
defense against betrayal.

—Tennessee Williams

THE SIXTH DEADLY SIN
ASKING FOR TOO MUCH TRUST

Before you accuse me (take a look at yourself).

— Bo Diddley

T HERE COMES a point in the execution of any performance goal where you must ask your employee culture to trust you—at the most, that everything will be better when the goal is achieved; at the very least, that the goal is going to last awhile before being replaced by another.

Chances are, you're not going to get all of that trust. Certainly, you're not going to get it all at once.

Management is focused on success, so it constantly looks forward, to what can be sold next. An employee culture is focused on survival, so it constantly looks backward, at what it has been sold before that didn't work out as promised. Understandably, the culture's memory is longer and more vivid. It may take a close look at what you're selling this time, but from a distance. With binoculars.*

Where could you possibly have lost trust with your culture—to such a degree that it greets new management plans with suspicion? If you're searching for the answer, start by looking in the place where you've most asked for the trust: company values.

BETTER ADD DANGER TO THAT LIST OF VALUES

Companies don't have values; people do. Every classic definition of values is that they are deeply held personal beliefs. In an organization with legitimate values, the person at the top brings their own values to

---

* A goldfish supposedly has such bad short-term memory that every time around the bowl is like its first. So if you get yourself a goldfish but have to leave it home alone every day when you head to work, don't feel guilty and start sprucing up the living room for your new pet. To the goldfish, it's always been *Hey, new couch! Hey, new couch! Hey, new couch!* Goldfish memory is actually a bit better than is rumored, though. They remember if something was good or bad even if they don't remember exactly what it was, and they'll alter their anticipatory behavior accordingly. One of the many differences between your goldfish and your employee culture is that your culture always remembers *exactly* what it was.

work and insists that others be allowed to do the same. Common values rise to the surface; they define how people inside of the company are treated and spill over to how people outside of the company are treated. It's a seamless, organic process.

What companies usually have are strategies—goals for increasing business. Nothing wrong with that except when they're sold as values: An employee culture understands the difference even if the company doesn't. One of the easiest ways to tell the difference is by watching what happens when pressure is applied to both. A strategy is a calculated method for achieving a result; under pressure of changing market conditions, an adept strategic team will change the strategy—it's the first thing that's sacrificed. A value is a deeply imbedded belief; under pressure, people will fall on it to protect it with their lives—it's the last thing that's sacrificed. There is a big difference between a company's value proposition and its values.

An employee culture cares so much about values because it assumes that they are reputable indicators of company convictions, wired as deeply as it gets. After all, that's what values are personally to the human beings who are in the culture: conscious and unconscious primary drivers of behavior.

Declare official company values, and the good news is that you will have gotten your employee culture's attention. Fail to vigorously protect them, and the bad news is that you will have gotten your employee culture's attention. There is a whole *subset* of potential sins within this Sixth Deadly Sin:

1. The values are posted as fact on websites and wallet cards, but are in fact aspirational statements, unregulated and unattached to performance realities.
2. The values were decided by a committee that hammered the passion out of them to reach consensus.
3. Company values bear little resemblance to what the culture perceives are the personal values of the CEO and the C-suite.

4. Senior management doesn't constantly talk about values, because coming up with them was the act of completion.

5. Those who ignore the values, including major revenue generators, are allowed to stay in their jobs without consequence or are buried elsewhere in the organization.

6. The company constantly celebrates what was done as most important, not how or why it was done.

7. There is no institutional support for what is considered most important—it is not systemically imbedded and reinforced, and there are perceived risks and restrictions to acting in the name of the values.

8. There is no authorization, even unstated, assuring the culture that it is safe if it acts in the name of the company values.

9. How the company represents its better self is inconsistent with how it talks privately about its products and customers.

10. Supposedly sacred internal values are used as external advertising messages and are then replaced by other advertising messages.

Should your company be guilty of these errors, it will have taken the most profound of human concepts—values—and pitched it to the most profound of human organisms—a culture—under false pretenses. Trust will be fractured at a deep level, not just of the company, but also of managers who've had to attach their own good names to this process.

You may not feel this on a daily basis, but you'll feel it when you need the most trust from your culture or need that trust the fastest. This will require a leap of faith when the culture has been given a host of large empirical reasons to mistrust. Your employee culture may occasionally act nuts, but crazy it isn't.

Remember that a culture isn't a closed system—well, it's closed to you, but it's open to new information. It may not trust you, but it wants to—it would be much better for the culture if it could. You can rebuild its confidence in the company and in you as a manager.

NOW, HERE'S HOW TO DO IT

1. AS A COMPANY: TRY NOT TO DECLARE VALUES. PROTECT THEM AT ALL COSTS IF YOU DO.

It's better if you don't officially state enterprise values. It may feel really good to broadcast, but it's the gateway drug to cultural detachment. When you are selling values, you are targeting your culture's deep desire for protection and affiliation. No matter how the values are positioned as a shared responsibility of all to uphold, they're perceived by an employee culture as a management manifesto, and the culture expects them to remain uncompromised.

Instead, let your employee culture declare them for you.

My company is often asked to determine the true state of a client's employee culture. When the culture is negative, one of the first things we look at is where its current critical perceptions were formed. This is most often traceable to a belief that the company declared values and failed to protect them. When the employee culture is in great shape—most willing to support a company plan—we find that it admits to being unaware of what the stated values actually are but is confident that the company will defend them.

Rather than telling your employee culture what the company values are, ask the culture to tell you: What does it think is sacred and uncompromisable? This is an opportunity for your culture to reinforce what it believes is special about the company and invite dialogue about where the values are strongest and where they are most vulnerable. Don't debate if what you hear is different from what you want to hear. Listen hard, and correct perceptions by altering the organizational behavior that created them: Start with where the perceptions began and recalibrate from there. Keep listening, especially after any possible test of the values or after any significant success.

The issue is what is genuine, not what is declared. Most enterprise mission statements are declarations of marketplace positioning, not company passion. Your company doesn't need to publish a mission statement to have a mission, and you don't need to write down values to make them real to your culture.

But you do have to appreciate the natural tension between these proclaimed enterprise sentiments and the real world of business that will attempt to constantly dilute them. Established values are difficult for companies that can rarely deal in absolutes within a shifting market environment. Safeguarding them is a constant and frustrating maintenance activity, a focus on down-in-the-weeds details. The weight of company intention can't be borne entirely by these innocent little values words; vigilance of the highest order is required to make the concept work.

Be sure, then, that yours is the kind of company that can take a stand in at least this one area: no shades of gray, no succumbing to pressure or temptation to compromise, no hesitation about company motives and response when they're violated. And get the trip wires, open communication, and fast response systems in place ahead of time.

If your company has already declared values, or believes it should in order to hold the culture accountable for performance standards, invite the dialogue anyway: Let the culture take a bat to the list if it needs to. It will help more than hurt.

And be sure to reposition strategies as different from values. Why does an employee culture insist it isn't "being told the whole story," to the dumbfounded amazement of the company's executive team, who can point to endless presentations that explained it? It means the culture has heard it but doesn't remember. It didn't stick because the culture thought it would soon be replaced. The goal wasn't anchored to anything permanent, so why pay attention?

Be clear about what is a strategy, which is necessarily fluid, and what is a value, which is willfully fixed. Show how the values are imbedded as key indicators within the strategy: how they're supported, how they're protected, how they will be celebrated. Make it clear that company accomplishment at the cost of company values will always be too high a price to pay.

2. AS A MANAGER: ASK FOR TRUST A LITTLE BIT AT A TIME.

As a manager, your job isn't to establish corporate values, so don't be worrying about that. Use the time you save to worry about making performance goals happen despite any cultural climate of skepticism.

Two principles will help you. The first is used in successful advertising and is known as the *staged call to action*. It's about bringing you along a little at a time to arrive at a purchase decision. A clever car campaign won't show you the new model and urge you to buy it. It will show you some exciting features of the new model and ask you to think about how great they are when you climb behind the wheel of your own car, which doesn't have them. Or it will ask you to go to the dealer for a test–drive: Don't buy it; just drive it. The campaign will move you forward a step at a time.

The second principle is my own, which I really use all the time: *Sanction the inevitable.* If things suck anyway, claim that it's part of your well-conceived strategic plan. In this case, it means that if you're not going to get the trust you want anyway, look great to your culture by not asking for it.

Let's combine the two principles to expedite trust:

It is small steps that will fortify trust, but the first step is a big one: You must admit that your employee culture may have a good reason to not trust you. As you've been told to do, you explain that everything will be bigger, better, and fixed forever as a result of the new company strategy. Should the culture believe this? Nah, given its experience it would be wrong to believe this, and you respect that. So you're not asking them to trust you about everything*—only about a few small things.†

Promise a couple of things that, over a short period of time, will definitely happen in the name of the latest plan. Promise a couple of things that, over the same short period of time, will definitely *never* happen in the name of the latest plan. Explain up front that when you deliver on all of these things, you are going to come back to the culture to negotiate for more trust. This places the culture in a position where it would be unseemly to refuse to give you the little that you've asked for, especially if it could be a new clue to its survival.

A culture deals in the real: It wants proof and truth. You may not be able to give it proof that a new plan will work out as promised. Give it the truth.

3. AS A CULTURE: TRUST IT TO BE TRUSTED.

Various stress fractures and dry rot may have caused an employee culture's trust to be less than weight bearing, but that can usually be reconstructed. One of the simplest ways is to give it a greater feeling of *being* trusted.

Your employee culture may disagree with you about how to stop a problem or create success. Maybe you're right as management with your ability to see further from up above. Maybe the culture is right from its close-up view of the daily workings of the business. Find out by agreeing to a short pilot period within a small organization. No matter what happens, you will have risked little and gained a lot.

---

* You shouldn't take this personally. It's less about you than about all the company plans you've had to sell that you might not even have bought yourself.

† Make them small things and don't promise them until you're sure you can deliver. Otherwise it will be about you and you *should* take it personally.

BUT THE POSTERS SURE LOOKED GREAT

Adelphia Communications

Revenue (peak) $4.36 billion (2005)

Revenue (current) $0

Officially declared values

Urgency. Accountability. Integrity. Respect. Ethical Conduct. Teamwork. Communication. Recognition and Celebration.

Values in action

"Adelphia Communications Corp. founder John Rigas and his son Timothy were convicted Thursday of conspiracy, bank fraud and securities fraud for looting the cable company and duping its investors." —NBC News, July 8, 2004

"The largest and longest-running bar tab in history."
—*New York Times*, July 9, 2004

Bear Stearns

Revenue (peak) $16.5 billion (2006)

Revenue (current) $0

Officially declared values

Access. Visibility. Flexibility. Entrepreneurialism.

Values in action

"This is not about mismanagement of a hedge fund investment strategy," said Mark J. Mershon, the head of the New York office of the Federal Bureau of Investigation. "It is about premeditated lies to investors and lenders."—"Prosecutors Build Bear Stearns Case on E-Mails." —*New York Times*, June 20, 2008

"The definition of a good trader is a guy who takes losses," [Bear Stearns' CEO] Alan Greenberg said. "The definition of an ex-trader is one who tries to cover up a loss."

Circuit City

Revenue (peak) $12.4 billion in 2007

Revenue (current) $0

Officially declared values

Respect. Teach. Engage (what you do matters). Simplify. Maintain highest integrity.

Values in action

Circuit City's most obvious failing was its customer service. In March 2007, it announced plans to lay off its highest-paid hourly employees and replace them with cheaper workers. That same year, then-CEO Philip Schoonover received some $7 million in compensation. A quick Web search on 'Circuit City complaints' brings up hundreds of thousands of entries."   —*Time*, Nov. 11, 2008

Countrywide Financial

Revenue (peak) $18.5 billion (2005)

Revenue (current) $0 (bought by Bank of America for $4 billion. Bank of America was sued for the purchase for $1 billion.)

Officially declared values

Honest. Accurate. Truthful.

Values in action

"Exhibit A for the lax and, until recently, highly lucrative lending that has turned a once-hot business ice cold and has touched off a housing crisis of historic proportions."   —*New York Times*, Aug. 26, 2007

Enron

Revenue (peak) $100 billion (2000)

Revenue (current) $0

Officially declared values

Respect. Integrity. Communication. Excellence.

Values in action

"It turned out Enron was good at inventing businesses, but terrible at the tedious work of running them . . . rules were for sissies. These were invincible innovators, who sneered at rules."—*New York Times*, Jan. 26, 2002

Lehman Brothers

Revenue (peak) $19.3 billion (2007)

Revenue (current) $0

Officially declared values

Build unrivaled partnerships with and value for our clients. Knowledge. Creativity. Dedication. Superior return for our shareholders.

Values in action

"Lehman Brothers was playing loose with its accounting even before the financial crisis, according to a report this week from a court-appointed examiner. The report details how Lehman regularly used an accounting gimmick at the end of each quarter to make its finances appear less shaky than they really were."
—*Christian Science Monitor*, March 12, 2010

Nortel Networks

Revenue (peak) $27.9 billion (2000)

Revenue (current) $0

Officially declared values

Customers are the driving force. People are our strength. Quality is in every aspect. Innovation fuels our future. Accountability brings clarity. Integrity underpins everything.

Values in action

"The Royal Canadian Mounted Police brought criminal charges on Thursday against three former executives of Nortel Networks, the telecommunications company . . . The charges stem from an accounting scandal that caused Nortel to fire or suspend the three men in April 2004." —*New York Times*, June 20, 2008

Peanut Corporation of America

Revenue (peak) $25 million (2008)

Revenue (current) $0

Officially declared values
Quality. Safety.

Values in action
"The company had no conscience in its production practices, sales, and distribution. That they would knowingly ship products tainted with salmonella to our nation's children almost defies belief."
—U.S. Senate Agriculture Chairman Tom Harkin

"The actions by the Peanut Corporation of America can only be described as reprehensible and criminal."
—U.S. Representative Rosa DeLauro

Wachovia Bank

Revenue (peak) $31.5 billion (2007)

Revenue (current) $0

Officially declared values
People as a competitive advantage. Ethics. What is right for our customers is right for us. Diversity and Inclusion. Leadership.

Values in action
"In a lawsuit filed last year, the United States attorney in Philadelphia said Wachovia received thousands of warnings that it was processing fraudulent checks, but ignored them."
—*New York Times*, May 20, 2007

Washington Mutual

Revenue (peak) $26.2 billion (2006)

Revenue (current) $0

Officially declared values

Absolute fairness, honesty, and integrity. Caring. Human. Dynamic driven.

Values in action

"In the end . . . the bank failed because its leaders abandoned its historical balance between growth and prudence." —*Seattle Times*, Oct. 25, 2009

"I never had a clue about the amount of off-the-cliff activity that was going on at Washington Mutual," said Vincent Au, president of Avalon Partners, an investment firm. "There were people at WaMu that orchestrated nothing more than a sham or charade. These people broke every fundamental rule of running a company." —*New York Times*, Dec. 27, 2008

THE SIXTH DEADLY SIN: ASKING FOR TOO MUCH TRUST

Management is focused on success, so it's always looking forward to see what can be sold next. An employee culture is focused on survival, so it's always looking backward to see whether the last thing it was sold worked out as promised.

1. Try not to declare company values. If you already have, protect them at all costs.

Better that you don't officially declare values and instead regularly ask your employee culture what it thinks the values are likely to be. If it's not what you want to hear, recalibrate policies and decisions to bring them into alignment. If you have declared values, do everything possible to protect them, including positive reinforcement for those who meet them, negative reinforcement for those who don't, and a celebration of how goals were achieved, not just what was achieved.

2. Ask for trust a little bit at a time.

Make small, short-term promises that don't require risk on the part of your culture to believe. Deliver on those, make some more, and momentum will increase as the culture collects proof points of your credibility.

3. Trust your culture.

One of the simplest ways to regain trust with your culture is to give it a greater feeling of *being* trusted. Even if you disagree with a culture's point of view on a particular subject, agree to a short, small pilot. You may learn something new about the business and your culture will learn to better trust your claims that you respect it.

BOTTOM LINE

Give Your Employee Culture CONFIDENCE

A great wind is blowing, and that gives you either imagination or a headache.

—Catherine the Great

THE SEVENTH DEADLY SIN
BIG KICKOFF. LITTLE PAYOFF.

'Scuse me while I kiss the sky.

—Jimi Hendrix

MOST COMPANIES handle the introduction of a strategy pretty well, promoting it big and hard at the outset. Most companies are pretty good at explaining the end goal of a new strategy: world domination. If it's clear where the strategy starts and where the strategy stops, you can't blame the employee culture for expecting that everything in between must have been figured out, too.

Since that's almost never the case, an employee culture perceives that it is being forced down an unlit, unpaved, and unproven road. The culture's entire reason for existing is to protect itself against such circumstances. Besides, every member of an employee culture has already had the delightful experience of taking their eyes off business as usual to support some New World Order and getting whacked on the head for it. Your employee culture is initiative-weary and -wary, preconditioned to resist another big new company plan.

THE MEETING AND THE DAMAGE DONE

Proclamations of major new goals usually start with good intentions— a desire to motivate a company's employee culture, not to mislead it. This often means premiering it at an All-Hands or Kickoff meeting. These are events that have to be experienced to be believed, although they're not always believed by the employee culture in attendance. In larger companies, the expense for these affairs is enormous and intense preparations begin many months before. The production values are stunning, although they tend to be wasted on employees just arrived from other countries, who look forward to catching up on their sleep through most of them. If held in Las Vegas, the staging and effects can be as complex as a Broadway show, and the sound system can rival a major touring band, although it will inevitably be used to blast some classic rock song rewritten with corporate lyrics, leaving a formerly beloved anthem transformed forever in the culture's now-traumatized memory.

In especially intense, high-performing companies, the pitch is aimed at the chronic insecurity of overachievers: "We had to go to Mars and *get that golf ball!* And we *did it!* Next quarter? *New planet! New ball!*" The intent of all of this Sturm und Drang* is to get the employee culture to pounce on the new goal like a chew toy, as if the culture were a frenzied corgi who has gotten into the chocolate.

SHAKEN, NOT STIRRED

Your employee culture may indeed respond to your goal introduction with enthusiasm, but never assume that has given you dependable cultural endorsement. The danger is that you have gotten typical buy-in, which means your culture agrees that it's a smart idea and could sell it to others. This is different from cultural buy-in, which means your *culture* has bought it and is committed to protecting it, course-correcting it, and representing it enthusiastically with its own good name.

It's a false positive: agreeing with something and buying something are not the same things to an employee culture. Cultural buy-in requires your employee culture to believe that the strategy will last awhile, that the risk-reward ratio is palatable, that it has the tools it needs to get this new job done, and that what executives say in big speeches usually comes true.

---

* It means Storm and Stress and comes from a late-1700s movement in German literature and music in which extremes of emotion were encouraged to offset constraints of rationalism, e.g., a rewritten Aerosmith song ("Sell This Way! Raise Hell This Way!") at your next All-Hands meeting used to offset the 163 PowerPoint slides the employee culture is forced to endure.

Full disclosure: Over the years, I have rewritten several classic songs as favors to clients for their big events, including, sigh, the aforementioned Aerosmith song, which included the aforementioned lyrics. If there's a rock-and-roll heaven, I'm going to hell.

DO THIS NOW

GIVE YOUR CULTURE ILLUMINATION

You are presenting serious goals, yet your employee culture will take them seriously only if you can provide that which is almost impossible: clarity about each step forward. How can you do that? You have to announce the thing at some point to gain the culture's focus that will begin to move it forward, without yet knowing the benchmarks, table stakes, metrics, resources, competencies required, or the circumstances you'll encounter along the way. This may be reasonable to management, but without this definition the employee culture will perceive the strategy as rushed and airbrushed.

Management is busy and can't be expected to know every tactical step that follows the announcement of a new strategy, but your employee culture doesn't always know this. The problem with selling a big initiative to an employee culture is that the culture has never created one itself. If it thinks a strategy is wobbly at the outset, it assumes the goal will follow a predictable pattern of uncertain in six days, forgotten in six weeks, and replaced in six months.

As with all business purposes, your culture is not trying to withhold its allegiance because it's uncaring. It may even prefer to be moved by the inspiration of an audacious performance goal. But it holds all truths to be self-centered and wants to know what it's getting itself into. A burning platform is inspirational—unless you happen to be standing on it.

Fourteen points? Ten big bets? The nine strategic imperatives? Your employee culture is busy, too, and any list of urgent priorities preceded by a number greater than three means that you've immediately begun to lose its attention and support. Each new priority requires opening a fresh investigation into the rules of survival, and an employee culture can't confidently monitor that many.

An employee culture will measure its response to an initiative in large part by how competent and complete it perceives the tactical plan to be; it's looking for signals that the new behavior is safe. Since the complete plan can't possibly be known ahead of time, the emphasis must be on ensuring its safety the best you can.

The key is to light the unknown road ahead a little bit at a time—as if you were holding a lantern down the darkened path, allowing the culture to see far enough ahead to proceed at least that far with confidence. Keep moving the lantern and the culture will keep moving with you.

NOW, HERE'S HOW TO DO IT

1. FORECAST THE CHOICE POINTS.

Over the next ninety days, where will your employee culture arrive at crossroads, with choices between supporting new goals and behaviors or old goals and behaviors that may still be required of it? Explain where these choice points will be encountered and the right, safe paths to take.

2. FORECAST THE CHOKE POINTS.

Over the next ninety days, where will your employee culture potentially be placed into situations where there is no clear choice between deciding on behalf of the new or the old? *Someone* will be unhappy with its choice. Explain where these "choke points" will occur, if you know them; if not, just explain that they may well occur. Either way, assure your culture that it's safe to raise a hand for help in those circumstances—management will understand that the employee culture is asking for clarification in order to move forward.

3. FORECAST THE SAFETY CHECKS.

Over the next ninety days, what are a few things the employee culture would definitely be doing if it were acting correctly in the name of the new goal? Make sure that these are behaviors or actions that the culture can obsessively self-monitor to assure itself of safety, without asking management.

■ ■ ■

You don't have to do this up front for the entire scope of the strategy, which is good, since not much has changed about your ability to do that since the previous page. You need only to light the road a few months ahead of time and keep updating to stay a few months ahead. If you can't do this, you have no right asking your employee culture to do anything for you.

Yet Another Cultural Learning Experience

NOT EXACTLY LEGEND THAT WAS INTENDED

▶ Oracle today is one of the world's three largest technology companies, offering hardware, software, and various database development and application tools. It is a competitive powerhouse, with most of the world's best-performing organizations as clients and annual revenues of over $40 billion.

This isn't about what Oracle is doing now. This is about what Oracle was trying to do in 1996, when my own company had just formed, and Oracle had just introduced a new company-wide strategic intent, designed to "enable the information age through network computing." Oracle had decided that four organizational transformations were critical to the success of the strategy:

- From Client-Server to Network Computing
- From Database Provider to Strategic Partner

- From Niche Player to Broader Market
- From Independent Organizations to One Team

And so was born the company's big Four Transformations initiative. With characteristic gusto, they unceasingly bludgeoned their employee culture with the change message. The Four Transformations—simple to understand but complex to execute—were listed on every poster on every floor in every building. The Four Transformations were listed on every screen saver on every computer. The Four Transformations were listed on every mouse pad on every desk.

The problem was that the Four Transformations had to take their place in line behind the Sixteen Thousand Other Transformations the Oracle employee culture had on its plate, none of which the company was willing to give up. Oracle was a notorious nonstop pressure cooker. Not a frothy place to work, except around the lips.

With all that relentless hammering, the executive team was sure the message had been nailed to the heads of every employee. But just in case a single part-timer in north Tibet had been living a life of self-imposed solitary penance in an Oracle mountainside monastery and missed the whole thing, they decided to do a telephone survey to confirm comprehension. Employees were called at random by an outside firm and asked nothing more obtuse than to simply name the Four Transformations.

The results were a disaster. North America scored only forty-three percent comprehension, France only six percent, and most geographies and business units notched somewhere in between. And this was a phone interview, with people called at their desks. They were leaning on the mouse pad that listed the answer while responding that they didn't know the answer.

This was about the time we were brought in to help convince the culture. We drew up a whole new plan, suggesting personal executive evangelism, different media, big and small events, transfers of competency, communications personality, cultural legends—a sixty-four-page summary of our tactical recommendations. Yet nothing was slowing down for the Oracle employee culture to make room for this, nothing was incenting it in any way to prioritize the initiative. It was Four Transformations, wrapped in Seven Deadly Sins.

The work was frustrating, and my company's project team was exhausted, physically and spiritually, by being unable to achieve our usual success. Came the day in our assigned visitor conference room on the Oracle campus when we had actually run out of ideas. "I can't think of one more way to sell this," one of my people sighed to a round of depressed, nodding heads and mutinous grumbling. "We ought to try mimes," I muttered, more to myself than to them and obviously as a joke.

"Yes! That's it! Mimes!" shouted my people, by now displaying *esprit de psychotic* episode. Everyone was so down at this point I figured, why not? Our company would foot the bill, I'd give everybody the day to play at this, and we'd come back reenergized. It had to be cheaper than a team dinner and drinks, and really, what could go wrong? We called an agency to get some professional mimes, scrambled a tech crew, and headed outside to set up the whole thing.

We decided to film on a small hill outside of the first building on the Oracle campus, where no one could see us from their office. The lights and cameras were put into place, each of the four mimes were given a big numbered sign and vague instructions to "act out one of the Four Transformations." (Next time you play charades, try to get the rest of the party to guess "Client-Server to Network Computing.") By the time we were finally ready to film, it was late afternoon.

Late afternoon, when Oracle people were leaving those offices to drive home.

The Oracle campus is next to the on-ramp of the 101 Freeway, the main artery connecting San Francisco with the southern part of Silicon Valley, so there was typically a rush out of the company's parking lots to beat the late-afternoon traffic. Not this time. This time, employees' cars were rolling to a stop in the street. "Huh," I thought distractedly. "That's interesting."

People began leaning half out of their car windows, staring wide-eyed at the mimes, which they assumed had been hired by Oracle, and shrieking at the top of their lungs, "I know the damn Four Transformations!" "I don't need any mimes to tell me how to do my job!" they were screaming. Some started climbing out of their cars, not to only get a better look, but very possibly to get crowbars out of their trunks.

The mimes managed to misinterpret this obvious crowd agitation as adoration and began to exaggerate their movements, which in turn were misinterpreted by already-incensed Oracle employees to suggest that they didn't understand the first mime presentation, so it was being repeated even slower and "louder" as edification for the obviously dim-witted.

"That's a wrap!" I shouted, and we hustled everyone into the equipment van, which sped away in the opposite direction.

All in all, I suppose it was an interesting experiment. It didn't help Oracle much, but they ended up changing the whole strategy the next year anyway. The mimes picked up some new hand gestures from the crowd that, for all I know, they continue to use to this day.

THE SEVENTH DEADLY SIN: BIG KICKOFF. LITTLE PAYOFF.

If you do a good job of introducing a goal and a good job of explaining the end result, you can't blame your employee culture for believing that everything in between has been figured out, too. When the culture realizes it's being forced down an unlit, unproven road, it will resist moving forward.

1. Forecast the choice points (update each ninety days).

Where will your employee culture reach a crossroads between doing things the old way and the new way? Explain the safe road to take.

2. Forecast the choke points (update each ninety days).

Where will your employee culture find itself with no easy way to make a choice between the new and the old? Explain that it's okay to raise a hand and ask for help.

3. Forecast the safety checks (update each ninety days).

What few things can your employee culture do to ensure its safety in the name of the new goal? Explain how it can verify on its own at any time that it is doing those things.

BOTTOM LINE

Give Your Employee Culture ILLUMINATION

The answer is "yes" or "no," depending on the interpretation.

—Albert Einstein

HOW TO SURVIVE YOUR EMPLOYEE CULTURE'S PRESSURE TEST

Mama said there'll be days like this.

—The Shirelles

HOW DO you measurably increase your employee culture's commitment? Start by recognizing that you are changing a belief system based on survival. It is a heritage of acute perceptions that has formed a point of view about what is real; perceptions that won't be breeched by an onslaught of business logic or material incentives. Transformation won't happen suddenly and will require constant maintenance.

That sounds like a lot of work, but as with most things it's easier once you know how to do it. Then it becomes your instinctive management behavior, advocated and protected by all that you've learned in this book. So that's done.

Not as such.

What can you expect from your employee culture when you've behaved exactly like you were supposed to for ten to twelve months—tromped unswervingly past the siren songs of the Seven Deadly Sins, stayed transparent and true, and consistently offered your culture equal parts respect and empathy?

You can expect your culture to go crazy on you and act like you've never done a single thing you've promised.

Don't be alarmed when this happens and don't be disappointed. This is a *good* thing. It means that your employee culture has taken notice of the consistency of your behavior and is beginning to suspect that it might be dependable and predictable. Your culture won't ever take this for granted, but it may take its opinion of your threat potential down a few DEFCON notches.

Before it does, it's going to be as sure as can be that this is a safe move. This is the part that will drive you nuts.

Your culture is going to pressure-test the strength of your commitment the only way it can: by walking away from your good efforts in an apparent dismissal of trust, as if it doubted your intentions or disbelieved in your leadership. It's a smart test: If you weren't serious about treating your culture right, this would be cause for abandoning your own commitment in disgust—you'd walk away from the culture and resort to an attitude of minimal expectations and micromanaging.

Grit your teeth, and hold steady through this test. It typically won't last long, and you'll come out the other side with real cultural momentum. Should your business ever get tested by real pressure, you'll be glad you passed this one.

WHEN THE PRESSURE DOESN'T KNOCK, IT CRASHES THROUGH THE FRONT DOOR

▶ Rackspace is a well-known and well-regarded IT hosting company, offering cloud, dedicated servers, and various combo plates. They are also well known and well regarded for the respect and affection given to their employee culture, and for how that translates to the fanatical support the culture offers its customers.

They were a client of my company for several years, and I know of many a wild and wonderful story about the commitment of management to their employee culture and the commitment of the culture right back to management. This one is my favorite.

Here's Lanham Napier, Rackspace CEO from 2006 to 2014, on his simultaneously worst and best hours on the job:

"On Monday night, on November 12, 2007, a DHL delivery truck crashed right into our Dallas data center. The driver went into a diabetic coma, jumped the curb, landed on our transformers, and knocked out all the power. It took the whole center out and canceled hosting services to a lot of our customers. We have an emergency response procedure and were immediately ready to go to backup generators, but then the fire department came and said, 'Look, the guy is still in the truck. We can't get him out unless you de-energize your building.'

"And so I was sitting on the other end of the phone in San Antonio going, 'Now what do I do? This was not in our script.' I said, 'Okay,' and then I told our team, 'All right, man, pull up the switch.' And what I should have said was, 'Can you give us a few minutes to do an orderly shutdown?' It was just a mistake on my part, and what it meant was that it caused trouble getting the chillers restarted, which took getting things back online to go from an hour recovery to, like, a ten-hour recovery, in some cases. But the dude was in the truck and we didn't know how bad he was, and I made the call.

"I felt like crap, man. I was feeling like, 'Dude, why didn't I do an orderly shutdown?' It didn't even occur to me in the moment. It was totally on me. Now this happened in the evening, after work hours for most of our employee culture. I was downstairs with our engineering teams in a darkened room, thinking I've just killed the company. And I remember walking up the stairs to the second floor, to the support floor, and I turned the corner and our whole company was there.

"They were all there, everyone, and we hadn't called them to come in. I didn't even think to do that. There were pizza boxes and food. They'd been there for hours; I just didn't know it. Their kids were in pajamas sleeping under their desks; whatever their personal situations were, they stayed there all night. And I've got to tell you, when I saw them there, I had tears in my eyes. 'It's going to be okay,' I thought. 'We're going to make it; we're going to make it through this.'

"And you know, that driver lived. We all survived."

Culture eats strategy for breakfast.

—Peter Drucker

PART 2
THE FOUR VULNERABILITIES

WHEN THE COMMITMENT OF YOUR EMPLOYEE CULTURE MEANS THE MOST

(You need meat.) Don't go no further.

—The Doors

YOUR COMPANY'S business performance is always vulnerable to the will of your employee culture, but there are two times when this is especially so:

➤ Business is on the way up
➤ Business is on the way down

This is when you need the culture to offer its maximum protection by adhering to your best judgment, and to its own, on behalf of company success.

▲ GOING UP

Scaling a great company culture when your company is growing fast:

You don't want the momentum of growth to diminish the spirit and quality of your employee culture. That could cause you to lose most of what—and who—has allowed the company to grow in the first place.

Keeping your employee culture united during mergers and acquisitions:

Just when you need the most unified and focused response from your employee culture, it will have been frozen in place. Major organizational changes call into question every rule of survival and emotional prosperity the culture depends on.

▼ GOING DOWN

Eliminating cultural complacency in a competitive market-place:

The day when your competitors relax their attempts to take your market share is the day when you won't need your employee culture's maximum innovation, rapid response, and disciplined execution.

The company is under pressure:

Should you ever stumble, fall behind, or get attacked, you'll need your employee culture to hang in, execute fast and well, and confidently represent the company's intentions with its own good name.

All of the solutions in this Vulnerabilities section are appropriate to apply to your own team, but this chapter addresses circumstances that affect the entire enterprise. These solutions are for you as a manager and for the company itself.

If you're losing your soul and you know it, then you've still got a soul left to lose.

—Charles Bukowski

SCALING A GREAT EMPLOYEE CULTURE AS YOUR COMPANY GROWS

Do you love me (now that I can dance)?

—The Contours

DOES YOUR growing company already have a healthy, supportive employee culture? Whether it was your values-based intuition (the right thing to do) or your market-based calculation (the right thing to do for the business) that got it, you sure don't want to lose it now. Dumb luck didn't bring you this far; smart instincts and an ornery point of view about how to run a business have earned you the right to grow. There is no mysterious rite of passage about what comes next, no magic revenue threshold that calls for a different philosophy. As you scale the business, it is important to scale what you do best.

The bigger you get, the sooner your company will be noticed as a looming threat on your competitors' radar screens, and the sooner they will swivel big guns in your direction. This is not the time to lose the heart of the business: what makes it great, what has attracted those who believed in it when it was just a promise. This is no time to lose the goodwill of your employee culture. More than ever, you'll need your culture to bust through front doors while watching your back door.

Of course you don't just want to compete as a much larger company; you want to win. A win that means the most is a win defined on your own terms. This is true if you plan on keeping the company, but it's also true if you plan on building, then selling it—building it right will give you the kind of market aura that causes a monstrous competitor to have to unhinge its jaws to swallow you.

When you already have a great employee culture, the key to competing against big companies is not to build another big company; it is to build a very big, small company.

1. STAY FOREVER YOUNG.

If you're moving from small to big, there will be continued pressure to fit into the professional slipstream and to prove to all, from customers to investors, that you are a safe bet. You won't be able to get away with some of the things that you once allowed your employee culture to do to blow off steam and celebrate wins, or the tolerance you might have had for individual eccentricity as a trade-off for sorely needed performance or special genius. More and more, your employee culture is going to hear, "Take that off—we're a business!" or "*Put that back on— we're a business!*"

If you're moving from midsize to bigger, there will be even more restrictions on individual judgment, even more process, even more layers, and even more determination to metaphorically dress your employee culture for success.

These kinds of constraints are a good way to build a company that operates to standard on a larger scale, but unless they're counterbalanced, they are also a good way to flatline the original feisty spirit of your employee culture. That spirit is just as important to enterprise performance now as it was back in the day.

Process, systems, and layers are all appropriate, but your company needs to pick places to dwell forever in the inappropriate, preserving the cultural personality and individual judgment that, while not disdainful of increased corporate control, remain sacred identity markers immune to taming. Your company must stay passionately, unapologetically, uncompromisingly, gleefully, and incurably crazy about some things. Don't make eye contact with us about these things, and don't ask us to turn down the music.

Walking the rolling deck between appropriate and inappropriate when the wave of growth hits is the magic that will astound your customers and confound your competitors.

• STOP THE STUPID

If you live in or have visited Northern California, you are likely aware of the Winchester Mystery House. It's an old mansion with a twisted history, the former home of Sarah Winchester, who was the widow of William Winchester, the gun manufacturer. Sarah was convinced that the ghosts of all who those weapons had killed haunted the house, and that only nonstop construction would appease the spirits.* She believed that if building ever stopped, she would die, and so, starting in 1884, she put her inheritance where what was left of her mind was, hiring crews to labor every day and night until her death thirty-eight years later, resulting in 160 rooms, 10,000 windows, 2,000 doors, seven floors, and three elevators. To confuse the ghosts, she added miles of winding hallways, stairs that went nowhere, and secret passageways that were forgotten soon after they were built.†

Segue dead ahead: As a company focuses simultaneously on growth and control, it constantly adds new policies and procedures. They're intended to speed the business as it gets more complex but often do just the opposite, adding layer upon layer of conflicting rules and processes, cumbersome procedures, and reports that go to no one for no reason, all to the anguish of an employee culture that was used to depending on its own common sense and commitment to get the job done.

Many of these policies are smart and necessary, but some are doubtless of dubious origin and intelligence. It's time to segregate them into two piles and burn one of them. This isn't meant to disrespect the need for process. Just the opposite: It is meant to reinforce the need for the right processes to help the company grow and protect the commitment of your employee culture.

---

* She could have moved to another house and left all that moaning behind, but that's just the way I think.

† Back *off*, Casper.

Start by requesting that your employee culture submit all policies, procedures, and decisions that it considers just plain dumb, redundant, time or money wasting; analysis that isn't ever analyzed; efficiency systems that are notoriously inefficient; procedures whose intention has never been understood by anyone; and any policy in violation of common sense and trust, or, worse, in violation of stated company values. Don't include just those that your employee culture thinks should stop but those it thinks should *not* have been stopped, like policies purely of benefit to your customers.

Provide a template to ensure that the submissions are addressable by senior management and that your culture doesn't perceive the request as simply soliciting rants. The template should require what the policy is, when it was implemented, which team or business unit it involves, what its negative impact is, and why it's way too dumb to live. It should request any recommendations for resolution and lessons that have been learned, like other ways the issue it addressed might have been better handled, and how to prevent something similar from happening again.

Add a reminder to steer clear of blaming anyone for the policy. The purpose here is to resolve the issue. The policy may have been flawed, but the issue it was aimed at was probably legitimate. The executive team has shown a willingness to initiate this process; the accountability from your employee culture is to provide a well-reasoned cure.

Give your employee culture ninety days to submit all recommendations, then give senior management 120 days to return orders to remove, revise, or retain. This will be a legendary proof point about how management came together to protect its employee culture from being punished by inefficiency as it tries to be accountable for success. After initial execution, this can become a gleeful annual process to blow out the pipes. Process and policy will have to make sense to stay intact.

● BACK THE WHACK

All of those bizarre little rituals, outside gatherings, contests that reward personality or pop culture more than performance, and the T-shirts, playlists, and cubicle souvenirs that your employee culture holds oddly dear? Like all things cultural, they are fraught with meaning. They confirm an employee culture's comfort with its workspace, the tolerance it believes it has earned from management, its delight in how it works and what it gets done, and its chosen heroes and villains. They are indicative of how a culture claims a company as its own, and it means it has made the blurring of work-life boundaries acceptable in part by dragging some of what is important in life into work.

Of course, your culture's expression of its comfort with being real can at times be inappropriate, unprofessional, goofy, and emotionally excessive. That's the way people are at home, with friends, at play, and about matters that mean something to them.

As organizations grow, the spirit this represents often becomes diluted—individuals who are bent that way carry on, but teams don't engage in it as much, managers don't notice it's missing as much, and companies don't approve of it as much. Is such spirit below the standards of acceptable, productive behavior? It is if "acceptable" means an uneasy no-man's-land that divides your culture from your company. If "productive" means you want your culture to work there, but not feel it lives there.

It's important to protect your employee culture's wilder rituals and celebrations. You can be moved or amused by them, but don't be disturbed. Blowing off steam is fine; it means pistons are pumping and the company is moving. Let your culture celebrate the sweat, celebrate the wins, celebrate whatever it wants to. These things are usually positive; an employee culture doesn't play at being unhappy.

As a company grows, prized cultural rituals and activities can get defunded for what are claimed to be budget conflicts but what are more likely the reprioritization of things now deemed irrelevant to an enterprise focused on the serious business of growth. Put that money back: Not everything the culture wants to do will cost, and what does cost shouldn't cost much. But even if it does, don't let that be an impediment.

License your managers to thrill. Explain the importance of endorsing the fun that the employee culture believes is important and imbed this importance right into managers' job descriptions. Fund the fun some so that managers can jump on opportunities to celebrate the spirit of the culture. Give each manager a regular budget of money and time to apply as needed, and insist they spend it. Don't try to replicate what the cultures do within their own teams on an enterprise-wide level, though; these things belong to the culture, not the company.

This isn't only about allowance in a material sense. It's as much about allowing the vibe of the tribe: some components of the business held sacred by the culture and everything else constantly subject to its benign irreverence. Those companies with the best employee cultures have a high degree of confidence in their employee culture's personality. Senior management doesn't recognize any danger in letting the employee culture be itself. The company likes the culture, and the culture likes the company.

In such companies, versions of the same personality are reflected throughout the management hierarchy. Executives in these companies are just as natural, passionate, and provocative as their people and are unafraid to show it. They get just as giddy about business done right, just as snarly about business done wrong, and are just as drawn to whack for whack's sake.

Your company's personality may be a bit more . . . tucked in . . . and your executives more reserved, but they're human, and something moves them to laugh uncontrollably, they have some guilty pop pleasures, they can't stop raging on about something. The point here is to let it be real, whatever it is. And if you in the C-suite are actually more fun and are passionate about a wider range of issues than you've thought appropriate to show your employee culture, drop the cosmetics and let those freak flags fly.* This is a signal that it's safe for your culture to be real, too.

2. INCREASE VIRUS PROTECTION.

To keep pace with growth, your employee culture will need to be increased from the outside. The bigger your own company gets, the bigger the companies you'll be recruiting from will be. Since no one inside your company will have seen the business any bigger than it is now, you'll want people with that larger enterprise experience. Those people will be drawn to you and that will be dangerous.

The danger won't show up wearing a THREAT T-shirt. It will come in the form of opportunities to hire people you need, often with impressive résumés. Sometimes those newcomers will be joining your good company from another good company, purely for the upside opportunity. But if you're renowned for having a fabulous employee culture, many will be joining to escape the downside of their current situation. Those new members won't hold your culture to its best standards; they'll hold it to a standard of "better than where I was."

This insidious erosion isn't always easy to see until you need to call your people to arms about quality or effort and find they don't come running anymore, they come stumbling and grumbling. It is staggering how quickly you can find that you don't recognize your own employee culture.

You can stop this problem before it starts by not confusing orientation with onboarding. The clearer you are about what you stand for as a special company with a special culture, the easier it is for someone to parrot that right back at you. People always seem more intelligent when they agree with your point of view; new members can enter into the culture having passed the open-book exam of an initial orientation pro-

---

* You're welcome for that image.

cess without truly being vetted. Create an onboarding process that extends ninety days and put some teeth into it, so when a new member is granted permanent status, you're confident they're the right fit.* It then becomes the entire culture's responsibility to ensure their success.

● SHOW WHAT IT MEANS TO BE A MANAGER

Maintenance of a great employee culture has a lot to do with how the culture is managed. Here, too, the threat of imported viruses is real and big. Managers will come to your company with points of view about supervising an employee culture that are contrary to what you want. These biases won't always be easy to see until they're in play; some of them are unconscious, and managers too can easily appear to be what a company wants when a company is very clear about what it wants. But your employee culture will see the difference and assume that the company sanctioned it.

To guard against this, establish firm criteria about how your employee culture is to be led and managed. Then prepare anyone assuming a management position at any level by helping them unlearn the job of management: an immediately applied development process that keeps what is right and resets what isn't. Use this process—figure a session of a couple of days—to acknowledge the competencies that they already have and let your company learn from them. Then examine what is in each incoming manager's tool kit—the skills, systems, and approaches they favor to build a team—and toss out the wrenches, hammers, and nose pliers.

This learning should be mandatory for all new managers coming into the company, regardless of level or experience, mandatory for those who are already in management positions, and mandatory for all promoted to the job of manager for the first time. Just make it mandatory.

---

* A committed employee culture will monitor this for you and expel any misfit, like the human body rejecting a goat's kidney as an attractive transplant option.

It may be harsh but it's a necessary litmus test: A constantly evolving company needs constantly evolving managers. If their egos can't handle some schooling, they are in the wrong place.* The right people will love the chance to get validation for what they believe is the better way to manage people.

Since the purpose of this learning is to help them to be successful in managing your culture, gift them with a survival guide as they graduate. With your employee culture's input, prepare a handy book (or app) that gives managers life saving info specific to managing in your company:

➤ Always do this and never do that
➤ Ten things that the culture believes that you definitely need to know
➤ How to start a fire (get things done) in the culture
➤ How to stop a fire (when things are getting done the wrong way)
➤ What intensity looks like in the company
➤ What humor looks like in the company
➤ What sentimentality looks like in the company
➤ What the culture expects from its manager
➤ What to do if the culture goes over your head to talk about you

This process isn't *How to Lead the Entitled*; as your incoming managers get some perspective and maybe some humility, that humility should extend right to your employee culture. Each manager should be ritualistically welcomed back by their teams with the message that the culture is eager to learn the benefits of their new manager's experience and is prepared to respond to the right kind of management.

All of this preparation isn't just for incoming managers. In the rush of growth, you will likely be promoting people as fast as possible from

---

* I'm still waiting for a client to take me up on the idea of putting a detox van in their parking lot for these sessions that shakes and smokes while managers are inside. Big sign painted on it: "For Those Drunk on Power." Still waiting.

within, often into management or senior management positions for the first time. They need the same prep for their employee culture and the same accountability from their employee culture.

THE OFTEN BONEHEADED HISTORY OF MANAGEMENT

▶ Current misunderstandings about what an employee culture is capable of are based on diminished management expectations and self-fulfilling beliefs that started long ago. The absurd history of early thinking wouldn't be such a big deal if it didn't affect today's relationships between managers and the employee culture. Amazingly, it may be hampering your own abilities to gain cultural commitment, without you even realizing it.

Read it and weep.

It was the best of times. Mostly it was the worst of times.

What has grown up to become "management" was born with the Industrial Revolution, circa 1750 to 1850. Before this, the world's economy had primarily been agricultural, with the centers of productivity spread among small farms. With the advent of rapidly growing machine-based manufacturing, the centers of productivity moved to the cities, and masses of job seekers moved with them.

This happened to be a time of severe economic class distinction: There were the rich, there were the poor, and there was nothing whatsoever in the middle. The minority rich, who held all the power and owned all the factories, were considered by all to be rich because they were smarter and more industrious than the poor. The poor were considered to be poor because they were stupid and lazy.

In between the rich and the poor was now jammed a new position called "manager," and that position was charged with getting results from an employee culture. People who everyone believed were stupid and lazy.

I mean everyone.

"Leave this hypocritical prating* about the working masses. The masses are rude, lame, unmade, pernicious in their demands and influence, and need not to be flattered, but to be schooled," said Ralph Waldo Emerson. "The mass never comes up to the standard of its best member, but on the contrary degrades itself to a level with the lowest," said Henry David Thoreau.

Frederick Taylor, inventor of the time-motion study and pioneer of the assembly line, enthused that "People are no more than mechanical parts of that assembly line. You don't spend time motivating them any more than you'd give positive reinforcement to a drill press." Elton Mayo, the father of the human relations movement, dismayingly noted that management was organized on the basic assumption that "workers were a contemptible lot."

Age of Enlightenment: The Dark Version

Back in the day, there was no history of employee management to study, no well-considered agreement about what worked and what didn't to ensure maximum employee productivity, and no thought about a higher level of employee fulfillment being connected to that productivity or even justified as a job condition. The science that grew up around management was as immature as management itself, and it was often evil science: cold, dismissive, and sometimes flat-out sinister.

By one hundred years in, it still hadn't gotten better, and just when employee cultures thought it couldn't get any worse, along came B. F. (Behaviorist. Fruitcake.) Skinner. Skinner believed that all human behavior was shaped by external stimuli and environment— it's what happens outside of you, not inside of you, that makes you act the way you do. His initial experiments were done on his own

* It means talking on and on about something. In this case, it means talking on and on about some lesser life-form known as "most working human beings."

daughter, but he soon moved on to working with rats and pigeons, since they were less likely to report him to the authorities.

"It is a mistake to suppose that the whole issue is how to free man," B.F. explained helpfully to management. "The issue is to improve the way in which he is controlled." In the now-classic studies during the 1940s, Skinner controlled the behavior of his animal subjects by rewarding them with food for pecking a button. Even when he removed the stimulus, pigeons would keep pecking, believing they would eventually get a reward. Companies of the time quickly seized on this concept of shaping behavior through basic reward and punishment. "Hey," they said, "we have plenty of buttons that need regular pushing! How much cheap food are we going to need?"

Skinner's findings gave management a concrete, understandable way to deal with the cause and effect of employee behavior. After determining the desired employee response, it became a matter of arranging the most fundamental stimulus to achieve it. That would be "fundamental" as in bribery and threat, not as in any higher level of emotional fulfillment. Skinner's ideas were used to create many of the era's organizational reward programs, disciplinary procedures, and management attitudes. You have no doubt experienced a compensation or performance evaluation process in your own career that's an extension of an early pigeon or rat experiment.

Let's move on.

Kurt Lewin, one of the pioneers of social psychology, formulated his famous change model for organizations in 1951. It included a fundamental first step, called "unfreezing," which was used to "motivate and make individuals or groups ready to change." It was swallowed without chewing by managers eager for the first-ever method for implementing change in an employee culture. Here are the steps:

1. Physical removal of the individual from accustomed routine sources of information and social relationships
2. Undermining and destruction of all social supports

3. Demeaning and humiliating experience to help them see their old behaviors as unworthy and thus make them motivated to change

4. Consistent linking of reward with willingness to change and of punishment to unwillingness to change

Feels warmer already, eh? Woof. Woof.

Theory Y Not

The ray of light that first scurried all the dust bunnies lurking under the stained sofa of management thinking (as it were) came about with a guy by the name of Douglas McGregor. His 1957 book, *The Human Side of Enterprise*, introduced a then mind-bending concept: An employee culture may actually want to work.

A manager's attitude depends upon their view of people, found McGregor. He divided management attitudes into two very different approaches and termed them Theory X and Theory Y.

Theory X was the prevailing management style in the 1960s. A Theory X manager, said McGregor, believes that employees are human beings who have an in-born aversion to work and will avoid it if possible. The manager must therefore use coercion, control, and the threat of punishment to harass workers into even mediocre efforts. A Theory X manager thinks employees have little ambition and actually prefer to be controlled. Otherwise, they'd be managers.

McGregor's other management type believes differently. A Theory Y manager knows that people can derive the same pleasure from work as from play, if the work is structured to provide psychological rewards. They believe that creativity and initiative can be found throughout the worker population and are not determined by job title. Theory Y, if you subscribed to it, meant that a worker's willingness to perform a job could be influenced and inspired by belief in their potential as a human being. Not too many people subscribed to it, and McGregor had to term anyone who did "the manager of the future."

The Song Remains the Same

Today's managers would never think of themselves as being Theory X types. After all, Theory X management is all about denying human potential. The unfortunate truth, as with most biases, is that Theory X behavior is persistent and lingers just under the surface of proclamations to the contrary. The history of management isn't really that old, and many of today's long-tenured managers learned how to supervise people from first- or second-generation descendants of the dark days; in turn, even if you are newer to management, you got some of this thinking when you were most eager to learn the job and were most impressionable. New managers often look to the senior-most executive in their company as a model, since that person should logically know most about how to supervise. Maybe they do, maybe they don't but either way they have probably been managing for a long time,

For all the good intentions and enlightened thinking that surrounds managers now, these early points of view are still imbedded throughout common practices of professional (and parental) authority that affect every manager. Even if you mostly escaped being influenced, that doesn't mean your employee culture completely escaped being on the receiving end. The dynamic between the two parties helps perpetuate the belief systems of both.

Some companies today are the same as all companies were yesterday: self-serving economic organisms that operate with a fundamental disdain of their constituencies. Employees and customers are unfortunate, unavoidable components that must be manipulated to assure financial success. If the Good Business Fairy descended from Planet Ten to the C-suite conference room of these organizations with a deal—"You can make your numbers and do it without employees and customers"—they'd be hacking off body parts to make the trade.

Because they don't really care about employees, such companies don't really know them. Because they don't know them, they don't know how to reach them, and efforts to motivate an employee culture are shortsighted, overtly manipulative, and fundamentally condescending. (Remember "Casual Day?" Turned out not to be an invitation for employees to spend Fridays in Mexico with umbrellas in their drinks but instead an opportunity to answer 175 emails by noon while wearing a pair of Dockers.)

The lesson that many managers learn in their formative years, directly in companies like these or as it unknowingly leeches into their DNA from exposure to generations of toxic manager thinking, is that management has to exist because an employee culture cannot fundamentally be trusted to protect the company with its own good judgment.

If a relationship is viewed as a test, the other side is bound to fail it. An employee culture will rise or fall to the level of empathy and respect it is given. You may not be one of those incorrectly thinking managers, or be working in one of those incorrectly thinking companies, but the people who comprise your employee culture have worked for other managers in other companies, and the culture's constant nervous obsession with its survival and emotional prosperity is a result of the inherited memory it, too, has built over the last couple of hundred years.

3. BE SURE TO TALK WHEN YOU CAN'T.

A growing company that heads toward its IPO may be mandated by law, investors, and common sense to keep certain information confidential. Sometimes this requirement will extend to not talking about it with the it with the employee culture. If transparency and intimacy have marked the relationship between the culture and management in the still small company, the employee culture will perceive the shutout as a signal that it can't be trusted or that management can't be. It will resent the former and could deepen its belief in the latter if there is also a recent flurry of new executive hiring to bolster the executive team pre-IPO.

The answer, as in everything having to do with your employee culture, is to tell the culture the truth, including the truth about why you can't tell it something.

4. DON'T DEMONIZE THE COMPETITION.

It's time to retire the small-medium business demographic once and for all; it's just ridiculous. Considering small and medium-size organizations to be the same is as much flawed logic for business-to-business as a business-to-consumer belief that people within an age range of eighteen to forty-five have the same preferences in style, viewing habits, and how they answer survey questions.

The driving concern of a small business is different from a medium one, and both are different from what drives a larger one. Small companies are obsessed with survival, medium companies are obsessed with growth, large companies are obsessed with protecting their status quo.

In pursuit of overtaking the next size up, a growing company will often demonize a larger competitor. This gets it off its own game and starts it acting like the competitor, right at the time it needs to be honing what it does uniquely and best. This isn't usually a good growth strategy, but the impact it has on the employee culture is even worse.

It is unhealthy energy for a culture, and should you do this in your company, you will be asking your employee culture to take its sense of self from taking down a competitor—to hurt others in another company who are linked fraternally in the Order of the Culture.

Your culture doesn't need a constant enemy to motivate it; that's cheap fuel, as unstable and unsustainable as benchmarking a culture's energy to revenue for revenue's sake. Trying to hurt another company means hurting the people within it, some of whom members of your own culture may actually know, given that it's the same industry, and all of whom your culture can empathize with. Besides, your employee culture is better motivated by a sense that what it does is special and important to the company and to those whom the company serves. This is where your culture's emotional resources need to be focused, and this is the best way to snuff the competition.

5. SANCTION THE INEVITABLE.

In a fast-growing, fast-moving company with a constant influx of new people in new positions, there are going to be a lot of things that aren't figured out: all sorts of tensions between authority and autonomy, and constant miscues and misinterpreted signals. Not everyone in the employee culture will have the tolerance for this kind of chronic chaos.

To avoid frying or losing your people, don't try to pretend that this condition is isolated or soon to be resolved. Instead, transform it into a primal source of your employee culture's energy: positive sense of self. Admit that any member of the culture could get a job at a more established, stable company where everything has already been figured out.

Then point out the only problem with that: Everything will already have been figured out. There is no opportunity to contribute, to innovate, and to solve problems that will affect the current state and future of the company. Explain that members of the company's employee culture ten and twenty years from now will benefit from the work this current culture does to create process and discipline where it's needed.

6. HONOR YOUR PAST TO PROTECT YOUR FUTURE.

It may seem that one of the perks of growing fast enough to force steady outside hiring is that you can finally swap out all of the legacy reprobates that whine about how your company's best days are behind it.

Don't do it. People whine because they care deeply about something, they can't stop it from being lost or damaged, and they can't stop caring. The whiners in your culture can be an invaluable enterprise asset.

Some longer-tenured members of your employee culture may simply be resentful of a time when the company was smaller, maybe looser, and when they had more direct impact and access to the top. But in many cases, they are self-appointed keepers of the flame who joined the company on the promise of its original purpose, and then kept the faith during the most uncertain of times. They are focused backward not to stop the company from growing, but to stop the company from growing past what they perceive it should stand for. They hold the genetic memory of your company and have a visceral sense of what is right or wrong, on or off, that your newer employees and managers couldn't possibly have.

There is a common tendency to disregard the dissatisfaction of older members of an employee culture in favor of the optimism of new recruits. The optimism of veterans is just as important, since the culture will continually check the satisfaction levels of members who've been around a while. If they sense it gets worse the longer you stick around, you'll see an increase in turnover among newer hires.

GIVE SOME HELP TO THOSE WHO MANAGE THEM

Of course just because these old-timers—no matter how young they are—were there when it all happened doesn't mean they personally made it happen. Sometimes their sense of ownership for results is way overstated, and stated loudly enough for everyone to hear. It can be intimidating to those who have to manage this outspoken group with its special aura of credibility, peer influence, and executive access.

Part of the education of your managers should be how to supervise tenured members of your employee culture: an explanation of why they are important; how to balance issues of tenure versus performance; an understanding of how veterans may see issues of growth, scale, and process; what gets them hot, what leaves them cold; how to sell change; and how to deal with their cultural influence.

PRESERVE THEIR EXPERIENCE

If the company continues to chart strong annual growth, this population will soon diminish in ratio to your overall employee culture. This may be the last generation of true veterans; in a few years, those that were here for a while won't recall the brave and funky history as something that happened to them, only to their forebears. Now is the time to begin preserving the experiences and wisdom and to choose what to have them mentor to the rest of the culture by creating your own museum. A museum that tells the history of the company to date, not just from the typical point of view of its visionary founders but from the point of view of the culture that helped build it. Think your entire employee culture won't respond to *that* kind of respect?

Your museum should start where your culture started, but this doesn't mean it should look backward. Your story is still being written and it is one of continued learning, strengthening, and progress. As such, it shouldn't speak only to victories, but to missteps that were course-corrected—especially those course-corrected by your employee culture.

Use this museum to give current members of your employee culture a sense of what it was really like back when, including what it was like to operate without the resources and reputation that the company enjoys today. Using physical space within the offices or digital space on your internal website, feature the company's original sentries in videos that explain the origins of stories, systems, and rituals that are known today. It means a lot more than some museums ever will.*

---

* When in New Delhi, be sure to visit the International Museum of Toilets—and ask the docent what grants it "international" status. In Croatia, visit the Museum of Broken Relationships—bring a date (or leave one there). In Berlin, visit the Currywurst Museum, where you can learn all about its history and "hear the sound of actual sausage cooking"—chills. Or in Austin, visit its thematic cousin, the Museum of SPAM—thrills. Stay on theme to its logical conclusion, and check out the Meguro Parasitological Museum in Tokyo—spills.

GIMME SHELTER: TACTICAL RECAP

SCALING A GREAT EMPLOYEE CULTURE AS YOUR COMPANY GROWS

The bigger you get, the sooner your company will be noticed as a looming threat on your competitors' radar screens. This is no time to lose the goodwill of your employee culture. More than ever, you'll need your culture to bust through front doors while watching your back door. This is no time to flatline the special spirit of your employee culture either. As you scale the business, it is important to scale what's best about it.

1. Stay forever young.

Constantly monitor the encroachment of unnecessary policies that tell your employee culture it cannot be trusted to use its own good judgment. As you increase what's appropriate, be sure to protect what's inappropriate—the passion, the exaggerated responses, the special sense of humor. Support but don't interfere with the strange rituals, celebrations, and decorations that are the culture's own.

2. Increase virus protection.

Be clear about what makes you special, extend the orientation process from days to months, and ensure that a new member's confirmation means that they truly understand and represent not just what the company does but how and why. Help managers new to your company recognize often-unconscious biases against respecting the power of an employee culture. Share exactly what it means to lead and manage the culture in your company. Act fast to remove managers who are obviously not cultural fits, but make it the culture's responsibility to help all other new managers become successful.

3. Be sure to talk when you can't.

Try not to reduce the transparency from management that your employee culture is used to, If you have to, explain why. Don't let the culture think you can't trust it or that you can't be trusted.

4. Don't demonize the competition.

Your employee culture doesn't need a constant enemy to motivate it. It's better motivated by a sense that what it does is special and important to the company and to those whom the company serves.

5. Sanction the inevitable.

Working in a rapidly growing company means a lot of processes and policies will be evolving as fast as the company does—or will be missing altogether. Don't try to pretend that this condition is isolated or soon to be resolved. Instead, transform it into a primal source of an employee culture's positive sense of self by explaining that this is its opportunity to create what doesn't exist and earn legacy impact, when future generations of the culture reap the benefits.

6. Honor your past to protect your future.

Don't dismiss the whiners; they are often the keepers of the flame and will alert you if it is flickering. Honor the past of your employee culture as an important signal to all of those who will join it in the future.

Between the idea and the reality . . . falls the shadow.

—T. S. Eliot

KEEPING YOUR EMPLOYEE CULTURE UNITED DURING M&A

Tonight there's gonna be trouble. Some of us won't survive.

—Thin Lizzy

MERGERS AND acquisitions can easily freeze an employee culture in place by calling into question every known rule of its survival and emotional prosperity—just about the time the company needs the culture's most fluid response.

The enterprise may not note the coming of the ice age. It may not even be that concerned about the distinction between a committed employee culture and an uncertain one, if the acquisition was intended to block a competitor from getting its claws on the company or to gut the acquisition for its assets and toss the hull, not to build a greater organization that exceeds the sum of the parts. It may not have time to sympathize even if it is aware: The company has to quickly begin a return on its investment, and plenty of beady analyst, industry, and media eyes are watching to see whether they should pronounce it a sound strategic judgment. Besides, the logic for the merger might be obvious: essential for the growth or even survival of the enterprise.

But as you now know, an employee culture is concerned about its own survival first. Its measurements are often different, and its dials are frenziedly seeking true north and safe harbor in the dizzying pitch of M&A reorder.

Many times an acquisition will go well, and the culture will absorb the changes without seeming to notice. But most times an employee culture *will* notice this:

If the acquired company was a former competitor and energy used to come from attacking it, it's confusing to both employee cultures: Now they're . . . *us*? If the founder of the smaller company was charismatic, chances are that person won't make an elegant transition to a new organization where they're not seated at the very top. If the founder leaves, the culture may feel they've lost their guiding light—or the guiding light took the money and ran. Some members of the employee culture might also have made a bunch of money from the deal, but some didn't: If both richer and poorer stick around there could be grating income disparities. Those who helped to build the smaller company will have to adjust their pacing to conform to how—and why—a larger company operates and may have to stem a leaking reason to believe.

As is standard cultural procedure, the acquired organization will reach out for information, from those in other companies that have been merged by the same enterprise and from members of other company cultures who have had any sort of merger experience. What comes back will often be grim tales that fail to calm an already twitchy group.

Meanwhile, the employee culture in the acquiring company will likely have to do more work to combine processes and goals, but it's doubtful that it'll be given any more resources, making its job harder and its patience shorter. The pressure will be on both cultures to integrate and cooperate in the name of the greater good while their every survival instinct is urging inflexibility to make sure their own people and processes emerge triumphant. There are sure to be reorganization and redundancies that affect both, and the cultures will be obsessively scanning the skies for vultures.

Let us review: Big money is noticeably spent on a merger or acquisition, which requires immediate flexibility and support from the employee culture to integrate the two organizations, but the culture is now hunkered down in its own cave focused on figuring out the rules of safety when pretty much all of those have just been called into question—who does what, who wants what, who stays and who goes, who reports to whom, and who are we now? That's too bad, because both companies' customer cultures are wondering the same thing, and this would be a really good time for the employee culture to represent enterprise intentions with its own good name. Ah, but it should all straighten out soon, because benevolent relationships are bound to develop among the existing and incoming cultures if they can just quash that anxious feeling that they'll soon be flung into the gladiator ring to see who survives.

Meanwhile, some key people have already decided to stay, some have decided to leave, and some have left emotionally even if they've stayed; it's the spirit of the culture that is departing. This would be the moment that the enterprise needs to claim confidently to the outside world that efficiency and success are intact and dependable.

If this were a trapeze act there would be a lot of casualties.

NOW, HERE'S WHAT TO DO

1. VALUE WHAT YOU BOUGHT.

An employee culture is a sizable asset in M&A: Its commitment can speed the integration of the two companies, bring the best of both to bear on the future, vouchsafe the new enterprise for customers, and send a signal to other acquisition targets that you are a great company to be acquired by. Assuming that the culture is committed.

Best then that you know ahead of time the state of the employee culture within the company you're acquiring, how this change is socialized and accepted, and any major distinctions between your culture and theirs. It should be part of the discovery process as much as financial due diligence. Spending the day on executive strategic chess moves won't get you very far if at night all the pawns move on their own back to their original positions.

2. PROHIBIT A CONQUEROR MENTALITY.

Mergers and acquisitions are generally not conducted between companies of equal size and potential. One of them is dominant, which is good strategically but not so good if it infects the culture of the ruling enterprise. This kind of arrogance and the condescension it brings will aggravate issues that you're trying to eliminate. It's also not the whole picture: You are allying with another enterprise to make a stronger market case, not buying another company because you felt sorry for it.

A competitive culture won't always make the distinction between what should and shouldn't be considered competition. Anything anxious and confused is fair game, and the tentative steps of the newly acquired employee culture may be seen as a natural target.

Your executive team needs to send the message of equality and value, often and loudly: Explain what the acquired company and the people in it have accomplished to make them such an attractive organization to pursue. Insist that diminishing this new company and its culture is the same as diminishing your own company and that it will not be tolerated. On the plus side, any aggressive examples by managers, employees, or teams to welcome the new culture should be noticed and applauded.

3. LET ACCELERATION BUILD.

The employee culture that is new to your company is going to be understandably cautious about how to perform in a way that best assures its survival and emotional prosperity. It is going to be evaluating information from a lot of sources, and between what the company says and what the existing culture says, a lot of the messages will be conflicting and unreliable.

It is going to have to learn the right way to behave and to deliver results. If your company tends to be unhelpful, impatient, or unforgiving toward those who need to tread tentatively, and to make some mistakes along the way to gaining competency, you will confound the learning process and ensure that the culture tends to be unhelpful, impatient, and unforgiving.

The incoming employee culture isn't moving slowly because it's simple; it's moving slowly because it's smart. Send a clear message of accountability to all in your existing manager and employee cultures to treat it that way, to show the tolerance and respect that will make performance acceleration a positive experience.

4. TREAT THE SACRED AS SACRED.

An acquired company's culture is going to be hypersensitive about the threat to what it considers sacred. Sometimes these are going to be big things, like its reputation for quality or innovation, its standards of customer support, and its positioning as a growing company to watch. Sometimes these are going to be less tangible things, like its access to levels of management, its familiarity with what rules can be bent or ignored to get the job done, and the emotional equity it has earned from existing relationships.

Sometimes these are going to be, well, human things. Be careful how you treat those people who have a position of success and influence, and instead transform them to cultural disciples who make the case for you. You can't be sure that anyone who leaves has a position of influence within the culture, so remember to bury your dead with dignity. The respect you show to those who leave is equated with the respect you show to those who stay.

Sometimes these are going to be small things that can't possibly mean that much, but they do: how the employee culture celebrates wins, strange little perks and weird rituals, special descriptive language, stories about key historical triumphs. They are key indicators to the culture about whether it is going to get respect and empathy from the new deal. Whatever you can keep should be kept, whatever you can improve should be offered, and whatever you have to eliminate should be done with some feeling.

Don't deny the acquired culture its history, but don't worry that it's stuck in the past: It's way too pragmatic for that. Ask yourself what would happen if you left things intact, and do that if you can. They'll be redefined naturally by the culture's new environment—all things in time.

The other danger of casually dismantling what was known by the culture in favor of what you believe to be better is that imbedded in what is sacred are solutions to problems that the company may have figured out better than you will. If your company is the bigger of the two, it's possible that the culture came up with creative but inexpensive workarounds. Documenting and comparing what's worked best in both companies is a great exercise for the culture and the enterprise.

5. FOCUS ON WHAT ISN'T CHANGING.

If there was ever a time to give an employee culture back its perspective—diminish the culture's concern that everything is subject to change and it has no way to predict its fate other than to fear the worst—it would be right about now.

To do this, focus first on what isn't changing: anything that either the new or existing—or combo of new and existing—employee cultures would dependably find the same about purpose, process, and pay.

Your employee culture is burning through a lot of energy as it seeks context, predictability, and sense of self amid the new and different. You need to replenish it, but since some of the questions the culture believes its life depends on you couldn't answer right now if your own life depended on it, give what you can in smaller steps. Explain all that you know and don't claim to know what you can't.

6. GET SOME FAST WINS.

Both your new and existing cultures need to know they can win together; they need to build trust with each other as much as with the company. Give them those opportunities, and not just around achievement of revenue goals, but around integration and common purpose. Use the wins to invent new celebrations of performance that both cultures can share. And react in a legendary way: Your employee culture needs some new legends to replace the old ones that are no longer relevant.

WHEN BAD THINGS HAPPEN TO GOOD COMPANIES

▶ By any corporate measure, EMC is a real good company. They're big: As the world's largest provider of data storage systems, they employ over 60,000 people. They're successful: As of this writing, their annual revenue charts at over $22 billion. They're smart: They have nimbly transitioned from owning their original data storage market segment to adding a credible share of information security and virtualization and are making a strong move toward private and public cloud apps. They're decent: Chairman/CEO Joe Tucci has an outstanding, eighty-nine percent approval rating on glassdoor. com, and the company has earned awards for quality of employee treatment and for social and environmental contributions.

This isn't an ad for EMC. Plenty of twist coming right up.

EMC is also real good at acquisitions. They've done over sixty of them, including the M&A Hall of Fame buy of VMware in 2004 for $625 million—current annual revenue is over $5 billion. It's a vital competence for EMC to have, since no successful company today can move slower than the speed of technology, including a technology company. The model of a successful IT hardware organization now includes positions in digital services, and that inescapable cloud. There isn't a better application of EMC's mighty cash reserves than to gain purchase in these areas, and purchasing other companies is the most direct way to do so.

So how does a real good company still end up making a series of bad moves around acquisition integration, and wind up with a cultural mess on its hands? More important for EMC—and even more important for you—what did they learn from the experience?

Perils of an Arranged Marriage

In December of 2003, hardware company EMC made its first major software acquisition, buying a company called Documentum, which specialized in digital document archiving. Documentum had recently earned $400 million in annual revenue; EMC paid $1.7 billion for it.

Like most growing companies, Documentum was proud of what it had accomplished and, for the most part, its current employee culture was who had accomplished it. The culture had a strong sense of ownership about the company it had built, and while it was exciting to be a tasty acquisition target of giant EMC, the implications of being swallowed whole and having its identity absorbed in a much larger company's digestive tract were not all that appetizing.

Whereas EMC is headquartered in Hopkinton, Massachusetts, about thirty miles outside of Boston, Documentum was in Pleasanton, California, about thirty miles outside of San Francisco. They had their own building in Pleasanton, and it was an extreme source of pride; the move from a rental space to its own building had confirmed its legitimacy and potential. The Documentum employee culture felt grand glancing up at the big "DOCUMENTUM" sign on the way in every morning. At least until the Monday morning when the sky was darkened by an enormous crane that had arrived to take it down and replace it with the one that proclaimed "EMC."

The installation took a week to complete, and for most of it just the words "MENTUM" remained on the building. EMC might as well have installed a flashing pink neon sign that proclaimed "ALL YOUR WORST FEARS HAVE COME TRUE."

The loss of its sign was a further indication of the diminishment of the Documentum employee culture's sense of self, which continued when it became apparent that it wasn't just that EMC had bought Documentum; *everyone* at EMC had apparently bought it.

Documentum was a client of my own company at the time, as was EMC later, and I heard this complaint constantly. Many bemoaned that the access they had always enjoyed was now difficult or impossible. "I used to be able to get any executive on the phone anytime I needed them," one member of the Documentum employee culture complained to me. "Yesterday, I was refused access to someone at EMC I really had to talk to—by their administrative assistant. When I complained, she said, 'We bought you.' 'Wow, you did?' I asked her. 'Did you use your credit card or just write us a check for the whole $1.7 billion?'"

The conquistador mentality that had spread throughout the EMC culture wasn't helped by the company's habit of reverentially referring to itself as "Core." "Think about it," I remember urging one EMC senior manager. "If you're Core, what does that make Documentum? Peel? These things mean something during sensitive times; you have to change that name." "We *have* thought about it," he said, "and we do have a new name." "Ah, great," I enthused. "What is it?" "We're Core. Deal with it," he said dismissively. Yum.

This attitude was never displayed or endorsed by CEO Tucci, nor by the rest of EMC's C-Suite. It was something that started deeper in the culture and initially went unnoticed from up above. The divide would have soon healed itself naturally as the two employee cultures became one, united for its own protection. But there were other tensions between the two groups, one of them being the fundamental differences between hardware and software companies.

The Ties That Blind

"Established hardware and growing software companies have completely different mentalities, and EMC didn't fully appreciate this at first," insists Mike DeCesare, who ran worldwide sales for Documentum and became EMC's EVP of field operations after the acquisition. "The only way hardware companies become big is by having a lot of market share in something that is mission-critical and reliably meeting that requirement. EMC storage competed through stability and service; it was a full relationship sell. At the time, Documentum competed on speed and innovation, which was a combination asking for trouble in that relationship."

Many of the EMC old guard were indeed troubled by the way Documentum staff thought, approached its business, and even dressed. In Hopkinton, everyone wore ties, and so soon came the pressure: All male Documentum sales employees should be wearing ties, too. At all times.

Says DeCesare, "We believed that Documentum customers expected us to be visionary and freethinking, and we felt the same way about ourselves. That's why we dressed the way we did; it was part of our identity." "I had to tell my team to wear ties," remembers a still aghast Trenton Truitt, a Documentum sales manager at the time. "Our employee culture was trying to be excited about being part of a bigger company. It was like announcing that the good news is you're playing in the Super Bowl. The bad news is you have to wear French Renaissance costumes."

Perils of a Deranged Marriage

Nowhere did the cultural conflict manifest itself more than in the sales organization. EMC's vision was that hardware and software would join hands and hearts in a client's lobby and ascend as a mighty united force to win business. The reality was that they couldn't even look at each other in the client meeting, because they'd scratched each other's eyes out in the elevator.

"You can't blame EMC for this," says DeCesare. "In the beginning, we were more a threat to the sales team than any sort of attractive partnership. When you have a ninety-nine-point-nine percent uptime claim and that kind of loyalty to and from your customers like they did, you take it seriously."

"EMC sales thought we were lazy and not making enough phone calls, but our sales cycle was radically different, serving different customers on a completely different end of a client's organization," insists John McGee, who was a vice president of sales at Documentum. "EMC thought we prized innovation over stability and saw us as a risk. They went nuts and boxed us out. We were the plague. They tried to control everything, and so *our* culture went nuts."

"Both cultures were very aggressive about winning, and all hell broke loose," says Trenton Truitt. "It was, 'It's my account.' 'No, it's *my* account.' We'd end up with fifteen people pulling up to the client in a van, everybody thinking, Who *are* these people?"

Boston Blue Bloods Meet the Church of the Rock-and-Roll Lizard

And so the stress continued to build and ironically came to a head with how the different cultures dealt with stress. EMC would get the job done, then button-down to ensure that whatever had happened didn't happen again. Documentum would get the job done, then party down to celebrate getting it done.

For Documentum, the biggest party of the year was always its annual Sales Kick-Off (SKO), a three-day extravaganza for the sales team to learn about new products and policies, meet peers they didn't often get a chance to see, and generally act like loons. Remember when feral beasts once roamed the earth, lunging at food and roaring at the sky for no apparent reason? So did the sales team, and they couldn't wait to get to Las Vegas and do it again. This was a software company.

Meanwhile, planning was in motion for the first-ever SKO event since they became EMC, which would take the place of Documentum's own sales event. It would be the first time that EMC had brought their entire organization together, including all of the acquired companies, all of the executive teams, and key people from partner and client organizations, totaling about 10,000 people. It was a big, critical event and in the planning meeting was CEO Joe Tucci and members of the EMC and Documentum executive teams, including Mike DeCesare. "You're not saying much," said Tucci to a noticeably glum DeCesare. "Do you have anything to add?"

"I'm like, 'To be honest, I do,'" recalls DeCesare. "'The agenda seems terrible. Eighty-seven different people presenting their slice of the world means this isn't going to be very motivating to anyone.'

Joe said, 'What do you think we should do?' 'Two words,' I said. 'Get Aerosmith.'"

"And [CFO] David Goulden looks over and goes, 'I actually agree. I think we should have a joint cultural liaison.' I said, 'I'm not talking about a joint cultural liaison. I'm talking about Aerosmith.' And Joe says, 'Well, how much you need?' 'A million bucks,' I said. 'Done,' he said."

Tick. Tick. Tick.

Of course, Aerosmith couldn't be the only stars; the Documentum employee culture looked to DeCesare, not Steven Tyler, for continuing inspiration. But a theme suggested itself* and it was decided that Aerosmith would come on during the first day, and on the second day the stage would remain set up the same, except this time, supported by a professional touring band and backup singers, DeCesare would surprise the audience by taking the microphone.

Tick. Tick. Tick.

DeCesare is a born presenter, and he swaggered out onstage, slugging look-alike ice tea out of a Jack Daniel's bottle and bellowing, "Sell this way! Raise hell this way!" to the frenzied delight of the Documentum part of the audience and the wide-eyed, stunned silence of the EMC part. The song screeched to an end, culminating in the three female backup singers turning away from the audience and bending over to reveal a large EMC in rhinestones on their respective panties.†

Tick. Tick. Tick. Boom.

"The reason I took such an extreme position about this event was that people down a level in the EMC organization were fighting hard to override our culture with theirs, and I felt like we had to fire back a little bit," explains DeCesare. "If I had any chance of making this asset work for EMC, I had to show my employee culture that I

---

* I suggested it, if you want to get specific.

† I did not—repeat, did not—suggest that last part.

was willing to stand up for them as aggressively as the EMC folks were willing to stand up for theirs. Our team couldn't lose its spirit and still perform the way the company needed us to.

"I knew that it would be incredibly uncomfortable for a lot of people in the room," he admits. "But I've got to tell you, the two thousand people who worked for me sure bonded with me that day. They understood what I was doing and why."

A Tale of Two Mikes

"I still get flashbacks," shudders Mike O'Neill, EMC's vice president of Integration Management, when I remind him of Documentum's 2004 wake 'em and shake 'em presentation in Las Vegas. To be fair, he wasn't in his current position when those backup singers were in theirs.

It's obvious that valuing and protecting the cultural component of acquisitions are lessons that have been learned by both Mikes and the companies they represent. And it seems that both have come to some of the same conclusions about how to do it.

Don't Touch Me There

"An acquisition typically starts with backslapping and belly bumping, then becomes head scratching and feet moving," says Mike O'Neill. "We want to answer how great outcomes can happen reliably. It is really more about culture than anything else—this is what we needed to learn about how to integrate and sustain and protect. The value of our acquisitions cannot really be sustained if we fail to understand what drives that value.

"We've learned a lot since Documentum," O'Neill claims. "There's a much better sense of the cultural differences and what we have to pay attention to, what sacred practices we need to leave alone." That's not the only thing EMC has learned to leave alone. "Do *not* touch the sales organization," O'Neill says emphatically.

To Protect and to Serve

"It is one hundred percent about the culture," declares Mike De-Cesare today. "I recognize this now, loud and clear." He left EMC to run worldwide sales for digital security company McAfee, which ironically was then acquired by Intel, but at least it resulted in his promotion to president of McAfee.

"At McAfee, every decision I make about an acquisition in the first twelve months is through the eyes of the acquired company," he says. "We're not just buying their technology; we're buying their culture. So I have to make decisions in the business that absolutely send a signal that I respect their culture, that I'm not looking to kill it, and that I want the best of what McAfee can bring to their business, but not in an overwhelming or suffocating way.

"My first step is to have the CEO of an acquired company report right to one of my direct reports on our executive leadership team, no lower than that. I want this new culture to feel that they have someone big and powerful standing up for them.

"My next step is to focus on the three or four things that you can really do to add value to their business, and do only those things. We will not look for economies of scale in the sales organization, though, because this creates anxiety and chaos that affects the entire business."

Cap Those Flames but Stay Hot

"Joe Tucci has always had a mind-set about acquisitions that is, in his words, 'We will do no harm,'" explains O'Neill. "On one level, I think it resonates, and on another level, it is unfortunately prohibitive. We're going to have to change *something* to deliver to the acquired entity what we promised we were going to bring to it, and the minute we do, we are seen by the employee culture as going back on that promise.

"To protect that intention, we now immediately put what I call 'fire spotters' into an acquired company. These are EMC people who understand our priorities, and they are especially empathetic individuals who will be fine-tuned to any violation or anxiety on the part of the employee culture. We also bring in someone from HR who clarifies that forty-five different things don't need to be done immediately; you only need to do these few, and we'll help you with them.

"Our job is to add value without suffocating the acquired organization and losing the personality of the company. The employee culture deserves the confidence that this thing won't be run out of some pasture in the back forty by people who are completely disconnected from their overall business.

"We want to do two things," O'Neill declares. "The second thing is that we want to continue to broaden our awareness of where the value is in an acquisition and how we sustain that value through culture." He pauses. "The first is that we want EMC to be a great company to be acquired by."

GIMME SHELTER: TACTICAL RECAP

KEEPING YOUR EMPLOYEE CULTURE UNITED DURING M&A

Mergers and acquisitions can easily freeze an employee culture in place by calling into question every known rule of its survival and emotional prosperity—just about the time the company needs the culture's most fluid response. The logic of the deal may be sound, for obvious reasons, but your employee culture operates on its own logic, for its own reasons.

1. Value what you bought.

An employee culture is a sizable asset—in this case, both the acquired culture and the culture it is being merged into. To minimize its value is to reduce the value of the acquisition. You bought it, now make sure it buys you by treating it with the respect you'd give to any business asset.

2. Prohibit a conquerer mentality.

Your executive team needs to set the strong standard of equality, often and loudly. The acquired employee culture built a company worth acquiring, and once the organizations are merged, they are under equal protection and deserving of equal respect. Start by learning from the acquired company, even if it is smaller—especially if it is smaller and had to do more with less.

3. Let acceleration build.

The employee culture that is new to your company is going to be understandably cautious about how to perform in a way that best assures its survival and emotional prosperity, when it's still trying to figure that out. Send a clear message of accountability to all in your existing manager and employee cultures that they should show the tolerance and respect that will make performance acceleration a positive experience.

4. Treat the sacred as sacred.

An acquired company's culture is going to be hypersensitive about the threat to what it considers sacred—big things and small things. They are key indicators to the culture about whether it is going to get respect and empathy from the new deal. Whatever you can keep should be kept, whatever you can improve should be offered, and whatever you have to eliminate should be done with some feeling. Whatever you can learn that will help make the new company better should be appreciated.

5. Focus on what isn't changing.

Your employee culture is burning through a lot of energy as it seeks context, predictability, and sense of self amid the new and different. You need to replenish it, but since some of the questions the culture believes its life depends on you couldn't answer right now if your own life depended on it, give what you can in smaller steps.

6. Get some fast wins.

Both new and old cultures need to know that they can win together. Give them the opportunity to get points on the board, and invent new ways to celebrate when they do.

Anyone who says you can't herd cats has never heard the sound of a can opener.

ELIMINATING CULTURAL COMPLACENCY IN A COMPETITIVE MARKETPLACE

Rust never sleeps.

LARGER COMPANIES commonly bemoan that they want their employees to act like entrepreneurs. Let's get this out of the way right now: No, you don't. Entrepreneurs are justly lauded for their ability to sometimes gather a handful of mud and twigs and, with unique vision and extreme tolerance for risk, use them to construct a great empire. Left unsupervised, though, they are equally capable of turning that empire right back into a handful of mud and twigs. Bringing entrepreneurs into a complex enterprise that favors control over creativity is like thinking, now that you've got your log cabin built, it would be a swell idea to get a few termites as pets.

Besides, it's not like entrepreneurs are drawn to a complex enterprise. Entrepreneurs want to do entrepreneurial things, not work within the shrouds of rules, layers, and process. What you really want from your employee culture is the entrepreneurial essence—strong sense of ownership, tireless support of what is most important, innovative solutions to seemingly intractable problems—applied to your organization's performance goals.

You want accountability.

An employee culture is willing to be accountable for its performance, but this can't be punishing to do. Your culture has to be able to reliably link behavior to its survival and emotional prosperity—it needs you to provide the proper tools, support, recognition, and consistency to make that link. Essentially, your employee culture wants you to be accountable, too.

1. PREVENT COMPLACENCY.

The opposite of accountability, and what a company fears most from its employee culture, is complacency: a culture that is uncaring, unwatchful, uncompetitive, and difficult to energize toward any new performance goal. A complacent culture is directly tied to its perceptions of the rules of survival and emotional prosperity being difficult to forecast and affect.

This is more often the case in larger companies, since growing companies would never dare to dream that their success is assured. Although a big company has bigger enemies and can't ever take market position and revenue for granted, an exaggerated threat message meant to be taken literally doesn't ring true for its employee culture. The culture fully understands the need to remain fiercely competitive, but it doesn't need a group degree in forensic accounting to figure out the company is not literally at the precipice of ruin.

If a company continues to cry wolf and flog its employee culture with the For Emergencies Only whip, claiming that it will soon be out of business with lives lost unless the culture works harder and sacrifices more—when the enterprise is known to have cash reserves greater than the GDP of a midsize continent, which its employee culture recognizes could comfortably feed every one of the estimated 160,000 wolves that inhabit North America and the combined continental landmass of Europe and Asia, so said wolves are actually passed out after another big meal rather than trotting hungrily after the purportedly limping company—it will stop responding to these constant exhortations to action.

This is true as well if your company continues to meet its numbers every quarter. A sense of inevitability trending toward inertia can grip your employee culture: The company will continue to make the numbers, and the culture will continue to get rewarded, by doing things the way they've always been done. The drive that the culture needs to keep the machine moving is predictable and measured, which can look a lot like complacency.

If either is the case—unconvincing threat or convinced of success—the culture's energy must be refocused: linked to something naturally regenerative to an employee culture. Beyond the size and revenue achievement, this is the use of the company's continuing power for greater good, finding new challenges that require a refreshing humility to achieve, and adoption of the spirit of generosity toward its industry that a true market leader exhibits.

2. GRANT AUTHORITY.

The companies with the most accountable employee cultures aren't the ones with the most controls; they're the ones that most trust the culture to use its own good judgment. Of course they have checks to protect against innocent mistakes of large caliber or abuse of the system—*доверия, но проверить**—but the emphasis isn't as much on those controls as it is on the confidence given to the culture.

Allowing a customer-facing employee culture to make customers happy no matter what it takes isn't just the best way to increase customer loyalty. It's the best way to increase cultural accountability, too. Give your culture the authority to resolve customer problems, and give it the ability to do something special for customers if it perceives the opportunity. If your employee culture isn't directly involved with customers, give it greater authority to protect the company's purpose and quality standards, which helps confirm its positive sense of self.

---

* Translates as trust, but verify. Just showing off with one of the two sentences I know in Russian, both of which mean pretty much the same thing. The other is *Что входит в этот суп?* (What's in this soup?).

Accountability without authority equals punishment. The more accountability you expect from your culture, the more authority it should have to accomplish what it is responsible for delivering. The more it accomplishes, the more it should be granted first-class citizenship within the enterprise.

● DECLARE THE EMPLOYEE CULTURE BILL OF RIGHTS

One of the recommendations that my company often makes to our clients is to implement an Employee Culture Bill of Rights. It is intended as a provocative C-suite declaration, proclaiming a spirit of respect for the value of its employee culture.

My company's international clients prefer other titles, since the Bill of Rights is an iconic American document, but I've always liked the implication. While the enterprise is hardly a democracy for its employee culture, the intention to protect this quality of life at work indicates that the culture has accountability for it, too. A democracy cannot remain vibrant if treated with complacency by its constituents.

The Employee Culture Bill of Rights serves as a declaration of the essential regard the company has for its employee culture. This is not a declaration of independence, but rather dependence: As a foundational document about life, liberty, and the pursuit of happiness, it depends on the participation of the employee culture to protect it with the kinds of behaviors worthy of continuing it.

This Bill of Rights has proven to be the stuff of cultural legend for three reasons. First is the relative audacity of an executive team to declare an intention purely of benefit for its culture.

The second legend comes from the intensity of the protection. The Bill of Rights shouldn't be announced to your employee culture without considerable thought given to how to protect its intent. A secure process is needed to allow the culture to report any violations, questions, or comments directly to the C-suite without threat of retribution, although instructions are to attempt to use regular

THE {COMPANY} EMPLOYEE
BILL OF RIGHTS

LIFE

You have chosen to work in a demanding industry, for a company obsessed with setting a new standard of impact. You have a right to be challenged constructively by this life at work, as well as the right to enjoy and explore your life outside of work. You have a right to be managed by someone who considers it important that you are able to balance life and work to help reach your personal and professional goals.

LEADERSHIP

You have a right to work for managers who behave like leaders. You have a right to know them – what they believe, what they are asking from you, and what you can ask from them. You have a right to direct contact with any of them without any chance of recrimination. You have the right to open and honest communication, even when the honest answer is they don't know or they cannot tell you.

RESPECT

You have a right to be treated with respect and decency at all times, including stressful times. People that you work with, whether they're inside or outside of our company, have a right to be treated this same way by you. You have the right to voice the truth as you see it about how to improve the organization, even if it's not the truth others want to hear. You have the obligation to hold yourself accountable for what you do but also the right to learn and grow from your mistakes.

ACHIEVEMENT

You have a right to a workplace where your contribution makes a difference. You have a right to discussion at any time about your objectives, performance and potential. You have the right to support or encouragement that helps you grow. You have a right to have the very best expected of you, backed by the confidence that you can deliver it.

IT IS THE INTENTION OF THE EXECUTIVE TEAM TO HELP TO ENSURE THESE RIGHTS WITH YOUR EQUAL COMMITMENT, THEY WILL BECOME A REALITY.

CEO signature /   COO signature /   CFO signature /

CTO signature /   CIO signature /   CMO signature /

EVP signature /   EVP signature /   EVP signature /

channels first—it remains the culture's accountability to help make this work.

Every regular operational meeting of your executive team should include a review of these reports, and not as the last item on the agenda, where it can be rushed or replaced. Protection of the Bill of Rights should be imbedded into job requirements for every manager, and there should be career and compensation implications.

The third legend comes from the effort. This is my favorite part, and not just because I don't have to personally do it. We strongly recommend that the document be produced as a single-sheet hard copy for each employee and that each of those copies be *hand-signed* by every member of the C-suite.

Many of our clients feature an employee culture numbering in the thousands or tens of thousands and the immediate reaction of the C-suite signatories to this is an inspiring, "What are you, *nuts?* No way." It can take many months before it is groaningly ready for presentation to the culture, but reaction to the signatures regularly proves second only to the document itself.

The entire process is a provocative action, followed by a significant action, followed by an outrageous action. But when the culture gets this announcement of intention and protection, then gets the document, and then finally gets that the signatures are real on every copy distributed, the company gets its hardwired cultural legend.

3. PROMOTE CURIOSITY.

A learning organization is a wonderful thing, but many companies are the exact opposite. They offer a development curriculum that few have time to attend and fewer have time to absorb. There is little opportunity for the culture to test new behaviors, and no tolerance for making mistakes. There is no pursuit of learning for anything other than to improve the fortunes of the enterprise, so no creative muscles are being stretched, and very little of what is learned is transferrable outside of the job, so its practice remains limited.

In these companies, which are essentially mediocrity factories, the driving message to the culture is to drive: Absorb as much as it can, do as much as it can, and keep moving. Ironically, the speed at which the enterprise moves will slow down an employee culture, since it becomes distracted by having to constantly recalibrate the rules of survival and emotional prosperity amid the blur.

There is a difference between getting bigger and growing up, and it's the difference between intelligence and wisdom. Wisdom is intelligence that has been seasoned by the lessons of experience. Intelligence understands the present; wisdom predicts the future. Intelligence can produce fast results; wisdom can produce lasting results.* The transformation from intelligence to wisdom in your company requires promoting introspection, challenge, and enlightenment in your employee culture. This is a formula for captivating and deepening its attention and increasing its accountability.

This means you can increase traditional employee development, but also encourage learning for its own sake, knowing it will give a return on its investment. So take a thought leadership position within your industry that challenges your employee culture to think bigger. Arrange for a tour of other companies in wildly different industries, and have the culture report back learning that is applicable to your company. Sponsor book clubs, music clubs, and any other group that members of your employee culture want to hoist a geek flag for. Present contest problems that require creativity to solve. Mix technical training curricula with humanities courses.

Whether it's standard skills-building training or something fruitier that you endorse simply to charge your employee culture's synapses, allow room to try, fail, and get stronger. Becoming newly competent at anything means dealing with the impatience, small victories, and de-

---

* Intelligence means knowing that a tomato is a fruit. Wisdom means knowing that you don't put it into the fruit salad.

termination that accompany the process. This will be a new source of energy for your employee culture, which will help fuel the energy it brings to the rest of the business, and it will remind your culture never to take other competencies for granted.

It will be the fuel for innovation too. Lack of innovation is not an indication of your culture's inability to innovate. It is an indicator of your culture's perception that innovation is unlikely to be encouraged or appreciated. Your employee culture is closest to customers, products and systems; it has plenty of ideas. These ideas will be multiplied if the culture is constantly fed new perspectives, metaphors, and systems for thinking, and new channels to communicate what it's thinking.

4. CREATE PERFORMANCE.

Consider all the things that managers have gotten people to do in the 3,500 years of recorded business history. Pretty impressive—unless you stack it next to all the things that leaders have gotten people to do in that same amount of time. The relationship between leaders and followers is humanity at its most potent. An employee culture will give it up for leaders in a way they'll never give it up for managers.

Management controls performance in an employee culture because it impacts skill; it's a matter of monitoring, analyzing, and directing. If you want to improve the skill of your culture, you should definitely manage it, but don't lead it. Leadership won't control anything. Leadership, which is a matter of modeling, inspiring, and reinforcing, *creates* performance in an employee culture because it impacts willingness.

The relative quality of performance from your employee culture probably has little to do with its skill. Those in the culture already know how to do their jobs—you hired them because they had that basic capability, and once they get an orientation to your products and procedures, they're skilled. From that point on, the quality and quantity of your employee culture's performance depends on its willingness to use that skill to the utmost, regardless of whether you're hovering over it like a supervisory gargoyle.

If you're trying to get more skill from already skilled people, you're pushing a dead button. This makes leadership more important than management: How can you control what you haven't first created?

Complacency doesn't just mark employee cultures that are less than competent; it breeds in employee cultures that are extremely competent. Such cultures are confident of success, enjoy the regular autonomy they have earned, and are entitled to all the material rewards they receive. The problem is what else to give the employee culture to ensure dependable commitment and a willingness to crank results up even higher.

Those that successfully manage the most competent cultures know that leadership and what it provides—meaning, vision, deep trust, and collaborative humanity—is the only solution.

LIGHTS, ACTION, CULTURE

▶ Montreal Canadiens' hockey goalie Jacques Plante once famously complained, "How would you like a job where every time you make a mistake, a big red light goes on and 18,000 people boo?" Multiply that by a factor of up to *three hundred million* and you have the spotlights that these employee cultures work under.

Here are four circumstances where an employee culture, sometimes just recently assembled, sometimes unknown to one another, have to perform live with balletic coordination and exacting attention to detail, when mistakes will be noticed, sometimes by the entire world, and remembered, sometimes for decades. They need to move fast, take directions accurately, act quickly on their own initiative, work as a team, and execute perfectly.

These four cultures have two things in common. First, they are comprised of very competent people; the circumstances under which they work wouldn't tolerate anything else—the job couldn't get done. Second, but as a result of the first, they are led more than they are managed.

CNN Scrambles to Assemble a Breaking Story

Forget the arguments about a partisan point of view. Forget the occasional humiliating misstep. Focus here instead on an employee culture that has to seize an urgent developing story of global importance right as it's happening, take fast feeds from different countries in different languages, double-confirm the facts, anticipate the arc of an unpredictable narrative, all the while balancing the possibility that some lives of their own team may be in jeopardy with a business imperative to get the story first when nobody owns it for more seconds than it takes to hit social media. And the world may literally be watching: CNN is available to over 360 million households in over 200 countries, not including airports and hotel rooms around the world (890,000 rooms in the U.S. alone), plus their website and the 268,559 sites that link to it.

While we're on the numbers, the eight words that forever raised the bar on expectation of news immediacy were uttered by a CNN reporter on January 16, 1991. As anchors of major networks sat comfortably behind desks in New York and Los Angeles waiting to narrate prerecorded film, a reporter on fledgling broadcaster CNN reported, *"This is Bernie Shaw. Something is happening outside."* Shaw was talking as he was moving from his room at the al-Rashid Hotel in Baghdad to the balcony, where he and two other CNN reporters were placing themselves directly in the line of fire to get the story. That war coverage was ultimately watched by more than one billion people and set the standard that the CNN employee culture still holds itself to in the event of a story of worldwide significance.

This is an expert employee culture under pressure.

Inside the Sweat Lodge

At CNN/U.S. in Atlanta there is the newsroom, where video and audio operators are bringing up various feeds—often from unstable hot spots in the midst of crisis—and actually writing the story that will go on air. Sitting next to them is the logistics team, who is coordinating satellite transmissions and fiber optics, which is near the international desk, where people are juggling dozens of ringing phones and blinking computers to coordinate with CNN teams and affiliates around the world. Since there is no way a single organization can have the exclusive on a huge story, the assignment desk is monitoring broadcasts from other news outlets worldwide on a wall covered by sixty screens while dozens of computer monitors are tracking user-generated information from sources who may be located where the story is happening but must be credible. Nearby, the logistics team is frantically working to ensure that crews are getting to the right places and, where necessary, that security teams are getting there with them.

Then there is the team in the control room, who actually puts it all on the air, cueing up graphics, coordinating with anchors and on-screen reporters, while CNN's other networks are doing the same around the world, and at the same time its mobile and website teams are working to get their versions of the story out.

"Adrenaline is high," says CNN's former president, Jim Walton. "We don't keep our people in those seats for more than a few hours, because we want them to remain on their game. The same goes for managers who are keeping them on their game; on big stories an executive producer might stay in the control room for four to eight hours, but they rotate in and out so there is constant coverage.

"It is very intense. I mean . . . it is *very* intense."

I ask Jim about management's role amid the intensity. "The executive producer is the master coordinator and final decision maker about what goes on the air, but they're working as much as supervising," he explains. "The rest of senior management is overseeing and giving guidance as to what story angles to take and making sure that we're getting it from all perspectives. Mostly we're trying to be available and stay out of their way while they do their jobs. Somebody needs to be sitting back from the madness of those rooms. It's our job to answer any questions, and give support as it's needed.

"We'll come down to make sure that everyone is all right, let them know that we understand how much pressure they're under, remind them that it's more important to get it right than to get it fast, and make sure they have what they need. But these are the teams who are doing it, and they're good at it," he insists. "Our job is to get out of the way, and let them do what they do best.

"Do we drill?" he says in response to my next question. "Don't need to. There are years and years of these major stories happening and years and years of experience in reporting them. You couldn't be in those rooms if you didn't know how to do your job. You'd melt from the heat."

When Your Passport Gets Stamped "Don't Go There"

"To a certain extent the people in Atlanta can do the best planning in the world," Jim explains. "But when you're in the field reporting the story and a firefight breaks out, *those* people are on their own. They've got to figure out whether to go around that darkened corner when there's been the sound of gunfire and explosions for the last hour."

This doesn't seem like something the network would highlight in the job description but for those driven to do it, it would *be* the highlight. "We put a lot of thought into who goes into a danger zone and why they do it. There are three types of people," he describes. "Those who truly are believers and they think it's important to witness history and report on it, and to hold those in power accountable for their actions. Then there are those who do it for fame and fortune, believing that if a big story happens, 'I'm going to be a star and good things will happen to me.' And there are those who are adrenaline seekers.

"We try to be aware of the leader's personality. Because there's a leader in every crew that goes into a hot spot, and they're going to make the call in the moment, not management in Atlanta. We want to be sure that they're going to listen when the cameraperson says, 'No, I don't want to go around that corner.'"

"Does a mania for the story ever cause the control room to have tension with the field?" I ask him. "Regularly," he responds. "In the control room, they want the pictures. They want that story. And you know, we've had instances where they wanted a live shot late at night, and you have to turn lights on for that. And the people on-site are saying, 'No, it's too dangerous. There are snipers here.' And there is tension back and forth.

"But somebody will always say, 'Look. It's over.' The people on-site always win. It's just people competing against their own standards, wanting to do better, and as soon as they stop and think about it, it's, 'I get it. Yeah, you're right. Be safe. We'll hear back from you when you can.'

"Even if they want to go, sending those people into possible harm's way is a really, really hard decision," he says. "At CNN, we have a volunteers-only policy and we won't send anybody into a war zone if they don't want to go. It probably doesn't surprise you, but there's never a shortage of people who want to go. It's exactly what you're talking about, that sense of self of an employee culture. These people are energized by it; the entire culture is energized by it. And it becomes the job of management to assess what to do."

That doesn't seem to be a highlight of a senior management job description either, and Jim agrees. "One of the longest nights that I ever had as president was when CNN suddenly got kicked out of Baghdad while the war was going on," he recalls grimly. "It meant that our people had to drive from Baghdad to the Syrian border, which was like six hours, while American planes were shooting at any moving vehicles in the area. We had a live camera set up at the checkpoint to confirm when they showed up, but we knew they might not make it. Yet they couldn't stay where they were—the Iraqi government was not in a tolerant mood. We had no control, no way to help them."

Call for You on Line Three, Jim. It's a Mr. It-Gets-Worse

"Hey, Stan, I'll tell you a great story about that war," Jim says. "I'm in the job of president only a couple of months. One day I get very credible confirmation that the hotel our people are staying at in Baghdad is a target because it's got communications equipment in there and so, get them out. I have a meeting right away with some of our people here and I decide the team in Baghdad will stay, but they'll move across the Tigris River to a different hotel.

"If Saddam doesn't let them do that because it's CNN and everybody else will wonder why CNN's moving, we'll pull them out of the country. If he takes them as human shields, we'll deal with that. It was big, big-time stress in Atlanta," he says quietly, remembering. "By the way, I had called our main Baghdad correspondent who was over there and talked to him about what he wanted to do, and there were six people there, and I talked to all six about it. They all wanted to stay, and I wrestled with whether they were just saying that because they didn't want their colleagues to think they were cowards. Do they really want me to pull them out? But I decided, okay, we'd go with their judgment and pull out only if we have to.

"Now, you'll love this," he says. "Ted Turner's out of the company at this point, but about a half hour later my assistant tells me Ted's on the phone. Someone in our meeting had called Ted to update him, so I say, 'Hey, Ted, what's going on?' and I hear, 'Damn it, Jim! You're going to ruin everything I built!' 'What are you talking about, Ted?' He's bellowing, 'You can't do this to me. You can't pull our people out of there!' I said, 'Ted, calm down. There's a war, they're in danger.' 'You're damn right,' he's screaming. 'Wars are dangerous. What do you expect? You can't pull them. We need people to witness history. You can't do this!'

"Then there's this pause, and he goes, 'I'm coming down to pick you up in fifteen minutes.' I asked, 'Why are you going to do that, Ted?' 'Because I'm going to take you down to Grady Hospital. We're going to go into the cancer ward, and we're going to grab some terminally ill patients, and we'll send them over there to cover the war for us.'

"'You are *kidding* me,' I say.

"No, that's Ted. He felt it was so important for CNN to witness that history and transmit it to the world that he was telling me if you'll feel bad about sending your own team, send these people because they're as good as dead anyway. I said, 'Come on, Ted, just relax,' and so then he says, 'Send me, send me! I don't have anything to live for anymore. My wife left me, I got fired, and I don't have any money left. Send me!'"

"Man, what did you do?" I ask him, not sure I want to know.

"What could I do? I just laughed and said, 'Don't worry about it, Ted. We haven't decided to pull anybody out. If they let us move, we'll move. If they don't let us move, we're going to extract them.'"

"Wow!" I exclaim. "How was your day at the office, dear?"

"Well, that's part of my job," Jim says. "It was pretty tough for those in the field that day, too."

THE SUPER BOWL IS ON, AND THE LIGHTS ARE OFF

"Camera 10, back up with the throw. Camera 22, stay with the man in motion. Camera 8, you've got this guy, follow him. Camera 15, I need you on coach reaction."

"I'm talking nonstop for three hours," says Emmy Award–winner Mike Arnold, lead game director for the NFL on CBS and the director of the Super Bowl. During those three hours, other numbers are talking too: Over 108 million viewers, justifying ad costs of $4 million for thirty seconds and igniting Internet gambling of over $93 million.

Mike Arnold isn't paying attention to any of those numbers. He is focused on fifty.

That's the number of television screens in the eighteen-wheel semitrailer parked outside the stadium. Inside the trailer, Mike is watching those screens intensely, directing editors, graphics, tape teams, and the camera teams on the field, all of whom are tracking the game as fast as it happens. He is making split-second coverage calls about which picture is going out on the air, live, to 180 countries.

Live. One hundred and eight million people. One hundred and eighty countries. Zero margin for error. This kind of make-it-or-break-it pressure would cause many managers to scream at their people—or to run shrieking for the hills. Not this guy: He's got the standing heart rate of an iguana.

A lot of his equanimity has to do with the quality of the team. The rest of it has to do with what little getting upset would accomplish. "They're all professionals," he tells me. "I use my own core team of twenty-five, and I cherry-pick the best of the rest. Everyone has been working football all year, so they intuitively understand the rhythm of the game. It's an honor to work the Super Bowl, and everyone knows it. Everybody wants to do their best."

"But even superstars need pumping up," I say. "That's true," he agrees, "but I don't do a lot of rah-rah before the game. I do tell them, 'Hey, you never know what will be the moment that everybody remembers from this Super Bowl. You could be the cameraman who has that or the tape guy who has the replay. If people remember it, they're going to remember it for a long time.' Then I counter the pressure by reminding them that once the kickoff happens, it's the same eleven players on eleven players, and they've all done this before.

"The game is going to be the game," he says. "We can only anticipate so much, and that's what makes it so exciting to watch. Sure, we can miss a key shot, but to get on my guys for it won't help and may not be fair. Remember, it's the quarterback's job to fake *everyone* out. I stay positive and supportive. If my guy misses a play, I'm not happy about it, and I may yell instructions, but I'm not yelling at my guy. What's the point of reprimanding someone in the middle of the action? I need them to focus on the game."

"Since a percentage of your employee culture is new, how do you rehearse?" I ask. "We don't just show up on Sunday to cover the game," he responds. "We watch a lot of films, visit the teams, and hold camera meetings. And then a week before, we bring a high school team into the actual stadium and have them run plays we think are going to happen in the big game, so we can block out camera angles." "A *high school* team?" I ask. "Of course, NFL players are a lot faster," Mike adds. Well . . . yeah.

"One of the things we do drill for is if someone runs onto the field," he offers. "Then we have a combustible situation that may be entertaining to some but might also be dangerous."

One of the things that Mike and his team never drilled for is what would happen if someone ran onto the field but they couldn't tell because nobody could even *see* the field: the midgame loss of power in Super Bowl 2013. "That was just surreal," he says. "Our cameras are shooting up in the lights and suddenly they lose the lights. Hey, what happened? When the lights went, we lost all of that power that went to the lights, which goes to a lot of our cameras, so we lost a bunch of cameras. We lost communications with our announcers in the booth, so they couldn't hear us. We were just flying blind, but we didn't panic. It was a fast team response: How do we get the cameras back? How do we fill the air with whatever we can?"

I venture that filming the Super Bowl must be akin to a tightrope walker who wisely doesn't look down until it's over. "This is just what we do," he says, all iguanaish. "You know what I'm amazed at? When you go to a restaurant with eight people and your waiter takes an order and doesn't write anything down. Then he brings it out, and it's right. How do they do that?"

He reflects for a moment and then sums it up. "The Super Bowl is organized chaos for three hours. I'm just the ringleader. It's a dream job."

THE CAMERAS ARE ROLLING.
THE BUDGET BETTER NOT BE.

In 1986, Frank Oz got his shot. It wasn't his first shot: He had joined Jim Henson's tiny troupe of puppeteers at nineteen, before *The Muppet Show* and *Sesame Street* were even born. Jim and Frank had grown those shows to legendary status, with Frank originating and performing many of the most popular characters, including Miss Piggy, Grover, Cookie Monster, Bert, Animal, and Fozzie Bear. He had also written, directed, or codirected several of the Muppet films, and had originated the voice and performed Yoda in *Star Wars.*

But now he was being given a major film of his own, out from beneath the safe umbrella of Henson and the Muppets. *Little Shop of Horrors* was rumored to be Warner Bros.' biggest-budget musical ever, and he was agonizing about how to direct every frame of it. In desperation, he called upon Howard Ashman, the award-winning writer and lyricist who had penned the film's screenplay. The two met for lunch in the Green Tulip restaurant at New York's Plaza Hotel.

"I was very analytical," he says. "This was my big movie and I was determined to do it right. I had pages and pages of notes and diagrams. Before Howard could even order lunch, I blurted out, 'I've got Audrey, this big plant from outer space, but there's also an ax murderer and a sadistic dentist, and the plant is eating this guy's blood, but there's singing and we have guest stars. Now, my first question is about the plant's motivation in this second scene and I . . .'

"Howard just stared at me and then he said, 'Frank. It's supposed to be *stupid.*'

"It was a Zen enlightenment moment. I had no question about what to do from then on. It immediately freed me to be myself."

And that is what Frank Oz has continued to do to this day. Not be stupid, since he is extraordinarily talented, but be completely who he is. If that means fully in charge but not full of himself, so much the better for him, his film crews and actors, and ultimately for his audience.

Like most directors, Frank likes to pick people he's worked with before for his films, but those people aren't always available when the movie is. He often has to go with a new crew, which can number in the hundreds for a major production. And then there is the separate culture of actors: human beings who are paid for their highly developed ability to be unbalanced to an often-exaggerated degree. The shooting schedule is always as compressed as possible, sometimes as short as seven weeks; even a major film is supposed to be completed within months. Out-of-control budgets can skyrocket by tens of millions of dollars. Every shot counts.

A newly assembled employee culture, with members who may not know one another. A subculture of actors. A tight shooting schedule. A ton of money on the line. Studio pressure. Really, what could go wrong?

Fortunately, you can't work on the crew of a major Hollywood film unless you're experienced and certified as competent. But competent is and competent does can be two different things. It's rare that big things go wrong on a professional set, but smaller missteps, willfully caused or allowed to happen, can force retakes that send the budget over the edge, threaten location availability, and lose the advantage of good weather for an outdoor shoot. And it can result in missing that perfect take, for even the best actors have moments when it works and moments when it doesn't.

How to Learn Nothing and Everything

Michael Burke is the chair of the renowned NYU/Tisch Department of Graduate Film, where Frank has occasionally tutored aspiring filmmakers. "What happens early on a major film set is people know whether the captain of the ship is competent, and they make the decision to just punch the clock or go for something special. All it takes is a couple of eye rolls among what you refer to as the employee culture, which everybody but the director sees. But if people believe in the director, that changes everything."

Directors usually set an immediate vibe on the set. Some are notoriously dictatorial, some are silent and brooding, some throw epic tantrums. Frank is collaborative, respectful, and funny. Where did he learn this? "Well, I suppose Jim Henson was my mentor," Frank allows. "He must have taught you the way to manage people, right?" I ask. "Jim never taught me anything, but I learned everything from him," insists Frank.

"Humanity is what I learned from Jim, except it was never about being humane for business reasons. It was just being humane, and it doesn't mean that I'm calculating what is required to get more out of people; it just so happens you get more out of people when you're humane. Jim helped us constantly, but he never told us what to do. He never told anybody what to do. Not once, not ever. He just lived it, and we emulated him. That spirit is still in me right now."

This Is a Drama. Aren't We Supposed to Be Tense?

"A film set is a pressure cooker," says Leslie Converse, who was Frank's assistant and then became his postproduction supervisor and a coproducer. "Frank immediately puts people at ease; if you've known him for an hour you feel you can trust who he is, that you've known him all your life. It's also really good that he swears as much as he does, usually when he first walks onto the set. You know where the boundaries are right away. And that's why people want to do their best for him."

This doesn't mean that he's Mr. Fluffy, using a hand puppet to implore, "Pweeze, everybody. Quiet on the set!"

"The job of a director is to make sure that everybody's making the same movie," says Rob Hahn, his cinematographer on several films. If they aren't, it is frustrating and tense. Frank is immaculately prepared and very disciplined and knows exactly what he wants," asserts Hahn. "But he has a willingness to hear suggestions from others, which most directors don't. Frank will also take an intuitive leap of faith if he believes in you. How could you not want to do your best for him?"

"Let me give you an example of Frank Oz," offers British actor Andy Nyman. "This will seem like a tiny thing, but it's so big," he insists. "In 2007, I get this call from the casting agent for a new film called *Death at a Funeral*, to be directed by Frank Oz. In the UK, the norm is to go into a studio and tape your audition, which will presumably be reviewed by the director and others—very impersonal. But the casting director tells me that Frank is going to be at the audition. I was up for other jobs at the time, but I didn't want to say yes to any of them and risk not working with Frank Oz.

"Frank's first words to me were, 'I'm sorry, I've got a cold and can't shake hands.' I was thinking, you're Frank Oz, I want to *lick* you. Then Frank says, 'Here's what we'll do. We're going to do the scene, and then we'll do it twice more and I'll give you my notes.'

"This seemingly small thing showed an absolute understanding of what is required of an actor. It was an astonishing level of respect, as opposed to the horrible audition where you sit in a waiting room listening to someone do their forty-five minutes and you do only two minutes and you're left in agony, feeling like a failure and wondering about your choice of careers.

"I don't know if Frank even recognizes the impact of what he does," he muses. "He just does it because he believes people should be treated fairly. And that's what he's all about: Never make something tense that doesn't have to be, keep it collaborative, and keep it fun. It is in total counterpoint to most directors."

The Art of the Pull-Aside

"Frank has what I call pull-asides," says Michael Burke. "He's really clear about how people should be treated and the level of respect that should be offered to everyone on the set. If somebody is doing something he doesn't like, he just pulls them aside, puts his arm around them, and lets them know this can't happen or they're going to be gone tomorrow."

"Yeah, I do that," Frank says. "There's no point in making a competent person feel incompetent. I have to nip things in the bud, though. Because I laugh and enjoy myself so much, people might think I'm not serious. They're always testing, always watching.

"I remember on *Death at a Funeral*, a few of the actors were late for the first day of rehearsal. They were five minutes late, but on a film set that means something. Since everyone else was there and waiting, I looked at my watch in an exaggerated way and said, 'You guys are late'—clearly not okay, but I kept it lighthearted. And then I went over to each of them separately and whispered, 'If you're late again, I'll rip your genitals off.' They figured I was kidding. But they weren't sure."

And in the End

"I'm just being myself, which is really the only person I know how to be," Frank insists. "I want to treat people kindly. I want to have fun, and I don't think it's fair that I get to be the only one. I hold myself to my own standards, and I hold the crew and actors to theirs." He stops suddenly, "Do you remember that old singer Perry Como? He was really popular and used to have his own television specials.

"The Muppets did a Perry Como show years and years ago. There was a famous opera singer on that same show, and what happened during those specials was two nights before you started shooting, you do a prerecord, so she was prerecording this aria and it's two o'clock in the morning and we were lying around in the hallway, waiting for our turn to prerecord our stuff. She is singing, belting out this beautiful song. I'm just a twenty-one-year-old, gangly, inexperienced kid, and Perry Como comes over and whispers in my ear, 'What's she screaming for? She's got the job.'

"Perry Como saw I was a young kid, and he wanted to make it easier for me and was just being inclusive. But ever since then I've thought, why am I screaming? I'm the director. I've got the job."

A ROCK-AND-ROLL ICON TAKES THE STAGE

Manchester, Tennessee, 7:55 p.m. on a steamy, sticky Southern night. It is the darkened main stage at Bonaroo, one of the largest music festivals in America. Over 100,000 people shift, stretch, and paw the ground expectantly in front of them. They have come to experience the music of a generation, of every generation most of them can recall. This might be the greatest show on earth.

Behind the stage is another crowd, this one numbering about 150. For most of them, work done, it is time for a last mental review of their careful preparations throughout the day. For some of them, it is time to take positions for the night that is about to begin. This is the employee culture—band and road crew—that works for Paul McCartney.

Only the best are hired to work with Paul, and it's a dream job. Well, there is this one nightmarish possibility: If something goes wrong in front of those 100,000 people, every one of them will recognize it. Instantly. They know every note and every word of every song as well as the people playing them do.

"Anything can happen," Paul's longtime rhythm and bass guitarist Brian Ray tells me. "Paul likes to rock. We are not playing to Pro Tools, pretaped material, or time references. We're not tethered to anything but each other up there. We're on natural monitors, speakers and boxes on the ground just like the old days.

"We are sharing a live musical experience like real musicians have always done, and it requires you to have visual and audio connection with each other," he continues. "It is an immediate, vital music experience for Paul's band. And it's not just us; we carry a regular road crew of about one hundred people, but we add fifty or sixty new crew members for each show—there are construction, security, lighting, video, riggers, sound engineers, guitar technicians, just so many elements. Our crew can make or break the course of a show at any minute within it."

I'm Down

"Once the show starts, our guitars are handed to us by human beings who are on the side of the stage tuning them, and there are a lot of strings, switches, and batteries that could go bad and change the show," he continues. "It's very real."

"How real is 'very real'?" I ask.

"Well, on this tour we played Glasgow," he says. "I've been starting the show alone on a twelve-string, just me onstage before the band kicks in and Paul comes out. A battery had fallen out of the guitar being delivered to me, which nobody realized. I'm on the stage in front of 40,000 people, it's the first song, and there's absolutely no sound. We're trying to figure out what could have gone wrong, trying this and that. Paul's just standing there looking at me, and I'm whispering to my guitar tech, 'Get me an electric guitar now—I need to start the show.'

"But that was one of sixty times we've performed that first song, and the only time something went wrong."

Listen to What the Man Says

"How do we all experience Paul? He is a great leader and a great boss. He wants the best out of people and he really gets it. Not because he's a tyrant in any way, because he certainly isn't, but because he stays on it. He throws down every time we play. He's going to step on the gas and reach deep every night, because he loves music and because he came from the clubs. That's still who he is."

"How much is he in control of the concert experience?" I ask.

"Everyone is aware that Paul is aware of every aspect of the show,"

Brian insists. "He's still driven, still that guy who's the best in Liverpool. He still wants to do mind-blowing work. He wants to impress. He still loves seeing the lighters in the air. He doesn't see his music as a museum piece; he wants it to be a living, breathing, vital thing. In concert, he just goes out there and performs like a human being who loves music, not like an idol who loves fame.

"And that example inspires all of us to do the same," he explains. "Everybody wants to be part of this . . . every single department backstage and onstage is making the eyeball shine on top of the pyramid. That thing at the top is Paul. We are there to help him put over his vision every night."

Good Day Sunshine

McCartney is renowned for being financially generous to his band and crew, but Brian doesn't want to talk about that; he wants to talk about this: "Paul is maybe the least cynical man on the planet. And the ones who share that worldview are the ones that stay with us the longest. It's a trickle-down thing. By his essence, I think Paul attracts people who carry that same sort of ethos of quality and of service to an audience and to music. That spirit. Everybody in the crew and everybody in the band pushes forward with that same sort of love of humanity and hope for a future." He pauses and then says quietly, "He has made me a better musician, and he has made me a better human being."

I should leave it there, but I can't. Paul McCartney is Brian's *boss.* Brian's *job* is to play Beatles songs to huge, cheering audiences. On behalf of every reader of this book worldwide, I ask, "How do you get a job like that?"

Brian Ray has worked as a professional musician for forty years—while most of us were listening, he was playing—including fourteen years as Etta James's guitarist and musical director, and in the studio with the late, great Willy DeVille ("He would tell me to make the guitar sound like the rusty springs in a whorehouse bed."). He's also a solo artist and records with his own band, the Bayonets. Got that, but let's get tactical: How does one ace a job interview with Paul McCartney?

"Sure, okay, let me explain," he says. "In 2002, Paul had hired a producer, David Kahne, who has also produced a basketful of number one records in his great career. He's the guy who had the vision to put together Paul's band. They had chosen the drummer, Abe Laboriel Jr., who is a buddy of mine, and he gave David my number. I didn't even have a cell phone, but I happened to be at home on Monday when the call came through to audition with Paul.

"I first met Paul the night before the audition, and it was as simple as, 'I want to make a toast to my friends here with me tonight at this dinner. I want to welcome my older friends, and I want to welcome our new friends, David Kahne and Brian Ray.' And the next day I played my first gig with him, although it was only one song."

"Well, that couldn't have been too hard," I say. "What was the gig?"

"The Super Bowl."

He adds, "The day after the show I was ready to say good-bye, and thank you, and it was a privilege, and I'll never forget it. Paul said, 'Welcome aboard. Stick with Abe and Rusty. They'll show you the ropes. I'll see you at rehearsal for the tour in five weeks.' And that was that."

"Well, that helps," I mutter.

"Great, man!" Brian says.

ELIMINATING CULTURAL COMPLACENCY IN A COMPETITIVE MARKETPLACE

An employee culture is willing to be accountable for its performance, but this can't be punishing to do. Your culture has to be able to reliably link new behavior to its survival and emotional prosperity—it needs you to provide the proper tools, support, recognition, and consistency to make that link. Essentially, your employee culture wants you to be accountable, too.

1. Prevent complacency.

An employee culture is unmoved by claims of enterprise-wide doom simply because the stock price falls a bit or a competitor runs a successful campaign. If your company is regularly successful, this may also cause complacency, since success seems assured. Instead link your employee culture's energy to something unchanging like quality, customer service standards, and impact on the world, and use financial performance as an indicator about how well those issues are being performed.

2. Grant authority.

The companies with the most accountable employee cultures aren't the ones with the most controls. They're the ones that most trust their employee culture to use its own good judgment. Allow your culture to earn its discretionary decision authority and to keep that authority when deserved.

3. Promote curiosity.

Business improvement, control, and innovation come from constantly learning better ways to do each of these things. A learning environment means tolerance for considering the new and different and the ability of your employee culture to make its suggestions heard, as well as opportunity for the culture to try, fail, and improve.

4. Create performance.

Complacency doesn't just mark employee cultures that are less than competent; it breeds in employee cultures that are extremely competent. Such cultures are confident of success, enjoy the regular autonomy they have earned, and are entitled to all the material rewards they receive. Those that successfully manage the most competent cultures know that leadership and what it provides—meaning, vision, deep trust, and collaborative humanity—is the way to increase the culture's willingness to use the skills it already has.

> Who are you going to believe, me or your own eyes?
> —Groucho Marx

MAINTAINING CULTURAL COMMITMENT UNDER PRESSURE

> Because you're mine, I walk the line.
> —Johnny Cash

SHOULD YOUR company ever come under serious pressure—financial, competitive, reputational—your employee culture won't decide whether to stand in support of the enterprise or fall back and watch what happens. That decision was made long ago. It's too late to develop the culture's most determined aid when you need it. This is when you'll know whether you've already earned it.

If your culture is already fully energized, has trust in the company's character, has legendary proof points of what is real, has a rock-solid belief that even under pressure certain things remain sacred and protected, is managed by leaders it considers credible, and takes its positive sense of self from the company's deepest noble purpose, then it means the pressure is on the company, not on what your culture considers most important. You can depend on the culture's commitment to see you through these tough times.

If these conditions aren't in place when the pressure hits, you can still increase support, but you have to *move*—fast and right. Don't assume that an obvious company crisis is enough to cause the culture to move for you.

You want to feel the power of your employee culture? If it hangs in there and makes sure your company does too, you'll never doubt it again.

NOW, HERE'S WHAT TO DO

1. CONNECT YOUR CULTURE'S SENSE OF SELF TO TOUGH TIMES.

If an employee culture is allowed to blame external conditions for internal performance, then aggressive and creative responses depart, and helplessness and cynicism take their place. The best organizations hold themselves as accountable for their problems as they do for their successes. Their victories are built upon learning from both and growing ever stronger—even under pressure, especially under pressure. This breeds the kind of employee culture that takes pride in its ability to meet, greet, and *spank* problems. Tough times? Tougher team.

Resolving a major company crisis becomes a prime source of the culture's sense of self, of its primal energy. Confronting issues and embracing new solutions is a small price to pay to get recharged.

USE WHO YOU ARE TO BEAT WHERE YOU ARE

A company crisis can spook your employee culture, especially if the company is used to an unbroken string of wins. Your culture can begin to question the company's ability to affect success and begin to question itself, too. Who are we now? Are we everything we thought we were? Just when it has to be most confident in its abilities, it will hesitate.

Amateur athletes treat a slump as a physical problem; professionals treat it as a mental problem. It's not the time to be losing your company's head when the enterprise is under pressure, and especially not the time to lose its heart. You want to be on your best game and send a signal to your employee culture that the company's DNA—character and passion—is unshakable, even when the business gets rattled. Revisit and reinforce that DNA for your culture now—say it clearly, and show it in how you approach resolution of the crisis. And then say it again and again. Don't just focus your culture on fixing the problem; remind it of who it is: Whatever gets us down doesn't matter; we get up stronger.

PROHIBIT EQUATIONS OF DENIAL

Really, chances are that something bad didn't just *happen* to your company; your company caused or allowed something bad to happen to it.

Drafting elaborate excuses about how forces of nature, acts of God, or world events contributed to the failure of your go-to-market strategy isn't just wasted energy but a dangerous message to your employee culture. If it doesn't own the problem, why should it own finding the solution? Don't be one of those companies that operate in a vigorous state of denial.

Like this one:

Should America's national anthem ever be updated, it won't likely include the stirring stanza, "Oh say can you see, the Peanut Corporation of America?" It wasn't the country's finest moment, and there isn't a Peanut Corporation of America anymore.

At its peak in 2008, Peanut Corporation of America accounted for 2.5 percent of the nation's processed peanuts. It may not sound like much, but that's a lot of peanuts, and a lot of major companies used Peanut Corporation of America to provide peanut butter for the foods they sold under their own labels.

Some bodies are unfortunately allergic to peanuts, but everybody is allergic to aflatoxin (fatal: one of the most toxic and carcinogenic compounds) and salmonella typhimurium (bad, but not fatal unless you're very young or very old). That's unfortunate, because both of these substances were routinely found in the products manufactured by Peanut Corporation of America, a company whose biggest achievement in its thirty-plus years in business was triggering the most extensive food recall in U.S. history.

Physical—and moral—hygiene just wasn't Peanut Corporation of America's thing. The company knowingly operated contaminated manufacturing plants that sickened and killed a bunch of people. While this was happening, it faked lab reports and obstinately refused to provide information to investigators, causing the Food and Drug Administration to invoke federal anti-terrorism statutes to get it. The company was ultimately charged with producing peanut butter that contained "filthy, putrid, or decomposed substances, as well as metal fragments." So metal fragments would be the good news.

In various Peanut Corporation of America plants, investigators found leaking water that had formed in "standing pools cluttered with bird feces," an air system that "drew dead rodents, rodent excrement, and bird feathers into the production area," and "live birds flying and walking inside the warehouse." Members of the employee culture later stated that conditions were "filthy and nasty" and claimed they wouldn't let their own kids anywhere near what was produced by those factories. One reported seeing a family of baby mice in a bag of peanuts, another saw a rat being dry-roasted.

The company's cowed and detached employee culture lamely claimed that management withheld knowledge of diseased products. Apparently the wrath of management wasn't withheld: In an internal email CEO Stewart Parnell raged, "These are not peanuts you are throwing away . . . It is money!!"

Faced with mounting evidence that the secret ingredient in its crunchy peanut butter wasn't, uh, nut related, the Department of Agriculture banned Peanut Corporation of America from all federal contracts, then realized maybe they should ban Peanut Corporation of America from all consumers, too. They ordered the company to clean up its act, and when that didn't happen, they ordered the company to shut down production and clean up its act, and when that didn't happen, they ordered the company to shut down, period. The company filed for Chapter 7 bankruptcy and liquidated its assets. They didn't get much for the "rodent dry-roaster" on eBay.

In 2009, Peanut Corporation of America finally issued a press release stating that "forced plant closings" had caused the company to declare bankruptcy:

FORCED PLANT CLOSINGS = BANKRUPTCY

Nuh-uh. This is an equation of denial, in which facts were minimized and rationalized in favor of a story that let the company off the hook in its own mind. An equation of accountability would have been:

> Nasty manufacturing plants + rat pieces in peanut butter x projectile vomiting + consumer deaths—wholesale customers + government inspections + 76-count federal felony indictment supported by 93,000 confiscated documents + forced plant closings x 2 = bankruptcy

Sorry about the segue here, but any claim by your own company that reduced customer spending has caused a decline in revenue is an equation of denial. Failure to anticipate or react to circumstances that *caused* reduced customer spending is what caused a decline in revenue. Any other story poisons your culture's willingness to solve problems as surely as feeding it rat-infested peanut snacks. The only equation that allows you to advocate and expect accountability from your employee culture before, during, and after a crisis is:

> This is what we did or didn't do = this is what happened.

2. EARN BACK TRUST A STEP AT A TIME.

If a company actually commits some atrocious violation of trust, a hole will have been torn in the fabric of the culture's belief system and will have to be painstakingly mended. If the violation was due to a breach of business ethics inside or outside of the company, the employee culture will back away from endorsing the enterprise, not just because its own sense of self has been impugned, but because of the enormous threat posed by not being able to take management at its word about fundamental behavior. Earning back trust will require a severe revamping of the people, positions, and policies responsible and plenty of time for the culture to reconsider its position.

Assuming your company isn't breezily fraudulent, the pressure on the enterprise may be enormous, but the process of ensuring cultural trust doesn't have to be. A company crisis creates uncertainty about the future, and your employee culture may be hunkered down and fearful, which can translate to angry. Do not be offended or defensive about this; your culture has to take care of itself more than usual now and resents having to do that, which is reasonable. Your focus is to get the culture to take care of the company, too. Bring your employee culture back a little at a time. You may not think you have that kind of time, but continue to deliver on small promises and momentum will quickly build.

3. REMAIN TRANSPARENT.

Under pressure, your employee culture will be hypersensitive to any management attempt to spin the facts. It goes without saying here— well, apparently it doesn't—but never lie to your employee culture, and never distort or withhold information. That you can't get away with it is one good reason: A culture is way too smart and way too focused on sniffing out what's real.

OPEN CLOSED DOORS

Any relationship disintegrates when motives become suspect. Presumably your executive team is comprised of smart and responsible people who care about the employee culture, and the culture has not reported any suspicions otherwise. But that doesn't mean the executive team's motives are known and understood, and they need to be to provide extra confidence during a crisis. There now needs to be greater transparency for your culture into how and why the executive team makes decisions. The culture needs to understand the motivations, principles, and processes of the group ultimately responsible for both the problem and the solution.

Some confidentiality, and even mystery, about how the senior-most team works is necessary and fine with your employee culture. It depends on you to do your business as you need to do it. The culture doesn't want to know everything; it wants context for the decisions that are coming its way, and it wants to know that the health of the culture is a constant priority when those decisions are debated.

No need to completely open the C-suite kimonos—your culture would prefer those to be buttoned all the way to the top, thanks anyway. But you can release an overview of monthly staff meetings within seventy-two hours, not as a reveal of confidential discussions, but showing some of what was considered a priority that might affect the culture and the pressure it's currently dealing with. You can regularly ask work groups to prepare reports for the C-suite to discuss in its monthly meeting and ask members or small teams to make brief presentations. Their individual experience will immediately be shared with the rest of the culture. This is a good idea, pressure or no pressure—it's a confidence builder for your culture to know that senior management has the prescience to plan for the worst times during the best.

CONSTANTLY POLL YOUR CULTURE

Your employee culture is your first electorate when it comes to a problem with your company's second electorate, your customer culture. Because many in your employee culture will be closest to many in your customer culture, it will have an important sense of external impressions of your company during troubled times.

And it will have ideas about how to improve these impressions. Some of the ideas will be good, some not so good, some gravitationally impossible, but all are worth hearing if only because it shows your culture that you want to hear them.

You can use technology to poll your employee culture about its perceptions of progress toward resolving current conditions. Use this same forum to solicit its suggestions and listen closely if it says it is lacking the tools or authority to help.

4. GIVE YOUR CULTURE SOMETHING TO SAY.

If there's major pressure inside your company, chances are people outside of the company are going to hear about it. That puts your employee culture in the middle, causing its members to represent what's happening to their family, friends, and customers—represent company intentions with their own good name when those intentions may be called into question by others.

CREATE LEGENDS

A legendary move or two by management when the company is under pressure will serve your culture by giving it compelling stories to tell. The first legends should be focused inside, on the culture itself, in recognition of the extra pressure it's attempting to handle. Consider a flagrant show of support for the potential of your people to help resolve issues; if appropriate, an apology to them for any situation that casts aspersions on their own abilities, or a public proclamation in local or national media of how proud you are of them.

TALK TO YOUR CUSTOMERS

Reach out to your customer culture with a message of support and affection for your employee culture when the company is under pressure. This demonstration of empathy for an employee culture that has to represent the company with its own good name and may be concerned about its own job future during a crisis is rarely, if ever, done. This is an outstanding opportunity to rally the support of your customers who are employees somewhere themselves.

If financial pressure on the company requires letting part of your employee culture go, the company should go out of its way in public statements to express appreciation for those forced to leave, as well as to explain how it is helping to ease the transition. If your press release about layoffs is focused on the benefit for shareholder value alone, the only positive reception will be from the analyst culture. That's an important culture for any public company, but it's far from the only culture that will decide how well your company rebounds.

TALK TO YOUR CULTURE'S FAMILIES

Pressure on your employee culture is going to jump the fence and follow it home. Let some enterprise support follow it home, too. Send a letter empathizing with any anxiety the family might be experiencing, reaffirm belief in the people of the company, and promise regular updates as the situation improves. If your employee culture has to work overtime to correct a problem, think about sending flowers or treating members' families to a night out.

WATCH WHAT YOU SAY

Be careful about what your company says to the media: Your employee culture is listening. If you take a defensive, victimized position and blame the world economy, competition, the weather, the collapse of the bee colony, or Christmas falling on a Thursday as the reason that trouble has found you, your employee culture is going to have a lot harder time believing that it should be accountable for helping to solve problems.

DON'T ASK YOUR CULTURE TO TALK FOR YOU

If a company causes itself some trouble, the company needs to step up to talk about it to the world, not use its employee culture as apologist or promoter. Advertising campaigns of this type are as uncomfortable for your customer culture to receive as they are for your employee culture to participate in sending.

WHAT PROGRESSIVE INSURANCE LEFT ON THE (ACTUARIAL) TABLE

▶ You just don't want this to happen to you if you're an insurance company. In November 1988, California voters approved Proposition 103, a ballot initiative that forced all insurers in the state to cut their car insurance rates by twenty percent across the board. The rollback was based on 1987 rates, and the law required insurers to refund the difference to consumers.

Prop 103 passed because many Golden State voters viewed insurance companies as, well, sort of soulless bloodsuckers that sold commodity products at inflated prices. The voters thought they had reason to be upset: California had some of the priciest car insurance rates in the country in those days, and customer service was not, let's just say, a driving force for most providers.

For Ohio-based Progressive Insurance, Prop 103 came as a body blow. Like most insurance companies, Progressive operated under thin profit margins. California generated a quarter of the company's revenue, and its business model there had just vaporized overnight. Glenn Renwick, who is now the company's CEO, was a rising star at Progressive in those days. "I'd been asked to go out to California and see what I could make of this," he recalls. "I had received the bill for the refund we were supposed to pay. It was more than our company's entire net income the year before."

What to do? In order to stay in business in California, Progressive needed to dramatically reduce operating costs in every way possible, including losing several hundred employees. That would have been inconvenient but not agonizing if Progressive was in fact a soulless, bloodsucking organization. But it's not. It is a close-knit organization that mainly promotes from within and rarely lets employees go. And now for reasons beyond its control, Progressive faced a stark choice in California: It could either slash costs or shut its doors. "It becomes very hard when you can no longer charge a premium that will allow you to effectively stay in business," says Renwick, who was given the miserable job of wielding the ax.

From an employee culture's point of view, layoffs are proof that its company's heart is a heart of darkness. They feature prominently in the scary stories that the culture whispers to itself around the campfire while savage drums and the muffled screams of former members echo through the surrounding jungle. No matter how hard management tries to sweeten the blow with severance packages and outplacement help, the point has been made: It could happen and our loyalty and good performance would not be enough to stop it.

Proposition 103 was a big story in California, which in those days meant that Progressive's employees were constantly reminded of their impending doom on the evening news. Renwick got to work—there really was no other choice for a public company facing this enormity of financial threat. He organized the RIFs into three phases over several months, and although he worked hard to communicate the reasons for the restructuring, anxiety levels predictably hit the red zone and stayed there.

It Happened One Night

Shortly before the first layoffs were scheduled to hit, Renwick happened to be working late and overheard two members of the employee culture talking in the hallway outside his office. "I wish they would just *ask* us," said one woman to the other. The thought struck him hard: In his efforts to be fair to everyone he had assumed a paternal responsibility for how the process would be implemented.

And so at midnight that same night, Renwick decided to tell his executive team that he was scrapping the entire involuntary termination plan that they had labored to design. In its place, he announced to the entire Progressive employee culture how many layoffs Progressive needed. He asked for volunteers for the first phase and suggestions for subsequent phases.

"We went to incredible extremes to get people jobs in other parts of the company," Renwick adds. "If they wanted to stay on past Christmas, we obviously didn't let them go in December. We couldn't change what had to be done, but we could do it in a way that was a good reflection of our culture."

It's not a squishy lost-kitten-returns-home-with-winning-lottery-ticket-in-her-teeth kind of story: Hundreds of Progressive employees still lost their jobs. But by listening to them, the company was able to bank a large measure of cultural trust and goodwill. "No one wanted to leave, but I got notes that I treasure to this day," Renwick says, "such as, 'My husband and I were going to start a small business. The severance will really help us,' or 'I was planning on going back to school, so I'm happy to leave in the first wave.' Mostly the letters, calls, and conversations said 'Thank you for listening when you didn't have to.'"

What was implied by the Progressive employee culture is, "We now know how you'll act toward us under pressure. Thank you."

The support of its employee culture came in handy over the next few years as Progressive addressed the deeper problem that had spawned Proposition 103 in the first place: the fact that its customers disliked insurance companies in general. In order to survive and grow, Progressive needed to change from a math-driven, transaction-oriented company to one that also cultivated customer relationships. And to build stronger relationships with its customers, it needed an employee culture that was willing to represent the company's intentions with its own good name.

Progressive had long been an innovator in the staid, heavily regulated U.S. insurance industry. Founded in 1937, it was the first insurance company to offer claims service centers and the first to offer lower premiums to safer drivers. After Proposition 103, the pace of innovation really picked up. During the 1990s, Progressive became the first car insurance company to service claims at the accident scene. It launched the industry's first 24/7 customer service support and was the first to allow insurance to be purchased online. Progressive also became the first insurance company to help customers make informed decisions by quoting the rates of its competitors. Their Snapshot technology collects real-time data on an insured car's hard braking and accelerations, allowing safer drivers to qualify for lower premiums.

The company has been equally groundbreaking about its own business. Since 2001, Progressive has been the only public company in the world to release monthly earnings statements. Rather than providing regular earnings guidance and then torturing the actual numbers to meet the expectations of Wall Street analysts, Progressive issues no guidance at all. Instead the $17 billion company simply releases those condensed financial statements every four weeks. "We're not going to put our thumb on the scale and manage accounting entries," says Tom King, a Progressive veteran who currently runs the company's international operations. "That's just not our culture." The results? Steady earnings growth and greatly reduced stock volatility relative to the market.

Next, the company set out to set the standard in customer service. You don't achieve transformation on that scale without a rabidly committed employee culture, and the payback to the company began to be measurable in how well it was able to shift.

These days Progressive is widely known for its quirky television ads starring Flo, a relentlessly cheerful salesclerk who works in a fictional "insurance superstore." During interviews with Progressive employees based at the company's bucolic (seriously) campus near Cleveland—which houses one of the country's best modern art collections and has "relaxation rooms" scattered throughout the offices where members of the culture can chill and reenergize— it became apparent that the employee culture identifies with Flo's manic zeal to help consumers save money on car insurance. "We are simple, easy, fun, someone you can trust," says Michelle Ferrara, a call center supervisor based in Tampa, Florida.

Chief Marketing Officer Jeff Charney gives those customer-facing members of the Progressive employee culture the opportunity to choose the ending for new commercials and will take the time to explain how the ads are made. "It gives them the inside scoop that is special and makes them stand out at a party or dinner table," says Charney. Other than inducing them to be responsible for turning the talk at a party to insurance ads, it's a nice thing to do.

Stand by Me

An employee culture will stand by the company only if the company stands by it first. The Progressive employees interviewed for this book described a demanding environment where honest mistakes are normally treated as teaching opportunities rather than firing offenses, just like in all those fable-story management books. Company-wide Communications Manager Angela Straub remembers a trauma-inducing moment when she spent a huge sum of money on a new marketing initiative and then realized that she hadn't actually gotten approval from the senior executive whose budget was going to be hit. Big whoops. "I was fully expecting to be fired," she says.

After consulting with her own manager, Straub death-marched over to the executive's office and explained the situation. "It was an honest mistake," the woman told her. "It's a big one, but you'll get the money that you need, and we'll make this right."

This vibe from the top is consistent throughout the Progressive executive team. CEO Renwick is a modest guy who stands in line for cafeteria coffee just like any other employee. He probably needs the caffeine, since he *personally signs* all 26,000 employee Christmas cards every year.

The Waters Rose. Didn't Touch the Humanity.

The real gift to its employee culture is Renwick's willingness to stand up for principle even when it costs the company money, although he is insistent that this is characteristic of the entire company, not only its chief executive. "Soon after Hurricane Katrina, a few of our claims managers and I were allowed to go in," he recalls. "I forget the number of acres that we had leased so that we could bring all the salvage vehicles out of New Orleans and put them in this field where they would dry and then, ultimately, salvage vendors would come and bid on them. This would be a significant number, probably millions of dollars.

"At the time, New Orleans was as horrific as you imagine it was—a sense of loss and helplessness was draped over the entire city and everyone in it. We're walking around and seeing a lot of cars that we insured, which were near totaled. And it occurred to me—and I'm going to make this into a very personal story because it affected me so much, but it's truly a Progressive story—it occurred to me that this was one time where you had to ask what is leadership?

"What I mean by that was we knew that, in some sense, these cars were going to come out of here one day. They'd be dry and they'd be painted, and they'd have new carpets in them. And someday, somebody in Iowa would buy that car and it will be okay. But it will never reflect the real history of what had happened here. We had to honor this; it was an event where you needed a human, values-driven decision process that is outside of the normal calculus of your P&L.

"That night I met with our people and we discussed it. 'I don't want any of these cars to ever leave New Orleans,' I said. We brought in three car crushers. We crushed every single car, from junkers to Mercedes-Benzes to Hummers. This was now *our* inventory we were destroying," he says.

"I'll never know how much we technically cost shareholders for not having gotten the salvage value. But it was the right thing to do and it seemed to me that if our company really has these values, then there will come a day when Progressive will be judged by which branch it took. There was nothing wrong with salvaging some of the cars. We were the only ones who cared and the only ones who would suffer. But it didn't feel right, and that was enough."

If You Could Care Just a Smidgen Less, That Would Be Fabulous

Ironically, sometimes a committed employee culture will overprotect the company and go against the very company principles it holds dear. In 2007, two investigators working for Progressive infiltrated a support group at an Atlanta church to gather damaging information about two church members who, they believed, were wrongfully suing the company over a car accident. The investigators secretly recorded church members talking about their most intimate issues, including sexual orientation, drug abuse, and abortion.

The day after this story broke in the *Atlanta Journal-Constitution*, Renwick publicly apologized on behalf of Progressive. The actions of the investigators were reprehensible, but they weren't necessarily illegal. Progressive could easily have stonewalled the whole thing and waited for the bad press to be replaced by some other company's bad press. Instead, Renwick created a new cultural legend. "What the investigators and Progressive people did was wrong—period," he said in a statement. "I personally want to apologize to anyone who was affected by this."

All's Well. Ends Well

Progressive continues to benefit to this day from these sorts of beliefs and actions, and even from that existential crisis it endured in California back in the 1980s. After Prop 103 nearly destroyed the company's business model, Progressive's management demonstrated respect by listening to its employee culture. In return, the culture helped transform Progressive into a profitable and renowned service business.

It's hard to imagine a better insurance policy.

GIMME SHELTER: TACTICAL RECAP

MAINTAINING CULTURAL COMMITMENT UNDER PRESSURE

Should your company ever come under serious pressure—financial, competitive, reputational—your employee culture won't decide to stand in support of the enterprise or fall back and watch what happens. That decision was made long ago. It's too late to develop the culture's most determined aid when you need it. This is when you'll know whether you've already earned it.

1. Connect your culture's sense of self to tough times.

Don't allow your employee culture to blame external circumstances for internal performance—and don't model it as management either. Instead, use the challenge of tough times to reaffirm the special character of your employee culture: Tough times? Tougher team.

2. Earn trust a step at a time.

Ask for trust in small steps and continue to deliver on what you promise. You may not think you have this kind of time under circumstances of unusual pressure, but it's the fastest way to gain reliable momentum.

3. Prohibit equations of denial.

There is only one equation to advocate with your employee culture: This is what happened or didn't happen = This is what we did about it.

4. Remain transparent.

Under pressure, your employee culture will be hypersensitive to any attempt to spin facts and needs to know how management is dealing with the crisis—not hear about it when the world does. The culture needs to see management, hear management, talk to management. Talk to the members' families too—if the company is taking public heat, they're feeling the pressure as well.

5. Give your culture something to say.

Help your employee culture advocate for the company under pressure by creating legends among your customer culture about how the enterprise is accountable, concerned, and decent. But don't put the burden on your employee culture to do the talking for you.

The lawn-cutter might just as well not have been there at all; the gardener will be there a lifetime.

—**Ray Bradbury,** *Fahrenheit 451*

PART 3
THE WHOLE POINT

Tryin' to make it real, compared to what?

—**Les McCann and Eddie Harris**

WHAT DO you want from your management career? Do you want to build a company, sell products, make money? These are very good things. Do you want to have a legacy impact on the lives of those who helped you do it? This is a great thing.

You don't have to trade off the good things for a great thing. But you have to want to do a great thing.

Knowing how your employee culture works and how to work it can be the pivotal difference between your career success and failure, or between your success and extreme success. But this isn't simply about your company or your career. This is about you and what you really want, whether you want to know your people and to know the positive impact you've had on them. If you step off the curb one day and are hit by a speeding truck, do you want your last thought to be, "Isn't that Shirley from accounting behind the wheel?"

Take a few quiet minutes to think about the one person who has had the biggest negative influence on your life. There is certainly someone, whether they have had a continuing role or whether they have touched you briefly, maybe without even realizing how they altered you and how you think of yourself. Now take a few quiet minutes to think about the one person who has had the biggest positive influence on your life. There is certainly someone, whether they have had a continuing role or whether they have touched you briefly, maybe without realizing how they altered you and how you think of yourself.

As a manager, you can be either of those people to your employee culture.

Culture is where the humans gather in business. You have constant, lingering impact on the members of your employee culture, inside and outside of work. You intimate whether they are worthy of inspiration or indifference; your actions color their prevailing view of the world as secure or anxious; and you are a role model of how the privilege of authority can be used for better or worse—authority that they will have when becoming parents and possibly managers themselves.

It is up to you if you treat what is most important to these humans with disinterest and depress their sense of who they are and what they deserve. Or if you treat them with the honor that humans have earned regardless of their position in the hierarchy of an enterprise, and lift their sense of who they are and what they deserve.

An employee culture's profound search for safety and meaning is a reminder that we all inhabit the same world; we all have these same concerns. The urgent questions you can help to answer for your employee culture—what do you do and what did you do today—have to be answered for you as well. Treating your employee culture with empathy, concern, and respect is not a performance tactic or a job responsibility. It is a mirror that reflects your own true humanity.

I hope that this book has explained how to move your employee culture as you need to, but far more than that, I hope that it has ignited anew the fire within you to do it for the right reason.

For nothing is fixed, forever and
forever and forever, it is not fixed.

   The earth is always shifting,
   the light is always changing;
   the sea does not cease to grind down rock.

Generations do not cease to be born, and
we are responsible to them because we are
the only witnesses they have.

      The sea rises, the light fails, lovers
      cling to each other and children
      cling to us.

The moment we cease to hold each other,
the moment we break faith with one
another, the sea engulfs us and the light
goes out.

                              —JAMES BALDWIN

"Be yourself" is the worst advice you can give to some people.

—Tom Masson

PART 4

RESEARCH NOTES AND TANGENTS

Thank you (falettinme be mice elf again).

—Sly & The Family Stone

CONTACT. LIFTOFF.

IF YOU WANT TO TALK

I'm always interested in hearing from you.

- ➤ EMAIL stan@employeeculture.com
- ➤ LINKEDIN linkedin.com/in/StanSlap
- ➤ FACEBOOK facebook.com/StanSlap
- ➤ TWITTER @slapcompany

IF YOU WANT TO TALK RESULTS

SLAP (the company) achieves maximum commitment in manager, employee, and customer cultures.

- ➤ Manager culture: We will achieve emotional commitment from your manager culture.
- ➤ Employee culture: We will achieve fierce commitment from your employee culture for any strategic or performance goal.
- ➤ Customer culture: We will achieve true brand status from your customers, including being branded for how you sell, not just for what you sell.

Our clients include Fortune 500 (you've heard of them) and rapidly growing companies (you will). We work successfully in any industry and in over seventy countries. No one has *ever* called SLAP work ordinary—methods used or results achieved.

I regularly give keynote speeches to audiences around the world. Happy to wake 'em and shake 'em for you.

WEBSITE: slapcompany.com
YOUTUBE: youtube.com/slapcompany

AT A LOSS FOR WORDS

When I pick up a new book, I always check out an author's appreciation section first. I want to see if they recognize that while writing is a solitary job, it's real hard to do without help from others. Read this one if you want; I realize it goes on for a while and most of it won't have direct value for you, but I could not have put this book in your hands without the support I was given during its writing. These people deserve their moment.

THANK YOU: MY WIFE AND LITTLE BOY

My wife spent many lonely days, nights, and weekends while I labored over pages. My five-year-old son had to regularly hear, "Not right now, honey," to his excited "Daddy, come play with me!" tugs on my leg. During the last month of writing, they left town to allow me the time and space to focus. And yet, knowing this was coming for over a year, I still cannot find the words to thank them for their faith and grace under pressure. They shake me with the power and accuracy of their love.

THANK YOU: THE RESEARCH TEAM

Seventeen years before a word of this book was written, research was begun on it in companies around the world. It took the form of proprietary solutions to help these companies, which were my own company's clients, achieve maximum commitment from their employee cultures.

This allowed me to hone accuracy and impact in the real world, and when it was time to write the book, I was able to call upon the experience of these many assignments. I also had access to candid recorded comments from over 15,000 members of various employee cultures that we'd captured over the years—more than enough to aggregate into patterns that support the book's findings. That work continues to this day in my company, and I used every finding I could grab, right up to the book's completion. When it came time to write the book, I added a lot of additional research to that experience. Experts in my own company did some, but I also went outside to people who are spectacularly skilled at it.

- ➤ Heading the research team was Richard McGill Murphy. He's a widely published writer on business and international affairs and, oh yeah, this: He holds a doctorate in anthropology from Oxford (based on field research in Pakistan), where he was a Fulbright Scholar. Richard's contribution is all over this book, and his dedication helped make it a reality. His deep knowledge of anthropology ensured that no matter how original my point of view is, it remains scientifically valid, which is good since the idea of angering a bunch of anthropologists is unnerving. Who knows what they've learned to do in the jungle?
- ➤ David Gorman, CEO of HackMart, provided critical thinking and support for several parts of the book. He made himself personally available whenever I asked, which was pretty much constantly. A special thanks to the very talented and very committed Kassondra Monroe, also from HackMart.
- ➤ Fred Arnstein gave his usual exacting, thoughtful opinions throughout, which invariably caused me to go back and confirm what I was sure I knew. I think he does this sort of thing just to mess with me, but he's the slap company's guy for statistical analysis, in which he holds a PhD, so I hesitate to mess with him.

- Rochelle Garner is a former senior reporter for Bloomberg, and she was able to bring both a pro journalist's critical eye and the ability to ferret out information that does want to be ferreted. Her expert contributions were fast, accurate, and often delightfully to the point.
- Dr. Rob Bogosian provided important detail about cultural silence. (His book on the subject is *Breaking Corporate Silence—How High Influence Leaders Create Cultures Of Voice*.) He also did an extensive dive into the body of existing literature about some of my book's key points—or tried to. Apparently there isn't much, which was gratifying to hear.
- The wisdom and experience of Julia Shumelda, who heads the slap company's facilitation and coaching teams, and who gets this stuff in the very fibers of her XXL heart, was always invaluable.
- Richard Greenberg's remarkable insights and relative (to me) calm was a rock-solid source of support. Richard: Wherever in the world our company has got you traveling to at the moment, thanks for that, for the consistently spectacular work, and for your deep and dependable friendship.
- Backing up the research team was fact-checker extraordinaire Delos Knight, detail-obsessed proofer Bob Christoph, and relentless epigram archeologist Kelsey Kennick. They made me look good despite myself—plenty of job security in that—and helped make this book credible for you.

THANK YOU: THE SLAP COMPANY

Company culture is my business, and over the years I've seen a lot of them. But in all that time, I have rarely witnessed one as committed as the people of slap. Thanks to everyone for who you are and what you do, and thank you, too, for your book contribution or book endurance. A special shout-out to those already noted; and also especially to Mikki Laurel for eagle eyes and mama lion protection; to Nancee Yago for extra faith and patience; to John Morrella for acquiring rights to about a gazillion epigrams and to the new and wonderful Heba Hamze. Once upon a time, thank you to Michael Plaut, Mike Zawitkowski, Sean Browne, and Andrew Wilson.

THANK YOU: PORTFOLIO

I am thrilled silly to have Portfolio, the business imprint division of Penguin Random House, as my publisher for so many reasons, not the least of which was their unhesitating willingness to go to the mat to help this book be all they believe it can be. This admittedly didn't always thrill me silly in the heat of the moment. But that heat was born of the extraordinary experience, wisdom, and humanity of the legendary Adrian Zackheim and his organization. How could any author not be deeply moved by the quality of this support? Thanks so much Adrian, and thank you to Natalie Horbachevsky, Niki Papadopoulos, Tricia Conley, Chris Sergio, Karl Spurzem, Hannah Kinisky, Margot Stamas, Jesse Maeshiro, Maddie Phillips, and Will Weisser. This is a Portfolio book. I love saying that.

THANK YOU: NILS PARKER

When Nils Parker got his talented mitts on what I thought was the final manuscript, it somehow became much better. Well not "somehow." It became much better because he applied an editing expertise so fast, sure, and right that it was stunning to experience. And a little disturbing: It took me a long time to write it, Nils. You could have had the decency to at least pretend to wait a couple of months until you figured out what had to be done.

THANK YOU: MARGRET MCBRIDE

Margret McBride is the best literary agent a boy could ever have. Hardcore in my corner at all times—no hesitation—and extraordinarily good at what she does, as a list of her bestsellers will attest to. She's just, ah, she's just delightful. I am crazy about her. Thanks also to the fabulously committed and resourceful Faye Atchison of the Mc-Bride Literary Agency.

THANK YOU: ALL WHO WERE INTERVIEWED

Interviews for this book were conducted with very busy people who went out of their way, sometimes repeatedly, to accommodate my manuscript deadline. Thank you to Mike Arnold, Elisa Villanueva Beard, Mike Burke, Leslie Converse, Scott Daggert, Mike DeCesare, Rob Hahn, Robert Hohman, Craig Jelinek, John McGee, Tom Mendoza, Lew Moorman, Lanham Napier, Andy Nyman, Alan Olivo, Bob Olson, Mike O'Neill, Frank Oz, Brian Ray,* Glenn Renwick, Jim Sinegal, Trenton Truitt, Jim Walton, Maggie Wilderotter, and Tyler Wirtjes.

Thanks also to Dr. Alison Arnold. At EMC, thanks also to Rick Devenuti. At Frontier, thanks also to Brigid Smith. At GoDaddy, thanks also to Kari Amarosso. At Glassdoor, thanks also to MaryJo Fitzgerald. At NetApp, thanks also to Danielle Grassi. At Progressive, thanks also to Kevin Ament, Charlie Baughman, Jeff Charney, Pawan Divakarla, Michelle Ferrara, Jacinda Jones, Tom King, Wanda Shippy, Angela Straub, and Erin Vrobel. Thank you to Lori Ruff, which is the same as thanking the entire world. Thanks to Alec Foege for being there at the beginning and Gary Stewart for staying up and flying up. William Barker, Steven Chean, Peter Martin, Patrick Milligan, and Thane Tierney: thanks for the deep thinking and intense jam sessions. A special thanks to the incredible Victoria Labalme (victorialabalme.com).

---

* Brian Ray's other job is being cofounder of the band the Bayonets, along with Oliver Leiber and an "ever-evolving, revolving cast of outlaws and ne'er-do-wells." Check 'em out at thebayonets.com and wikipedia.org/wiki/The_Bayonets.

THANK YOU: THE READERS' GROUP

Many of those already named read manuscript drafts, but thanks also to Lynne Marie Auzenne, P. Beihl, Sherry Benjamins, Tim Burch, Lucas Burt, Diane Cooley, Dan Cousins, Thomas Fakhoury, Heather Guild, Jay Golden, Barbara Gordon, Mark Halladay, Paul Hawkins, Andrea Huff, Ian Huschle, David Jamison, Adrian Jones, Kip Knight, Bruce Lee, Neville Letzerich, Ramola Lewis, Armen Markarian, Mimi Mehrabi, Mike Mikulay, Amy Mendenhall, Regina Miller, Dan Parisi, Lynette Reed, Janet Rolle, Lauren Saginaw, Gary Selick, Nina Simosko, Brian Smith, Erica Smith, Maggie Spicer, Dave Swinkin, Mark Thompson, Stacy Tyler, Betsy Utley, Gerardo Valencia, Brian Winchar, and Jene Yoder, and for their insight/incite. Thank you Sue "Birdi" Burish for being such a bright light during some dark and funky times.

THANK YOU: MARKETING TEAM

The first rule of great marketing is don't say something until you stand for something. The second is to pick an outstanding team to say it. Thanks so much to Anthony Bear (bear@humanitymedia.net) for the website; Seth Combs for the evangelical campaign; Chris Johnson at Simplifilm (Chris@simplifilm.com) for the video; and Natascha Thomson at Marketing Accelerator (nathomson@marketingxlerator.com) for SEO.

THANK YOU: PERSONAL SUPPORT

It takes a village to stop a cow from wandering off in the night and from becoming a cow in the first place while glued to a chair writing for eighteen hours a day. I'm blessedly in good health and pretty fit, but the hours on this book would mess with anyone's well-being. These committed people helped keep me healthy and productive: Eduardo Dolhun, William Grossman, Josh Schiaretti, and Stephen Seligman.

THANK YOU: OTHER KINDS OF SOLID SUPPORT

Rik Kirkland; Greg LeClair; Sarah Wotherspoon; David and Todd Moss, Eric Black, Alphonso Aviles and all the rest of the great folks at 24hourtek (a name I took literally); Wayne Ng; Clare Kuo; Liz Wiseman, and of course Dean and Cheryl Radetsky.

Thanks to Judy Ranzer, the world's best travel agent (judyranzer@gmail.com); Theron Kabrich of San Francisco Art Gallery, home of the world's best music photography (sfae.com). And thank you so much to Steve Berson (steve@bersonfinancialgroup.com), the world's best accountant and a best friend at all times.

THANK YOU: AL SATTERWHITE

Al is the legendary photographer who has shot Muhammad Ali, Steve McQueen, Hunter Thompson, Keith Moon, and Tom Waits. I figured that portfolio of personalities made him an obvious choice for my author photo. I'm still stunned that he agreed to do it. He is too.

THANK YOU: MATT HALEY

Photo-realist Matt Haley did the engine graphic on the front cover. He's a scary mix between illustrator and illusionist. Jodi Smith did a version too and it was a growling, prowling beast of an engine. It was a tough choice and I thank you both.

THANK YOU: WORDS

A big thanks to everyone along the way who transformed cuneiform into the English alphabet. Twenty-six letters that seem so innocent.

Writing a book is a consuming and exhausting experience that's hard to describe. But the thrill is hard to describe, too. Not just the thrill of completing the manuscript or hitting the bestseller lists—way before that. The thrill of a perfectly executed sentence that you are the first to ever see as it comes into the world. If the thought of this doesn't get your nose open, you probably shouldn't be writing. It's not for everybody; many people are well adjusted and don't need to do it.

I wrote this book in my company's San Francisco offices, in our library at home, and at Goldeneye in Jamaica. The one you want to check out is Goldeneye. It was originally the home of author Ian Fleming and is now owned by Chris Blackwell, who last year turned it into a small resort: only twenty rooms and the Fleming house. In Fleming's house is the original desk where he wrote all thirteen James Bond books—James Bond did not exist until he was created at that very desk. I got to set my laptop right where Fleming set his typewriter. What a rush.

Now, Chris Blackwell: Back in the day, his mother was Ian Fleming's lover and—how's this for a traumatizing childhood event?—the inspiration for Pussy Galore. She once even gifted Fleming with a boat she named Octopussy. *(MOM! Ewwww!)* When he was twenty-one, Chris's own small sailboat got wrecked and he washed up on shore injured, only to be taken in by Rastafarians who nursed him back to health. This gave him a spiritual connection to that culture and he went on to found Island Records, the label that brought Bob Marley and reggae to the world (he also signed U2 when they were a bar band in Dublin). It was his birthday when we were there, and he invited us to dinner. Man, oh, man, does this guy have some stories.

Goldeneye is gorgeous and secluded—heaven for introverts. I've worked with enough rock stars and Hollywood folk to be deeply unmoved by close proximity to most, but our last night there, hanging at the bar with Chris, Win and Régine of Arcade Fire, and Bob Marley's daughter, drinking Blackwell Dark Rum (yeah, the guy has his own rum) as the waves lapped nearby and the warm Jamaican breeze tickled the trees, I began to give serious thought to ditching everything, moving there, and becoming a goat farmer. A couple of keynotes, a couple of goats: I could make it work.

And finally, I can't imagine a better compliment to a writer than this one from George Painter about the work of Violet Trefusis: "It's like being driven at 90 mph over an ice field, by a driver who knows how to skid for fun."

THANK YOU: MUSIC

I most often listen to music while I write: two playlists that I've named *Manic* and *Depressive*. As of this writing, there are a ridiculous 5,787 songs in the first and 6,033 in the second. Many different genres and geographies are represented, but they have in common a visceral passion. I owe a big thanks to all of these tracks for keeping me on track.

Usually I just put one of the two playlists on Shuffle and let it do its thing, but I found myself playing one song—*The '59 Sound* by The Gaslight Anthem—over and over, and it kind of became the anthem for this book. Not because of any particular weight or relevance but because of what it does: It pumps you up, moves you along, then settles you down into a better place than you were before. It is immediately intimate and you have the sense that the writer knew exactly where he was going from the beginning and wanted to take you with him.

I wanted to take you somewhere with this book.

"Any kind of apathy in a songwriter pisses me off." —Brian Fallon, The Gaslight Anthem.

SELECTED
RESEARCH NOTES

SOURCES, DATA POINTS, RELATED & VAGUELY RELATED FACTS,
WEIRD SCIENCE AND ANTHROPOLOGICAL JUNGLE CRED

"IF SOCIETY LACKS UNITY BASED UPON THE COMMITMENT OF MEN'S WILLS TO A COMMON OBJECTIVE, THEN IT IS NO MORE THAN A PILE OF SAND THAT THE LEAST JOLT OR THE SLIGHTEST PUFF WILL SUFFICE TO SCATTER."

Emile Durkheim, *Moral Education: A Study in the Theory and Application of the Sociology of Education.* Free Press of Glencoe, 1961 (English translation of *L'Education Morale*, originally published 1903)

"A society is composed of people; the way they behave is their culture."

Melville J. Herskovits, *Man and His Works: The Science of Cultural Anthropology.* A.A. Knopf, 1949

"Among animals, man is uniquely dominated by culture, by influences learned and handed down. Some would say that culture is so important that genes…are virtually irrelevant to the understanding of human nature."

Richard Dawkins, *The Selfish Gene* Oxford University Press, 30th Anniversary Edition, 2006 (originally published in 1976)

Subject: Culture as an actor
Date: Thursday, June 6, 2013 at 9:23:43 AM Pacific Daylight Time
From: Richard M. Murphy
To: Stan Slap

I would also fill out the culture discussion just a touch. I like the image of MM turning on a spit, don't get me wrong but I think it would be helpful to add just a few paragraphs explaining how/why anthropologists developed their concepts of culture and how you see those concepts applying to modern business organizations. I totally agree tha ve *don't want to slow the book down -- it's just a matter of quickly establishing your authority as a business* ~~n~~ *thropologist so that readers buy into the journey they're about to take.*

END FINAL VER. FOR BOOK .... IN NOTES?

HOW ANTHROPOLOGISTS THINK ABOUT CULTURE

There is a distinguished intellectual history of people searching for insights into how power relationships work in societies. A surprising amount of early anthropological theory is judged as credible today and when it has been superseded is still respected as the best rational thinking of its time.

Respect is a key word in the study of culture. Even when anthropologists labored in service to power, they were still motivated by respect for the peoples they were observing: they were still driven by learning for learning's sake: and they still believed in humanity's ability to prove non-stop fascinating, resilient and impressive.

Their ethnographic studies focused on native tribes in primitive cultures; I have focused on employees in modern corporate culture. Issues of comparison, relativism, context and diffusion that mark the thinking routes of anthropology are valid in both—there's little difference between a group of natives who studied animal entrails to determine what the gods had in store for them and an employee culture that studies management emails for the same purpose.

****

Before there were anthropologists there was plenty of thinking about culture. Originally it was about growing stuff: In Roman times the word "culture" referred to a cultivated field or piece of land. Cicero (106 BC-43 BC) was the first to use the term in a spiritual sense with his concept "cultura animi," or cultivation of the soul, which presumably involves the yanking of weeds from your very essence.

In the 17th century, Europeans started using the term culture with reference to self-improvement through education. For the German philosopher Samuel von Pufendorf (1632-1694), culture referred to "all the ways in which human beings overcome their original barbarism, and through artifice, become fully human." Essentially, fake it 'til you make it.

Meanwhile, over in drizzly London, Thomas Hobbes (1588-1689) was publishing *Leviathan* with its sunny idea that human beings originally lived in a state of nature, which made life "nasty, brutish and short," so they created a social contract in which they surrendered some of their freedom and autonomy to a central authority in exchange for protection.

Hold that thought—or have your central authority hold it for you—because culture is now becoming a social concept, related to "civilization".

It was the 18th century and still the Age of Enlightenment in Europe. In Germany the burghers of Konigsberg were setting their watches by loony OCD professor Immanuel Kant who power-walked to his lectures within *seconds* of the same time every day. Kant favored an individualist definition of culture as "man's emergence from his self-incurred immaturity." At this point culture was still about education but not for long because Kant's sparring partner Johann Gottfried Herder (1744-1803) gave Kant's individualist perspective that social spin,

"Culture, or civilization ... is that complex whole which includes knowledge, belief, art, morals, law, custom, and any other capabilities and habits acquired by man as a member of society."
—Edward B. Tylor, Primitive Culture: Researches into the Development of Mythology, Philosophy, Religion, Art, and Custom. Cambridge University Press, 2010 (originally published 1871)

claiming culture is "the totality of experiences that provide a coherent identity, and sense of common destiny, to a people."

Under the influence of Herder, European scholars like Wilhelm von Humboldt (1757-1835) fell madly in love with the notion that humanity can be divided into distinct national cultures, each of which shares a worldview. This idea caught on like Jerry Lewis in Europe because it lent credence to the emerging concept of nationalism, which was quickly replacing older ideas like the divine right of kings and religion as the main organizing principle for European society. Suddenly, those self-consecrated kings were either dead or figureheads and European nation-states were building colonial empires that stripped natural resources from the natives while infusing them with European innovations like restrictive underwear and croissants.

Naturally European (and later, naturally American) imperialists used this as the intellectual justification for abusive expansion, considering it *mission civilisatrice*, or in America, Manifest Destiny, which is the belief that expansion by subordination is justified and pretty much inevitable. Soon enough the natives were forced to attend school, which they clearly needed to do, and along the way not only developing a lust for designer purses they couldn't possibly afford on a native's salary but far worse, political ideas of their own. Wait a minute! When we taught you all that history about the French Revolution and independence we didn't mean you should internalize it. Well, well, well: Look who was paying attention in class after all.

We're in the 19th century now and suddenly the British, French, Germans and Americans had new empires to administer and lots of complicated native cultures to reckon with. They needed to understand those natives in order to rule them effectively so the urgent call went out across the lands: *Let's get us some anthropologists!* Before you know it French ethnographers were studying the Berber and Arab tribes of Algeria while the Brits fanned out across Eastern and Southern Africa, and the Americans raced to publish monographs about the Sioux, Cherokee and Comanche tribes before the U.S. Cavalry could kill them all.

As anthropology gained credibility and became an academic discipline, intellectual rigor increased and great thinkers were attracted to the field. They started pondering how to make meaningful comparisons between discrete cultures, thus setting up one of the lasting fundamentals of anthropological observation: comparative analysis.

TRANSLATION: YOU WOULDN'T BE THE FIRST MANAGER IN HISTORY WHO REALLY WANTS TO UNDERSTAND A CULTURE — AS SOON AS POSSIBLE, BEFORE THE NATIVES NOTICE.

When grad students asked Sir Evans-Pritchard for advice about how to do anthropological fieldwork, he had one stock reply, according to Oxford legend: "Always bring two folding tables into the field. That way your bearer won't have to disturb your notes when he brings you dinner."

—Richard McGill Murphy, personal communication from his personal trove of E-P lore when studying anthropology at Oxford

Enter Sir Edward Evans-Pritchard (1902-1973), one of the Original Gangsters of British social anthropology, as it were. Evans-Pritchard published groundbreaking ethnographic studies of social organization and religious practice amongst Nuer and Azande tribesmen in Sudan, and his influence on the field is so huge that modern anthropologists still refer to him by his initials. In 1965, O.G. E-P wrote that "There is no other method in social anthropology than observation, classification and comparison in one form or another." Basically, the anthropologist has to conceive the society that they study in light of at least one other, their own. This seems logical now but was breakthrough thinking at the time and this is what modern anthropologists still do: They compare cultures, looking for distinctions and similarities.

These comparisons can illuminate both cultures, like when the French anthropologist Louis Dumont (1911-1998) contrasted the hierarchical caste tradition of India with the Western tradition of individualism. In the world of Indian caste, the ranking principle is that purer castes outrank less pure castes. This is in contrast with Western individualism, a form of social organization based on the assumption that all individuals are morally equal [true if the bar is set really low]. From an anthropological POV, this brings both cultures into play on more or less equal terms.

TRANSLATION: YOUR EMPLOYEE CULTURE IS BEST UNDERSTOOD ON ITS OWN TERMS. NOT IN TERMS OF COMPANY GOALS, THE PERSPECTIVE OF YOUR MANAGER CULTURE OR HOW THE COMPANY MAY PREFER TO DEFINE THE CULTURE'S CHARACTERISTICS TO MAKE ITSELF LOOK GOOD.

Still famous in anthropological circles is E-P's example of the Azande granary, which he used to distinguish African and Western theories of causality:

In the early 1930s, E-P lived among the Azande of the Congo and southern Sudan. The Azande were a farming people who believed that witches among them were responsible for many of life's misfortunes. The Azande built wooden granaries on stilts to protect the grain from insects. Because there were few trees and little shade in Zandeland, local Azande would often hang out underneath the granaries, gossiping and playing the African hole game. Every now and then a granary would collapse on top of some Azande, injuring or killing them.

The Azande always blamed these disasters on witchcraft, although they understood that most granaries collapsed because termites gnawed through their wooden supports. Of course the termites ate the supports, they said. But a termite-infested granary could collapse at any time. From an Azande point of view, only a witch could make it collapse at the precise moment when people were sitting underneath the damn thing.

Westerners would call this bad coincidence. The Azande didn't believe in coincidence and called it witchcraft. Both conclusions make sense within the cultural logic that produced them.

"A man once lost a diamond cuff-link in the sea and twenty years later, on the exact day, he was eating a large fish – but there was no diamond inside. That's what I like about coincidence."
—VLADIMIR NABOKOV

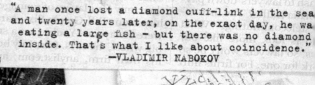

MAN OF
THE YEAR

The comparative method works for illuminating both cultural differences and similarities. Writing in the 1920s, the great German-American anthropologist Franz Boas (1858-1942) insisted that uniformity of process was essential for comparability, writing that "Only those phenomena can be compared which are derived psychologically or historically from common causes." At around the same time, the Yale anthropologist and linguist Edward Sapir became known for the important principle of *diffusionism*, which asserts that resemblances between geographically discrete cultures happen as the result of historical, well, obviously, diffusion.

Stripped of anthro-babble, diffusionism means that cultures around the world resemble each other because of ideas that spread through human contact, which is why many cultures around the world were found to be a lot alike in lots of ways. Famed American anthropologist Ruth Benedict (1887-1948) wasn't buying it and pushed back on Sapir's theory by arguing that no cultural trait can be understood in isolation. Dimensions like language, art and personality must be analyzed in relation to each other as parts of a unified cultural whole. She had a point but so did Sapir.

This brings us to *structuralism*, one of the more broadly useful concepts produced by social anthropology. It was most closely associated with the recently late French anthropologist Claude Lévi-Strauss (1908-2009) who argued that human beings everywhere display common cultural characteristics based on common mental structures. From his perspective there was no essential difference between civilized and "savage" thought.

Lévi-Strauss focused especially on the study of North and South American myth and totemism, showing how common concepts such as the opposition of raw and cooked food and the elaborate process of exchanging women (not as raw or cooked food) produced different but comparable practices in cultures that had little in common historically or linguistically, like indigenous communities in the Brazilian Amazon vs. the Pacific Northwest.

The human beings who comprise cultures have brains wired the same way, no matter where they are in the world, he said. Lévi-Strauss called this same basic brain process, which produces the same types of social structures, myths and superstitions in every culture, a "common grammar." This means that different cultures exhibit similar characteristics: Superficial differences are generated by a common underlying logic.

TRANSLATION: THE PURPOSE AND THINKING PROCESS OF AN EMPLOYEE CULTURE IS ESSENTIALLY COMPARABLE FROM COMPANY TO COMPANY, REGARDLESS OF COUNTRY, INDUSTRY OR BUSINESS UNIT.

Diffusion says that historical circumstances and the spread of information unite cultures. Structuralism says that common cultural logic can be traced even without a historical connection. Add relativism and you have the three anthropological power chords.

Structuralism has proven a strong tool for cross-cultural analysis, but by focusing on cross-cultural transformations of specific practices, institutions or legends, the work of Lévi-Strauss and others ascribing to his beliefs tends to sort of flatten the contexts in which social phenomena are imbedded. That's not completely a criticism: The literary theorist Paul de Man advocates in his 1971 book *Blindness and Insight* that any strong reading implies a degree of blindness in other places.

...ure is an historically transmitted pattern of meanings embodied in symbols, a system ...herited conceptions expressed in symbolic form by means of which men communicate, ...etuate and develop their knowledge about and their attitudes toward life."
...ord Geertz, The Interpretation of Cultures. Basic Books, 1977

BRAHMINS
KSHATRIYAS
VAISYAS
SUDRAS
PARIAH

Context is vital in determining the meaning of any event, practice or institution in particular society, which is what forms the basis for meaningful comparison. This mean always arises from what anthropologists call *segmentary opposition*, which is a snotty te for—wait for it—context. Writing in 1983, Dumont argued that value is "normally segmenta in its application." He just meant that theories are generally clearly defined in opposition other theories. In a 1967 article, the British anthropologist Julian Pitt-Rivers (1919-2001 a probably not necessary to point out that he was British) said that social solidarity "is not.. innate property of a social group but a function of its relationship to that which is conceptua excluded from it."

TRANSLATION: YOUR EMPLOYEE CULTURE ESTABLISHES SOLIDARITY BY CONTRASTING ITSELF WITH YOUR MANAGER CULTURE.

In modern corporate cultures, just like in the classic field studies of social anthropolo context is determined not only by time and place but by human beings and their behav Pitt-Rivers did his major fieldwork in Andalusia, where he found that notions of honor va according to social class, the type of community and its size. Rigid typological definiti of "honor" had limited explanatory value in Andalusia, where lower-class villagers defi "honor" in terms of female chastity, while for aristocrats "honor" meant flouting the sex rules that constrained their social inferiors.

"Flouting" sounds like a fabulous dirty word all by itself, but that's not the point meaningful cross-cultural analysis of honor in Andalusia would require a comparison of th respective social contexts. The same is true for a comparative analysis of leadership, strat implementation and cultural resistance in the enterprise.

TRANSLATION: YOUR EMPLOYEE CULTURE'S PERCEPTIONS ARE DRIVEN BY THE CONTEXT OF ITS CIRCUMSTANCE

[Sadly, for the ruling class of Andalusia,] it's not the 19th century anymore. Today corporations that are a dominant locus for cultures, and the social classes within are define being an executive or an employee. Noted British-Czech anthropologist Ernest Gellner (19 1995) insisted that while primitive societies were mostly about structure, modern societies mostly about culture.

"In modern society," wrote Gellner in his 1965 book *Thought and Change*, "culture beco of utmost importance—culture being, essentially, the manner in which one communica ...In simple societies culture is important, but its importance resides in the fact that it reinfo structure—the style of being and expression symbolizes, underlines the substance, the effec roles, activities, relationships. In modern societies, culture does not so much underline struct rather, it replaces it."

TRANSLATION: YOUR EMPLOYEE CULTURE IS DECIDING THE SUCCESS OF YOUR STRATEGIES & PERFORMANCE GOALS AS YOU READ THIS SENTENCE.

WE ARE AMUSED BY YOUR IMPERTINENCE AND HAVE DECIDED TO LET YOU LIVE.

jolly   twit   scoff
chaff   tease   bait   flout
banter taunt   cod
        tantalize   rag
        tantalise rally
              ride razz

"We need, in every
community, a group of
angelic troublemakers.
BAYARD RUSTIN

KINDNESS IS
[...]T ABOUT THE
[...]YOU CAN D[...]

MARGARET MEAD
XXL
MUSTANGS

LOOKS GOOD ON THE COFFEE TABLE
IF YOU'RE TRYING TO DATE ANTHROPOLOGISTS

Austin, J.L., *How to Do Things with Words*
Cambridge, Harvard University Press, 1962.

Barnes, R.H. "The Leiden Version of the
Comparative Method." JASO 16, 1985.

Benedict, Ruth, *Patterns of Culture*
Routledge & Keagan, London, 1935.

Bloch, Marc. *Land and Work in Medieval Europe*
Berkeley: University of California Press, 1967.

De Man, Paul, *Blindness and Insight: Essays in
the Rhetoric of Contemporary Criticism*
Minneapolis, University of Minnesota Press, 1983
(orig. 1971).

Dumont, Louis. *Homo Hierarchicus: The Caste
System and Its Implications.*
University of Chicago Press, 1980 (orig. 1966).

---. *Essais Sur L'Individualisme: Une Perspective
Anthropologique Sur L'Ideologie Moderne*
Paris, Éditions du Seuil, 1983.

Eggan, F.W. "*Social Anthropology and the Method
of Controlled Comparison*"
American Anthropologist v. 56, 1954.

Evans-Pritchard, Edward E. *Witchcraft, Oracles
and Magic Among the Azande*
Oxford, Clarendon Press, 1937.

---, *The Nuer*
Oxford, Clarendon Press, 1940.

---, *Kinship and Marriage Among the Nuer*
Oxford, Clarendon Press, 1951.

---, *Nuer Religion*
Oxford University Press, 1956.

---, *Theories of Primitive Religion*
London, Faber & Faber, 1965

Gellner, Ernest, *Thought and Change*
London, Weidenfeld and Nicholson, 1964.

Geertz, Clifford, *The Interpretation of Cultures*
New York Basic Books, 1977.

Herskovits, Melville J. *Man and His Works*
New York, Knopf, 1948.

Leach, Edmund, *Rethinking Anthropology*
London, Robert Cunningham & Sons, 1961.

Lévi-Strauss, Claude, *La Pensée Sauvage*
Paris, Plon, 1962.

---, *Le Cru et le Cuit*
Paris, Plon, 1964.

Mead, Margaret, *Coming of Age in Samoa*
New York, William Morrow, 1928.

Pitt-Rivers, Julian. "*Contextual Analysis and the
Locus of the Model*".
European Journal of Sociology, v. 8, 1967.

Pocock, David, *Social Anthropology*
London, Sheed & Ward, 1988 (orig. 1961).

Radcliffe-Brown, A.R., "*The Comparative Method
in Social Anthropology.*"
London, Huxley Memorial Lecture, 1951.

Tylor, Edward B. *Primitive Culture: Researches
into the Development of Mythology, Philosophy,
Religion, Art, and Custom*
Cambridge University Press, 2010 (originally published 1871).

Velkley, Richard, *Being After Rousseau:
Philosophy and Culture in Question*
Chicago, University of Chicago Press, 2002.

POST HOC ERGO PROPERTY HOC
Noted naturalists (like Darwin) and scientists (like Hawking) believe that the egg came before the chicken. Yet Aristotle advanced the ideas of "potentiality," which means that something is possible, and "actuality," which means the potentiality has become real. The purpose of the egg is pretty much to *become* a chicken, *whereas* the chicken is the chicken. And so the IDEA of the chicken, which is the egg, would seem to come before the chicken. But wait: Anything could happen to something classified as "potential," vs. the reality of said chicken being right there in front of you on the ground or the grill.
Aristotle sez the chicken came first.

Barely 1 in 5 employees are (21%) are engaged on the job * 71% of all employees are not fully engaged * 8% of all employees are fully diseng
– Towers Perrin, 2007 * Professional services and construction companies report the highest level of employee engagement, and travel and reta
record the lowest. * – Temkin Group, 2013 * 70% of employees who lack confident in the abilities of senior leadership are not fully engaged * 8
employees dissatisfied with their direct manager were disengaged * Companies with engaged employees outperform those without by up to 202%
B is lost annually due to employee turnover (Bureau of National Affairs) * –Employee Engagement Infographic by Dale Carnegie Tr
www.dalecarnegie.com * 38% of staffers would rather have more work on their plate, sit next to someone who eats loudly, and take on a longer con
than work next to their boss. * 46% say that even though they sit close to their co-workers they mostly communicate with them through email
phone. * 24% say they spend more time in meetings talking about work than actually doing it. * – "New Ask.com Study Reveals Workplace Prod
Killers" PRNewswire, May 7, 2013 * 64% of people said they have more to offer in skills and talent than they are currently being asked to demo
at work * Organizations with higher engagement levels outperformed the total stock market index * Organizations with higher engagement
shareholder returns 22% higher than average *Organizations with higher engagement level achieved twice the annual net profit * Organizations
top quartile of employee engagement scores had 18% higher productivity * Companies with engagement ~~~~~ he top quartile averaged 12%
customer advocacy * 84% of "Worlds Most Admired" Companies stated their efforts t~~~~~~~~~~~~~~ ngthened customer relations
Engaged employees in the UK take an average of 2.7 sick days per year, wh~~~~~~~~~~~ has 6% lower average engag
levels than other large economies (Kennexa, 2011) * Bottom 10% in emplo~~~~~~~~~~~~~r * Companies with high le
engagement show turnover rate 40% lower than companies with low levels o~~~~~~~~~ Whitepaper, November 12, 2
88% of those who reported that they are highly engaged also reported that t~~~~~~~~ es to the organization's suc
There is a clear connection between engagement and retention. The more en~~~~~~~ ~nt of employees plan on s
with their current employer. * 41% reported that in order to advance in their ca~~~~~~~ ~ ~uic~ St
on Employee Engagement" Clarfit.com, March 01, 2013 * Companies with en~~~~~~~ recovered from the recession at a faster rate. * There is a point of diminishing~~~~~~~
their time working remotely are the most engaged, at 35%, and they have the~~~~~~~
working remotely seems to h~~~~~~ ~~~~~~~

> **Have A Jamage! Day!**

> "When buying a use
> punch the buttons on t
> If all the stations are roo
> there's a good chan
> the transmission is sl
> —**LARRY LUJACK**

> "The totality of beliefs and sentiments common to the average members of a society forms a determinate system with a life of its own. It can be termed the collective or common consciousness."

–Emile Durkheim, The Division of Labor in Society. Free Press, 1997 (English translation of De la Division du Travail Social, originally published 1893)

2013 * Engaged employees are ...
mpany even if it's not expected. * En

Surve~~~~
relatio~~~
on sta~~~
Custo~~~

Thank You for choosing Re~~~~~
in Bridgewater. Today your server was
thinking about ending your life.

~an six times as likely to recommend a friend or relative apply for a j
~~~rted that th~~~~ ~o
ye~
~rt
ay

> "If you're after makin' honey, don't go killin' all the bees."
> —Joe Strummer

STRANGE CULTURAL PRACTICES

CAGANERS (Spain)
Christmas tradition: Hide small statuettes of people defecating in the nativity scenes of friends and family to try and find. Started in 17th cent

BISHNOI (India)
Most committed animal rights culture in the world. Followers of eco-frier Hindu guru, Sri Jambheshwar Bhagwan, since the 15th century. In 174: 363 Bishnoi men, women and children gave their lives to protect trees from cutting by the king's men at Kherjarli. Women breastfeed orphane

LU (Vietnam)
Believed only savages, wild animals and demons have long white teet Blackening assured the person would not be mistaken for an evil spirit Blackening of teeth certifies that a woman is grown and ready for man Red sticklac, a resin from secretions of tiny aphid-like insects that sucks sap of a host tree, diluted with lemon juice or rice alcohol and stored the dark for a few days. Three applications, every other day for a we Very painful—can only drink liquids through a straw.

TORAJA (Indonesia)
It is essential that that the spirit of a dead person meet their relatives so they can guide him on his journey into the afterlife. The dead bod would be supported so that it "walks" back home from wherever it h died, no matter how far that was. Those accompanying the decease warn people they meet on their path not to talk directly to the dead man. Also practiced on animals.

TIDONG (Borneo)
For three days and nights following the wedding, both the bride an groom are prohibited from any bathroom activities—from urination

"In theory everything works. In practice, there is no theory." –Yogi Berra

> Magick is the Art and Science of causing Change to occur in conformity with Will.
> —Aleister Crowley

The first time that the United States has ever been at DEFCON 2, the second-highest level of military readiness considered the "next step to nuclear war," was in October of 1962. It happened almost to the minute of James Brown recording the *Live at the Apollo* album. Brown took to the stage at 11PM on October 24. At 10:52 PM that same night, no doubt in preparation for what he was about to unleash, the U.S. Strategic Air Command was ordered to drastically increase nuclear defense readiness. Some might say too little too late.

"THE ONE THING THAT CAN SOLVE MOST OF OUR PROBLEMS IS DANCING."
-JAMES BROWN

Policy Resistance to change in dynamics systems, AKA fixes that fail and fixes that backfire. Whenever a system has two or more actors, you have two or more goals. If you try to introduce a third goal, there will be resistance.

LOCUS OF CONTROL: A central principle of social-learning in human psychology. First theorized by Julian Rotter in '54. Refers to extent to which people believe they can control the events that affect them.

"Locus" is Latin for location. People with an internal locus of control believe that every action causes a reaction. This translates to a belief that it's up to them if they want to have control over what happens.

An employee culture has an external locus of control—the control over events that decide its survival and emotional prosperity is located outside of the employee culture, not within it. It has been repeatedly proven that people with an external locus of control tend to be more stressed and depressed.

DANGER
Do not hold the wrong end of a chainsaw

N5D WE
RAY. XCELLENT VID
GEOMAGNETC STORMS RE DN
13 0

here is no such thing as inner peace.
here is only nervousness and death."
—FRAN LEBOWITZ

Your strategies may be rocket s

Locus of control has been considered as one of the dimensions of core self-evaluation—how somebody conducts essential self-appraisal—joining neuroticism, self-efficacy and self-esteem. It has been seriously theorized that all four dimensions are measuring the same factor. *IT SOME MEASURES THE REGULAR STATE OF AN EMPLOYEE CULTURE.*
(See: Timothy Judge, Amir Erez, Joyce Bono, Carl Thoresen, "Are Measures of Self-Esteem, Neuroticism, Locus of Control and Generalized Self-Efficacy Indicators of a Common Core Construct?" *Journal of Personality and Social Psychology*, 2002)

WEEEEE!

"If everything seems under control, you're just not going fast enough."
—MARIO ANDRETTI

> "To wax poetic is honorable, to blather inconsequentially is not. But honor is as much an attitude as it is an act. To be self-possessed is more honorable than to be dumbfounded. And to respect the honor of others is in itself honorable."
> —Steven Caton, *Peaks of Yemen I Summon: Poetry as Cultural Practice in a North Yemini Tribe*. University of California Press, 1990

REAL ENTERPRISE EVENT THEMES

Refuse To Lose

Growing Global!

We Are The Champions!

We Are Still Family

Keep Your Eye On The Ball

Focus And Fire!

Let's Rock!

Let's Roll!

Let's Rock And Roll!

Beat Them Bad

The Power Of Synergy

In It to Win It

Faster! Stronger! Longer!

Higher, Deeper, Wider!

Land It And Expand It!

More! More! More!

This Time It's Personal!

SUNSET. & DONT 4GET. Y OUI MET! ...VEHOS... RUST 17 25 10 48

> "...a culture's chance of uniting the complex body of inventions of all sorts which we describe as a civilization depends on the number and diversity of the other cultures with which it is working out, generally involuntarily, a common strategy."
> —Claude Lévi-Strauss, *Race, History and Culture (1996).*

> "SOMETIMES REALITY CAN BE TOO COMPLEX TO BE CONVEYED BY THE SPOKEN WORD. LEGEND REMOLDS IT INTO A FORM THAT CAN BE SPREAD ALL ACROSS THE WORLD."
> JEAN-LUC GODARD

> "Augustine was quite clear that power, the effect of an entire network of motivated practices, assumes a religious form because of the end to which it is directed, for human events are the instruments of God. It was not the mind that moves spontaneously to religious truth, but power that imposed the conditions for experiencing that truth."
> —Talal Asad, "*Anthropological Conceptions of Religion: Reflections on Geertz*," Man (18) 1983.

Steve Cropper ENTERPRISES INCORPORATED

AVENUE SOUTH

WHEN THE GOING GETS WE THE WEIRD TURN PRO. — HUNTER S. THOMAS

PEOPLE GET READY   **THERE'S A TRAIN A COMIN.'**   **CURTIS MAYFI**

Stan Slap
To: Mike DeCesare
Re: WALK THIS WAY EMC VERSION

WALK THIS WAY: EMC VERSION

Back East acquisition forces a transition
We hear the voices of Hopkinton say
Tighten up and button down; we'll call at 4AM so be around
You've got to be changin' your ways

We run the software business; it just isn't in us
You bought us to win
Don't be putting our souls at risk 'cause the best part of winning
The drinkin' and the grinnin'
We do business with a little twist
Like this!

Walk this way, talk this way, get in this way, win this way
Compete this way, beat this way
Sell this way, raise hell this way
With an ESG twist
Like this!

> "PRIMITIVISM IS RARELY BETTER THE SECOND TIME AROUND."
> —ROBERT CHRISTGAU

TOP 10 WORST SONGS TO PLAY AT A COMPANY OFF-SITE

1. Bad Reputation
2. Chain Of Fools
3. Won't Get Fooled Again
4. Don't Fear The Reaper
5. Flirtin' With Disaster
6. Go Your Own Way
7. Bad Company
8. Running On Empty
9. Crazy Train
10. Whipping Post

First Posted: 08-18-10 01:52 PM
Updated: 08-18-10 02:32 PM

Shenzhen, CHINA (AP) – Following a string of suicides at its Chinese factories, Foxconn Technology Group...installed safety nets on buildings to catch would-be jumpers. Now it is holding rallies for its workers to raise morale at the heavily regimented factories.

The motivational rallies are titled "Treasure Your Life, Love Your Family Care for Each Other to Build a Wonderful Future."

(= WORK HARDER)

"'Obnubiliate' means to make unclear."
Eugene Ehrlich, *The Highly Selective Dictionary*, HarperCollins 2009)

"WHERE ARE WE GOING?"
"PLANET TEN!"
"WHEN ARE WE GOING THERE?"
"REAL SOON!"

—Lord John Whorfin to workers; workers' response: *Buckaroo Banzai*

(= LIVE BETTER)

HUFFPOST

Stretches All Desk Workers Should Do Today

Posted: 06/14/2013 2:49 am EDT

By Katherine Schreiber

We know sitting all a desk all day is best for us. But not everyone has a company gym or workweek that allows for morning and afternoon fitness classes. So here are muscles made most stiff by sitting. No gym equipment or extended lunch

Neck And Shoulders. Hunching over keyboards strain... ch your arms behind you, and interlock your... shoulders. Draw your chin down to... (low suit.)

Flexors A... ...keeping the knee directly above ankle. Keep ...ing and ef... ...you, gliding the knee forward. You may feel a stretch in ...for support. Hold for 30 second. Switch sides. Repeat.

m Greatist: ...Day Gift Ideas for Your Fit Dad: ...Recipes: ...ly Unexpected ...Care About a D...

Reach out ...your gaze

...the origin ...ingers to ...body. Hold for...

> "Bureaucracy is the kinship of modern man."
> —Ernest Gellner, *Thought and Change*. Weidenfeld and Nicholson, 1964)

Woody Guthrie's 1942 New Years Resolutions

to write me

Resolutions

them my own

NEW

Wednesday, June 19, 2013 5:19:25 PM Pacific Daylight Time

Subject: Culture vs. Culture
Date: Wednesday, June 19, 2013 5:16:09 PM Pacific Daylight Time
From: Richard M. Murphy
To: Stan Slap

We didn't talk about it in quite those terms (body/environment), but they make sense now that I thi Through most of the book you personify the culture as an individual actor, you say "the culture nd Z." My take is that this is a perfectly legitimate rhetorical device as long as you flag it for us gument. Strictly speaking, however, the culture is not an actor but rather a set of individuals culturally patterned ways.

I think you just need a line or two in the Margaret Mead section saying "In this book I through it were a person. I get that a culture is in fact blah blah blah..."

1. WORK MORE AND BETTER

2. WORK BY A SCHEDU

3. WASH TEETH IF ANY

Victor Hugo finished The Hunchback of Notre Dame against severe deadline pressure from his publisher. Toward the end of 1830 he only had a few months to deliver the final manuscript and every week he was late he would be fined 1,000 francs. So he put himself under house arrest, which consisted of locking up all his clothes. If he couldn't get dressed he couldn't go out — not much else to do but work on the book. He met the deadline.

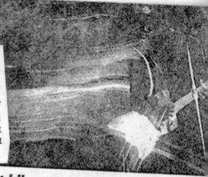

Bo Diddley's Guide to Survival

Alcohol and Drugs Only drink Grand Marnier, and that's to keep the throat from drying up in a place where there's a lot of smoke. As for drugs: a big NO!

Food Eat anytime, anything you can get your hands on. I mean it!

Health Whenever you get to feeling weird, take Bayer aspirin. I can't stand taking all that other bullshit.

Money Always take a lawyer with you, and then bring another lawyer to watch him.

Defense I can't go round slapping people with my hands or else I'd go broke. So I take karate, and kick when I fight. Of course, I got plenty of guns - one real big one. But guns are for people trying to take your home, not some guy who makes you mad. I used to be a sheriff down in New Mexico for two and a half years, so I know not to pull it right away.

Cows If they wanna play, and you don't wanna make pets out of 'em, and you can't eat 'em - then get rid of 'em.

Women If you wanna meet a nice young lady, then you try to smell your best. A girl don't like nobody walking up in her face smelling like a goat. Then, you don't say crap like "Hey, don't I know you?" The first thing you ask her is: "Are you alone?" If she tells you that she's with her boyfriend, then you see if the cat's as big as you. If you don't have no money, just smell right. And for God's sake don't be pulling on her and slapping on her. You don't hit the girls! If you do this, you can't miss.

Hearing Just don't put your ears in the speakers.

QUI-MOVE N2 SCORPIO. DEI
6 u 9 3 ¤ 66

"The development of the concept of the calling quickly gave to the modern entrepreneur a fabulously clear conscience—and also industrious workers; he gave to his employees as the wages of their ascetic devotion to the calling and of cooperation in his ruthless exploitation of them through capitalism the prospect of eternal salvation."
–Max Weber, *The Protestant Ethic and the Spirit of Capitalism*, 1905

When the American anthropologist Jon Anderson did fieldwork among the shtun tribes of Eastern Afghanistan in the 1970s, he found that Pushtun leaders, khans, were also mediators rather than dictators. For the Pushtun, a khan is somebody who "feeds the people" and "ties the knot of the tribe."

Woody Guthrie's 19-

15. LEARN PEOPLE BET
16. KEEP RANCHO CLE
17. DONT GET LONES
18. STAY GLAD

"To have humanism we must first be convinced of our humanity."
—Thomas Pynchon

21. BANK ALL EXTRA M
22. SAVE
23. HAVE

FISHERMAN'S

"It's always a pleasure
to find something
that matters."
–DON CORNELIUS

☮, ♥✊

sert his authority
doubts about his leadership in a
morning conference call with
Wall Street analysts.
"Our goal is simple: It's to create value for our shareholders
and for our debt holders, for our
clients and for our employees,"
Mr. Fuld said in the call. "On
many fronts on this cycle we did
not achieve this goal. This is my
responsibility. We've made a
number of changes. It's now my

ght for
placed
than a
to as-
ease

PEOPLE STRATEG
(not for wide co

mary:
7 Marketplaces People Strategy has 54 elements pillars:
1. People Development
2. Talent Management
4. Communication and Engagement
4. Accountability, Assessment and Recognition
"Great Place to Work"

develop and execute this People Strategy?
It's the right thing to do to drive better business results.

"People are out there doing bad things
to each other. That's because they've
been dehumanized. It's time to take the
humanity back into the center of the ring.
...Without people, you're nothing.
That's my spiel."
—JOE STRUMMER

dependence of Lehman.
Some analysts said Lehman's
mortgage assets might deterio-
rate further.
"The general question is, Have
Continued on Page 2

ears into six fig-
eers.
gy problem is
economic im-
the electricity
y, a consult-
l engineer-
ains why
n't go

31. LOVE EVERYBODY
32. MAKE UP YOUR MIND
33. WAKE UP AND FIGHT

THIS MACHINE KILLS FACISTS ➤
THIS MACHINE SURROUNDS HATE
& FORCES IT TO SURRENDER ➤
THIS MACHINE FLOATS ➤

The beaver has a house
but it's on the top of the hill.
Bears live on the hill.
Go through the maze and help
beaver get to his house.
The mountain is his house and you
need to help him get to his door.
SRS

UNITED STATES DISTRICT COURT
SOUTHERN DISTRICT OF NEW YORK

I HAVE A LEGAL TEAM: MLK OWNED THE SPEECH & DIDN'T TAKE KINDLY TO ITS BEING USED WITHOUT PERMISSION.

- - - - - - - - - - - - - - - - -

MARTIN LUTHER KING, JR.,   :   63 Civ. Action 2839

        Plaintiff,   :

     -against-   :

MISTER MAESTRO, INC. and TWENTIETH   :
CENTURY-FOX RECORD CORPORATION,

       Defendants.   :

- - - - - - - - - - - - - - - - X

[stamp: U.S. DISTRICT COURT FILED DEC 16 1963 S.D. OF N.Y.]

STATE OF GEORGIA)
) ss.:
COUNTY OF FULTON)

    MARTIN LUTHER KING, JR., being duly sworn, deposes
and says:

    1. I reside at 563 Johnson Avenue, N.E. in the
City of Atlanta, Fulton County, in the State of Georgia.

    2. I am the plaintiff in the above captioned
action and I am represented by my attorney, CLARENCE B.
JONES, ESQ., a member of the firm of LUBELL, LUBELL AND
JONES, with offices at 165 Broadway, in the Borough of
Manhattan, County of New York, in the State of New York.

    3. I am submitting this affidavit on the advice
of my counsel, p   nt to a request therefor by the Honor-

             ited State

"IN MY COUNTRY WE GO TO PRISON FIRST AND THEN BECOME PRESIDENT." —NELSON MANDELA

    4. I am President of the Southern Christian
Leadership Conference (hereinafter referred to as "SCLC"),

"It is only the opposition between tribes that gives most
cultural events their value. Such opposition can be
expressed or exemplified but it cannot be explained,
and accounts of conflict to do not warp the symmetry of
honor by showing change and subordination."

- Paul Dresch, *Tribes, Government and History in Yemen*, Oxford
University Press, 1994

Classic Bayard: August 28, 1963. Early morning on the day of the March on Washington and the Mall is deserted—alarmingly so to members of MLK's senior team. This event is supposed to demonstrate the massive reach of the racial equality movement and if it's sparsely attended it will be a public humiliation that could destroy credibility. They whisper furiously to Bayard, who is in charge of planning the event. Sniffing a potential disaster, members of the press gather around him and inquire provocatively where the projected crowds are. He pulls a piece of paper out of his pocket and then checks his watch. "Everything's going according to plan," he responds mildly, apparently reviewing his event schedule with satisfaction. As the press wanders off, an assistant asks what's on the piece of paper. "Nothing," Bayard replies. "I was terrified," he recalls years later about the blank page.

I HAVE A DREAM BY THE NUMBERS

2 MONTHS
Time MLK gave Rustin to plan the entire March on Washington event, including the program, the security, the food, the travel, the celebrities and the hundreds of portable toilets.

On March day, all D.C. **liquor stores were closed** for the first time since Prohibition.

Amount the event cost to produce
$133,329
(about a million bucks in today's dollars).

All city jail prisoners were transferred out of town to make room for the **anticipated mass arrests**.

Rustin assigned Rachelle Horowitz to manage all of the transportation for the March on Washington event. Her response: "Are you *crazy*? I don't know anything about transportation. I can't *drive!*"

Number of government-deployed police for the event
24,900

All **elective surgery was cancelled** in local hospitals and extra plasma was stockpiled.

"Let's just win."
—*Margret McBride*

5,900	POLICE
4,000	NATIONAL GUARD
15,000	MILITARY PARATROOPERS

Judges were instructed to **prepare for all-night bail hearings**.

"I believe in social dislocation and creative trouble."
–Bayard Rustin

Number of volunteer fire marshals Rustin trained in nonviolent mediation for the event **4,000**

**RECORDED ARRESTS: 0
RECORDED INJURIES DUE TO VIOLENCE: 0**

ial fact is every way of acting, fixed or not, capable of exercising on the ual an external constraint; or again, every way of acting which is general hout a given society, while at the same time existing in its own right ndent of its individual manifestations."
Durkheim, *The Rules of Sociological Method*. Free Press, 1982 (English translation ègles de la Méthode Sociologique, originally published 1895)

What traits do you most appreciate in others?

TOLERANCE

What traits do you most appreciate about yourself? EMPATHY & THE ABILITY TO JOIN OTHERS IN LAUGHING AT MYSELF (GUESS THAT'S THE SAME AS EMPATHY)

What traits do you most dislike in others?

EDITTLEMENT, ELITISM, CONFORMITY, COMPLACENCY.

What traits do you most dislike in yourself?

CONSTANT SELF CRITICISM

What is your present state of mind?

DISTRACTED & FOCUSED

What event in history do you most admire? WOMEN'S SUFFRAGE, TIANAMEN SQ. STONEWALL, MOHAMMED BOUAZIZI'S LAST STAND

How would you like to die?

FAKED

What is your motto? PERSONAL! THINK DEEP, LIVE SHALLOW
PROFESSIONAL: ET IRRUMABO CUM EAM ARREPTUROS MUND!

*Pseudocide is the act of faking a person's death in order to start a new life and/or escape in his/her responsibili
Pseudocide in itself is not a crime but depending on the reasons and circumstances, e.g. faking death in order t
avoid paying debts can send the person in a jail but a pseudocide committed in order to start a new life and not
avoiding any debts or crime is completely legal.* —From Wikipedia, the free encyclopedia

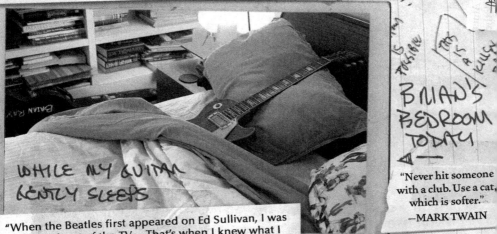

WHILE MY GUITAR
GENTLY SLEEPS

BRIAN'S
BEDROOM
TODAY

"Never hit someone
with a club. Use a cat,
which is softer."
—MARK TWAIN

"When the Beatles first appeared on Ed Sullivan, I was
there in front of the TV. ...That's when I knew what I
wanted to do when I grew up. Years later, I slept
with my 1968 Goldtop Les Paul and would wake up
gazing at it like I would my girlfriend. Every night
I dreamt of doing what I get to do now."
—BRIAN RAY

https://www.youtube.com/watch?v=uZt1xK

STANDING HEART RATE OF AN IGUANA: 20-3

"Most of what we call management consists of making
it difficult for people to get their work done."
-Peter Drucker, *The Essential Drucker: The Best of Sixty Years of Peter Drucker's Essential
Writings on Management.* HarperBusiness reissue, 2008)

A BAT CAN EAT 500
INSECTS IN A SINGLE HOU

ROCKLAND PSYCHIATRIC CENTER

NY STATE ARMORY

with you in Rockland, where we are great riters on the same dreadful typewriter."
—**Alan Ginsberg,** *Howl*

'Know something, sugar? Stories only happen to people who can tell them. " **ALLAN GURGANUS** "A writer lives in a state of astonishment. Beneath any feeling he has of the good or evil of the world lies a deeper one of wonder at it all. To transmit that feeling, he writes. " **WILLIAM SANSOM** "I was working on the proof of one of my poems all the morning, and took out a comma. In the afternoon I put it back again." **OSCAR WILDE** "A writer is working when he's staring out of the window. " **BURTON RASCOE** "I try to leave out the parts that people skip." **ELMORE LEONARD** "You must write every single day of your life...You must lurk in libraries and climb the stacks like ladders to sniff books like perfumes and wear books like hats upon your crazy heads...may you be in love every day for the next 20,000 days. And out of that love, remake a world. " **RAY BRADBURY** "You have to develop a conscience and if on top of that you have talent so much the better. But if you have talent without conscience, you are just one of many thousand journalists. " **F. SCOTT FITZGERALD** "I seat myself at the typewriter and hope, and lurk. " **MIGNON EBERHART** "A writer is someone for whom writing is more difficult than it is for others. " **THOMAS MANN** "When genuine passion moves you, say what you've got to say, and say it hot. " **D.H. LAWRENCE** "People who devote their lives to the studying of something often come to believe that the object of their fascination is the key to everything. " **JONATHAN HAIDT** "The difference between the right word and the almost right word is the difference between lightning and lightning bug. " **MARK TWAIN** "What we find in books is like the fire in our hearths." **VOLTAIRE** "Write what should not be forgotten. " **ISABEL ALLENDE** "Even the most productive writers are expert dawdlers. " **DONALD M. MURRAY** "You have typewriters, presses. And a huge audience. How about raising hell? " **JENKIN LLOYD JONES** "I, like Solzhenitsyn, believe that words will crush concrete. " **NADEZHDA TOLOKONNIKOVA** "Words have weight, sound and appearance; it is only by considering these that you can write a sentence that is good to look at and good to listen to. " **SOMERSET MAUGHAM** "I do not put that note of spontaneity that my critics like into anything but the fifth draft. " **JOHN KENNETH GAILBRAITH** "Easy reading is damn hard writing. " **MAYA ANGELOU** "To me, the greatest pleasure of writing is not what it's about, but the inner music the words make. " **TRUMAN CAPOTE** "A writer only really ever has-or cares about-one kind of power, which is the power to engage readers. " **A.O. SCOTT** "You philosophers are lucky men. You write on paper and paper is patient. Unfortunate Empress that I am, I write on the susceptible skins of living human beings. " **CATHERINE THE GREAT**

The Russian word for "sock" (сущ) is pronounced "no sock."

James Maxwell and Second Law of Thermodynamics.
Maxwell's demon, how the processing of information drains energy:

2DS

"One of the most famous responses to this question was suggested in 1929 by Leo Szilard, and later by Léon Brillouin. Szilard pointed out that a real-life Maxwell's demon would need to have some means of measuring molecular speed and that the act of acquiring information would require an expenditure of energy." — **Wikipedia.org/wiki/Maxwell's demon**

1. **Museum of Broken Relationships**
   Cirilometodska ulica 2, 10000, Zagreb, Croatia
   +385 1 4851 021
   http://brokenships.com/

ONE USED EARRING c.1997

2. **The Hobo Museum**
   51 Main Ave S, Britt, IA 50423
   (641) 843-9104
   http://www.hobo.com/museum.html

3. **Sulabh International Museum of Toilets**
   Sulabh Bhawan, Dabri Palam Rd, Mahavir Enclave, Palam.
   New Delhi, DL 110045, India
   +91 11 2503 1518
   http://www.sulabhtoiletmuseum.org/old/

"My mandolin fingerpicking technique is a blend of Pete Seeger, Earl Scruggs and total incompetence." —Jimmy Page

4. **Museum of Bad Art (MOBA)**
   580 High St, Dedham, MA 02026
   (781) 444-6757
   http://www.museumofbadart.org/

5. **The Plagiarism Museum**
   Bahnhofstrasse 11
   42651 Solingen
   www.plagiarius.com

"Mankind are so much the same, in all time and places, that history informs us of nothin new or strange in this particular. Its chief use i only to discover the constant and universa principles of human nature."

David Hume, *An Enquiry Concerning Human Understanding* (1748

slap Your strategies may be rocket science. Perfect. We're in the rocket scie

10/27 - w/DAVID & RICHARD R&T MTG
1. ORGANIZE FRAMEWORK
2. TITLE
3. TOOLS

DINNER
Served from 5pm

ENTREES
Red Beans & Rice—Oh So Nice

This is Howlin' Wolf's new album. He doesn't like it. He didn't like his electric guitar at first either.

SANCTION THE INEVITABLE

From the Back Story

Winter's Tale

. . . When writing *Winter's Tale*, I lived in Manhattan and Brooklyn and was obsessed with every aspect of the city, to the point of walking, wandering really, ten to twenty miles a day to gather sight, sound, and incident, as if every view, every ray of light that would come from the west at sunset from beneath a lid of black cloud and turn the city gold, every face,

I never practice my guitar. From time to time I just open the case and throw in a piece of raw meat.
—Wes Montgomery

yone can make the
mple complicated.
ivity is making the
plicated simple."
CHARLES MINGUS

(1991) *More Than a Fake Book.*
nesota: Hal Leonard.)

trust

OCCURRENCE OF "TRUST" ACROSS ALL ENGLISH BOOKS IN GOOGLE BOOKS' COLLECTION
Source: Google Books Ngrams Viewer   http://books.google.com/ngrams

C, n. A blackguard
e faulty vision sees
s as they are, not as
ought to be. Hence
custom among the
ians of plucking out
ic's eyes to improve
sion.

ose Bierce, The Devil's Dictionary,
olishing Company, 1911

Dear Optimist,
Pessimist, and
Realist,
While you guys
were busy arguing
about the glass of
water, I drank it.
Sincerely,
The Opportunist

ORACLE INCITE GMM VIDEO SCRIPT DRAFT (CONTD)

nswer: GMM is an intense several days, filled with presentations about the next major
eps in achieving our strategic intent. Senior management presents latest thinking, issues,
d organizational requirements. Work teams assemble throughout the days to turn strategic
itiatives into executable action plans. Each GMM has a theme; this year's is "Taking
harge of Transformation."

KELLY (contd.)

he competition is intense to see who gets to go to Oracle'S GMM. Mostly because of the
umors about what happens here. Mostly by those who've never been. So, if you're feeling
eft out, let us clear it up for you Our Incite team has compiled a list of the key distinctions
between what people think a GMM is all about and what really happens.

CUT TO SCREEN/KELLY V.O. READS

WHAT PEOPLE THINK	WHAT REALLY HAPPENS
Limo service at airport	Sorry I'm late. I took the wrong bus.
Huge fancy hotel	Reservation lost by (completely booked) huge fancy hotel
Huge fancy hotel suite	Why do I always have to share a room with Wally?
P.A.R.T.Y.!!	P.O.W.E.R.P.O.I.N.T.!!
One on one time with Larry	Tip: Bring your own binoculars. Rentals are expensive.
Huge fancy dinners	Chicken a la Roadkill

	✓	Name	Time	Artist	Album	Plays
5452	✓	Jumpin' Jack Flash (Live)	5:00	The Rolling Stones	Flashpoint	82
5453	✓	Daylight	5:28	Coldplay	A Rush Of Blood To The Head	84
5454	✓	Wake Up This Morning (Acoustic)	4:03	Alabama 3	The Last Train To Mashville	84

> If you're going to try, go all the way. Otherwise don't even start. This could mean losing girlfriends, wives, relatives, jobs. And maybe your mind. It could mean not eating for three or four days. It could mean freezing on a park bench. It could mean jail. It could mean derision. It could mean mockery, isolation. Isolation is the gift. All the others are a test of your endurance. Of how much you really want to do it. And you'll do it, despite rejection in the worst odds. And it will be better than anything else you can imagine. If you're going to try, go all the way. There is no other feeling like that. You will be alone with the gods. And the nights will flame with fire. You will ride life straight to perfect laughter. It's the only good fight there is.
>
> — HENRY CHINASKI

						86
						87
						92
						101
						106
						107
						109
						119
						119
						123
						131
						132
5467	✓	Deliver Me (Slight Return)	2:17	Sonia Dada	Sonia Dada	135
5468	✓	Purple Rain	8:41	Prince	Purple Rain Original Soundt...	141
5469	✓	Watch The Sunrise	3:45	Big Star	#1 Record/Radio City	146
5470	✓	I'll Be Your Shelter	4:53	The Housemartins	London 0 Hull 4	151
5471	✓	Nux Vomica	5:30	The Veils	Nux Vomica	161
5472	✓	Lean On Me	4:29	The Housemartins	London 0 Hull 4	162
5473	✓	Everyday I Write The Book	3:52	Elvis Costello And The Attractions	The Very Best Of	171
5474	✓	Be My Baby	2:41	The Ronettes	Phil Spector Back To Mono	177
5475	✓	Abbie Hoffman vs. Pete Townshend (Liv...	0:15	The Who	30 Years Of Maximum R an...	192
5476	✓	Wicked Rain/Across 110th Street	8:15	Los Lobos (w/Bobby Womack)	The Ride	197
5477	✓	When Tomorrow Comes (Live Acoustic)	3:22	Eurythmics	Live 1983 - 1989	225
5478	✓	Go Go Go	3:01	The 88	Not Only... But Also	226
5479	✓	The '59 Sound	3:13	The Gaslight Anthem	The '59 Sound	1843

The Indians feel it is necessary to teach the exploiters a lesson to prevent their return.

7 AUG 2014.
CENTRO DO GUILHERME, BRAZIL.
REUTERS/LUNAE PARRACHO

1, 2 … 10!

E BRIDGE IN HERE? THIS IS A BOOK ABOUT THE PERFORMANCE
OR SO CHILL OUT.

evenue. Improve margins. Don't just make market share; take it. Up
eputation. Better product quality. Get to market faster. Put major d
u and the competition. Become one united team across business

nployee could argue with the irrefutable logic of these corporate
a perfect world, your own employees would immediately gra
emselves wholeheartedly to achieving them.

ipe the drool from your desk and say "hi" to reality.

rld, neither business logic, nor management authority, n
etitive urgency will convince an employee culture to ac
its own. In the killing field between company concep
any a failed strategic plan.

VOX POPULI, VOX DEI

When small men cast large shadows, you know the sun is setting. AMERICAN PROVERB

The tortoise breaths; it is only its shell that prevents our noticing it.
NIGERIAN PROVERB

It is the pot that boils, but the dish gets the credit.
CAMEROONIAN PROVERB

The cork is always bigger than the mouth of the bottle.
ESTONIAN PROVERB

A PESSIMIST IS SOMEONE WHO'S LIVED WITH AN OPTIMIST.
AMERICAN PROVERB

Painting the pipe will not clean out the well.
English proverb

Be always a little afraid so that you never have need of being much afraid.
Finnish Proverb

WHEN TWO ELEPHANTS TUSSLE, IT'S THE GRASS THAT SUFFERS.
ZANZIBARIAN PROVERB

They must have clean fingers who would blow another's nose.
DANISH PROVERB

No one can blow and swallow at the same time.
GERMAN PROVERB

Never show your teeth unless you can bite.
IRISH PROVERB

Those who want the last drop out of the can get the lid on their nose.
Dutch Proverb

When the hands and the feet are bound, the tongue runs faster.
GERMAN PROVERB

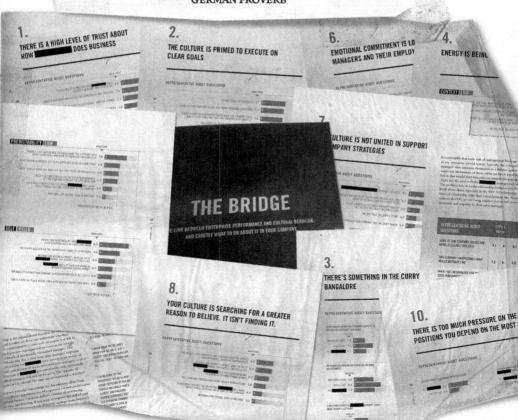

I had a lover's quarrel with the world
—*Robert Frost*

Aimer, c'est agir.
—*Victor Hugo*

CITATIONS

Page 109

"Adelphia Owner John Rigas found guilty." *The Associated Press.* 2004.
http://www.nbcnews.com/id/5396406/ns/business-corporate_
scandals/t/adelphia-founder-john-rigas-found-guilty/#.VD_soSLF98E

Meier, Barry. "2 Guilty in Fraud at Cable Giant." *The New York Times*, July
9, 2004, accessed October 16, 2014, http://www.nytimes.com/2004/07/
09/business/media/09rigas.html?module=Search&mabReward=relbias:
w,{%222=%22:=%22RI:12=%22}=&pagewanted=2

Thomas, Landon Jr. "Prosecutors Build Bear Stearns Case on E-Mails." *The
New York Times*, June 28, 2008, accessed October 16, 2014. http://www
.nytimes.com/2008/06/20/business/20bear.html?pagewanted=all&mod
ule=Search&mabReward=relbias%3Aw%2C%7B%222%22%3A%22RI%
3A12%22%7D

Siconolfi, Michael and Michael Rapoport. "Former Bear Stearns Executive
Alan 'Ace' Greenberg Dies." *The Wall Street Journal*, July 25, 2014,
accessed October 22, 2014. http://online.wsj.com/articles/former-bear-
stearns-chief-alan-ace-greenberg-dies-1406309249

Page 110

Hamilton, Anita. "Why Circuit City Busted, While Best Buy Boomed."
Time, November 11, 2008, accessed October 16, 2014. http://content.
time.com/time/business/article/0,8599,1858079,00.html

Morgenson, Gretchen. "Inside the Countrywide Lending Spree." *The New
York Times*, August 26, 2007, accessed October 16, 2014. http://www
.nytimes.com/2007/08/26/business/yourmoney/26country.html?pagewa
nted=all&module=Search&mabReward=relbias%3Aw%2C%7B%222%2
2%3A%22RI%3A12%22%7D&_r=0

Keller, Bill. "Enron for Dummies." *The New York Times*, June 26, 2002, accessed October 16, 2014. http://www.nytimes.com/2002/01/26/opinion/enron-for-dummies.html?module=Search&mabReward=relbias%3Aw%2C%7B%222%22%3A%22RI%3A12%22%7D&pagewanted=print

Page 111

Trumbull, Mark. "Lehman Bros. used accounting trick amid financial crisis –and earlier." *The Christian Science Monitor*, March 12, 2010, accessed October 16, 2014. http://www.csmonitor.com/USA/2010/0312/Lehman-Bros.-used-accounting-trick-amid-financial-crisis-and-earlier

Austen, Ian. "3 Ex-Nortel Employees Are Accused of Fraud." *The New York Times*, June 20, 2008, accessed October 16, 2014. http://www.nytimes.com/2008/06/20/technology/20nortel.html#

Page 112

Times Wire Services. "Schools, disaster victims, may have gotten tainted peanut butter." *Los Angeles Times*, February 6, 2009, accessed October 16, 2014. http://articles.latimes.com/2009/feb/06/nation/na-salmonella-fema6

"Calls for criminal probe in peanut recall begin." *The Associated Press*. January 28, 2009, originally found on Associated Press http://www.nbcnews.com/id/5396406/ns/business-corporate_scandals/t/adelphia-founder-john-rigas-found-guilty/#.VD_soSLF98E

Duhigg, Charles. "Biking the Elderly, With a Corporate Assist." *The New York Times*, March 20, 2007, accessed on October 16, 2014. http://www.nytimes.com/2007/05/20/business/20tele.html

Page 113

DeSilver, Drew. "Reckless Strategies Doomed WaMu." *The Seattle Times*, October 25, 2009, accessed on October 16, 2014. http://seattletimes.com/html/businesstechnology/2010131911_wamu25.html

Morgenson, Gretchen and Peter S. Goodman. "Saying Yes, WaMu Built Empire on Shaky Loans." *The New York Times*, December 7, 2008, accessed on October 16, 2014. http://www.nytimes.com/2008/12/28/business/28wamu.html?pagewanted=all

Printed in the United States
by Baker & Taylor Publisher Services